THE GENEROSITY OF THE DEAD

Medical Law and Ethics

Series Editor
Sheila McLean, Director of the Institute of Law and Ethics in Medicine, School of Law, University of Glasgow

The 21st century seems likely to witness some of the most major developments in medicine and healthcare ever seen. At the same time, the debate about the extent to which science and/or medicine should lead the moral agenda continues, as do questions about the appropriate role for law.

This series brings together some of the best contemporary academic commentators to tackle these dilemmas in a challenging, informed and inquiring manner. The scope of the series is purposely wide, including contributions from a variety of disciplines such as law, philosophy and social sciences.

Other titles in the series

Ethical Issues of Human Genetic Databases
A Challenge to Classical Health Research Ethics?
Bernice Elger
ISBN 978-0-7546-7492-4

Issues in Human Rights Protection of Intellectually Disabled Persons
Andreas Dimopoulos
ISBN 978-0-7546-7760-4

The Legal, Medical and Cultural Regulation of the Body
Transformation and Transgression
Edited by Stephen W. Smith and Ronan Deazley
ISBN 978-0-7546-7736-9

Bioequity – Property and the Human Body
Nils Hoppe
ISBN 978-0-7546-7280-7

Altruism Reconsidered
Exploring New Approaches to Property in Human Tissue
Edited by Michael Steinmann, Peter Sýkora and Urban Wiesing
ISBN 978-0-7546-7270-8

The Generosity of the Dead
A Sociology of Organ Procurement in France

GRACIELA NOWENSTEIN
University of Groningen, The Netherlands

ASHGATE

Published by
Ashgate Publishing Limited
Wey Court East
Union Road
Farnham
Surrey, GU9 7PT
England

Ashgate Publishing Company
Suite 420
101 Cherry Street
Burlington
VT 05401-4405
USA

www.ashgate.com

British Library Cataloguing in Publication Data
Nowenstein, Graciela.
The generosity of the dead : a sociology of organ procurement in France. -- (Medical law and ethics)
1. Procurement of organs, tissues, etc.--Law and legislation. 2. Procurement of organs, tissues, etc.--Law and legislation--France. 3. Procurement of organs, tissues, etc.--Moral and ethical aspects. 4. Procurement of organs, tissues, etc.--Moral and ethical aspects--France.
I. Title II. Series
344.4'404194-dc22

Library of Congress Cataloging-in-Publication Data
Nowenstein, Graciela.
The generosity of the dead : a sociology of organ procurement in France by Graciela Nowenstein.
p. cm. -- (Medical law and ethics)
Includes index.
ISBN 978-0-7546-7432-0 (hardback) -- ISBN 978-0-7546-9118-1 (ebook) 1. Donation of organs, tissues, etc.--Law and legislation--France. 2. Donation of organs, tissues, etc.--Social aspects--France. I. Title.

KJV5372.N69 2010
344.4404'194--dc22

2010025630

ISBN 9780754674320 (hbk)
ISBN 9780754691181 (ebk)

Mixed Sources
Product group from well-managed forests and other controlled sources
www.fsc.org Cert no. SGS-COC-2482
© 1996 Forest Stewardship Council
FSC

Printed and bound in Great Britain by
TJ International Ltd, Padstow, Cornwall

Contents

List of Figures and Tables

Figures

Tables

Note to the Reader

Most of the informants who have contributed to this research were nurses and intensivists in charge of procurement activities in French hospitals, fulfilling respectively the functions of hospital coordinator and referent physician. They are referred to as Hospital Coordinator (HC 1 to 13) and Referent Physician (RP 1 to 12). Each of them is also referred to as 'she', whether male or female. More generally 'she' is adopted as the neutral form instead of he/she.

BDPD stands for Brain Dead Potential Donor.

Capital letters are used in interview quotes to mark a stress in the voice of an interviewee.

Unless otherwise noted, I am responsible for all translations from French (legal and academic texts, press articles and quotes from interviews with informants). The translation of quotes from interviews has not been an easy task. Interviews by nature have broken sentences and include colloquial expressions. I have tried to be as faithful as possible to the originals.

> Mais, pensait Mme Michaud, on habille et on pare bien les morts qui sont destinés à pourrir dans la terre. C'est un dernier hommage, une preuve suprême d'amour à ce qui fut cher.
>
> Irène Némirovsky, *Suite française*[1]

1 'All the same, thought Madame Michaud, you dress and adorn the dead who are destined to rot in the earth. It's a final homage, a supreme proof of love to those we hold dear' (Némirovsky 2007: 37).

Acknowledgements

My acknowledgements go firstly to my informants; all those professionals, physicians, nurses, hospital directors and members of transplant institutions, who were so patient and generous in sharing their time, knowledge, impressions and emotions with me. Without their contributions this work would not have been possible. As this book is written in English, it will not be fully accessible for a number of them, who will not have the opportunity to comment on or disagree with my analyses and conclusions. I apologise for that.

I also wish to thank Simone Bateman, John Griffiths, Stéphanie Hennette-Vauchez, Martin Kohli, Massimo Mazzotti, Gianfranco Poggi and Donald van Tol, who commented on different aspects or versions of this book. My thanks go also to my colleagues at the Department of Legal Theory at the University of Groningen; Marc Hertogh, Heleen Weyers and Nicolle Zeegers, for their stimulating conversations. Thanks also to Toni Marzal, for his help in translating many of the quotes originally in French, and to Marike van der Meij, student assistant at the University of Groningen, for her help concerning the study of the public debate on organ donation in the Netherlands.

Para Nora y Benjamím

Introduction

French law stipulates that those who do not opt out of organ donation during their lifetime automatically become potential donors after death:

> The removal [of organs for transplantation] may be carried out if the person has not objected, during her lifetime, to such a removal. This objection may be declared by any means, and in particular by recording it in the appropriate automated national register.
>
> If the doctor is not directly aware of the wishes of the deceased, she must seek to ascertain from those close to the deceased whether she objected during her lifetime to the donation of organs ….[1]

Here is how the head of an intensive care unit describes the situation in French hospitals:

> … normally the law should allow us, from the moment there is no clearly expressed wish on behalf of the deceased, to assume that, implicitly, he is in favour of organ donation, which is not at all what happens in practice. … in practice, we abide by the advice expressed by families. This happens, whatever the motivations behind their response may be, whether we think they are good or bad …

This book is about the tension between these two approaches to decisions concerning post-mortem organ retrieval.[2] However, this is not to say that it is a study of a 'gap' between law and practice. Rather, it is a study of the relationship between the two, dealing with the flexibility of rules, legal and non-legal, as well as the dynamic relationship between the legal and non-legal rules themselves. These issues are explored through a study of how organs (and tissues) are made available for transplantation in France, in particular how the circulation of organs is organized and regulated within the country.

The relationship between law and practice is examined on the basis of the assumption that, whatever formal or normative differences one may posit between legal and non-legal rules, nothing allows us to take any differences for granted when it comes to understanding the practical fate of a legal rule. One must keep

1 Loi n° 2004-800 du 6 août 2004 relative à la bioéthique, article 1232-1.
2 Living donation is thus not dealt with in this book.

in mind that legal rules are generally applicable in contexts where non-legal rules are also likely to organize and regulate social action and interaction, and which rules are binding in practice often does not depend on their legal character but on local culture and local power relations. Thus the relationship between a law and social life can only be studied in context and with particular attention to the 'shop floor of social life', namely 'that concrete social situation where the social action and interaction that are the subject of legal regulation takes place' (Griffiths 2003: 19).

What is a rule? A rule is a general statement about how to interpret, and what to do in, certain situations. Each instance of the mobilization of a rule thus entails a move from the general to the particular. If we are interested in the effect that a rule may have in practice, we need to look at the relationship between the general statement and the case; in other words, at the process whereby a general statement becomes case-application. The meaning of a rule is neither unique nor fixed: knowing it does not amount to knowing the meaning of each of its terms and establishing its global meaning once and for all. Generally, the meaning of a rule is likely to vary according to the particular cases to which it applies. This is so because the meaning of words is flexible and social life is not made up of repetitions of the same situation. The meaning of a rule is also likely to vary according to the context in which it applies, namely to the characteristics of its field of application (Moore 1973). This does not mean to say that there are no regularities in rule application, but that these are the result of social practice and are not fixed in an initial general statement. Because a general statement can comprehend neither all the possible cases of its application nor the specificities of the social context where such cases will arise, it is only the study of the specific situations in which a rule applies that will give us the keys to access the subtleties, and regularities, of its meaning (Bloor 2002).

This book examines the procurement of cadaveric organs in France through the prism of the professionals in charge of the decisions to retrieve organs and of the organization of procurement processes. Some may find its content at times unsettling. The topic has its crude sides and this book contains detailed accounts of tragic situations involving loss, death, corpses and body parts. The use of this material is not gratuitous, nor is it done to shock the reader. It is due to the fact that to understand organ transplantation today, aspects of organ procurement that are generally kept in the shadows must be made visible. Most discussions about how to respond to the ever-increasing demand for organs tend to leave precisely that which is fundamental to the activity of transplantation and the problem of shortage to one side: the origin of the organs. This is not to say that there is an attempt to hide the fact that organs come from recently deceased people. It is the implications of this fact for all participants in the situation of organ retrieval that are often overlooked. Nevertheless, these are important, for it is differences in how these situations are dealt with by those involved that explain the most enduring regional and historical variations in procurement rates.

In these situations, the shock and pain of those who have brutally lost a loved one are confronted by the needs of the community to have access to the body of the newly dead person as a source of healing material. Thus, to pose the question of organ retrieval entails the re-enactment of fundamental socio-political relations: between the individual and the state, between the individual and the community, between the individual and her network of close persons, between this network and the state and between fellow citizens. It also entails the mobilization by participants in these situations of representations about death and dying, about body and personhood, about medical authority and biomedical expertise.

Existing laws regulating organ retrieval establish the conditions under which organs from the dead can become available. They are based on the principles of gratuity and voluntariness and structured around systems of presumed or of express consent, also known as opting-out or opting-in systems. Both systems amount to the regulation of a form of generosity or solidarity by the state. The evolution of practice in French hospitals since the first law of presumed consent was enacted in 1976 (involving movement toward active participation by the relatives of the potential donor in the decision-making process) reflects broader social changes in the legitimacy and scope of projects of social engineering with the law. This evolution also reveals the changing conceptualization in French society of the relationship between the individual and the state, and between the private and the public spheres. It also reflects recent changes in the status of medical professionals as figures of authority and agents of state policy. Last but not least, the distance between a formal legal approach that presumes 'the consent of the dead',[3] and the approach that in daily life guides the physicians and nurses in charge of decisions to retrieve organs, makes the tension between the formal legal conceptualization of persons as isolated individuals, and the more sociological view of persons as embedded in relational networks, particularly salient. While the law considers potential donors as individual legal actors, in practice in most cases, it is the network of affective relationships of the potential donor that is central to decision making about organ retrieval.

Chapter 1 presents a brief history of the biomedical revolution that in the 1960s made organ transplantation possible. The activity of organ transplantation was surrounded by an aura of fascination at the time, for it seemed a biomedical miracle rendered possible by an enchanted form of generosity: the gift of life. As transplantation activity increased, human organs became a scarce resource and shortage a problem to be managed, leading in many countries to the enactment of laws and development of policies. Comparisons in procurement rates have regularly been made since the beginning of the activity, revealing national differences that are very high. The reasons for these differences have been and still are endlessly discussed in the international arena, which is mainly composed of medical, legal and ethical actors. These discussions often appear rather detached from shop-floor reality and often focus on legal factors. Closer to practice, some authors stress the

3 The expression is from sociologist Paterson (1997).

importance of organizational factors for understanding variations in procurement rates. Both approaches tend to place little or no importance on the situational aspects of the question, particularly on the relational factors that influence the decision-making process in hospitals.

Chapter 2 discusses how French political and legislative authorities have responded to the 'demand' for organs produced by the development of transplantation medicine. In the 1970s, the nationalization of corpses was rejected and the presumption of the generosity of the dead was presented and adopted as the best solution to the problem. The first law of presumed consent was approved in 1976 in an atmosphere of faith in biomedical progress and in the law as a tool that would enhance this progress. Solidarity and the development of bioscience marched side by side, as the protagonists in a perfect French republican tale. In the mid-1990s and 2000s the law was discussed in parliament on two occasions, with legislators appearing increasingly disenchanted. The law had failed, it was said: the presumption of consent was not being applied in hospitals, where families were generally acknowledged to have the final word on retrieval. Nevertheless, the principle of presumed consent was not contested and was re-confirmed twice by the French legislature. The history of presumed consent in the French parliament has thus moved from a position of faith in social engineering with law to disillusioned support for the law as text.

During the 15 years that followed the enactment of the first law in 1976, organ transplantation moved from being a new experimental technique to something closer to a routine therapeutic treatment. Organ procurement practices similarly followed a process of normalization, moving from heterogeneous to standardized practices. Chapter 3 examines this process. Until the mid 1980s, local retrieval practices were very different, depending on the hospital where the decision was taken as well as the staff in charge at a specific time. Sometimes organs were retrieved without letting the relatives know. At times, relatives would be informed in advance that organs were going to be taken before the body of the deceased was released. Sometimes relatives would be asked by hospital staff about the wishes of the deceased or about their own wishes with regard to the fate of the corpse. In some hospitals an intensive care physician would talk to the relatives about organ retrieval, in others it would be a transplantation surgeon, or an intensive care nurse. However, since the early 1990s these procedures have occurred in the same way in all French hospitals: the relatives are consulted by a specialist nurse and/or an intensive care physician, and they enjoy a paralegal right to veto organ retrieval. This chapter provides contextual and structural historical keys to understanding this evolution.

Chapters 4, 5 and 6 reveal in detail how physicians and nurses describe the situation in which decisions about organ retrieval are made. Such situations are considered quite exceptional by those involved in the daily routine of intensive care units, and as particularly difficult to manage and cope with for all involved. The fact that potential donors are in a state of brain death is the first difficulty that participants must face (Chapter 4). While relatives are told that their loved one is dead, what they see is a body that is warm and that has a heartbeat, with blood still circulating and lungs being filled with air pumped by an artificial respirator. The announcement of brain death is a counter-intuitive expert statement that can only be accepted if the relatives trust those who make it.

While families need time to comprehend what they are being told, to digest and reflect upon what is being asked of them, the medical, organizational and institutional times are constrained (Chapter 5). The brain-dead body is unstable and needs close monitoring. The process of organ retrieval requires tight organizational procedures: one potential donor implies the possibility of many organs and tissues to be retrieved, each organ or tissue will be extracted by a different team, often coming from different hospitals all over the country, and all this needs to be coordinated with the central transplantation agency which allocates the organs. As one of the nurses interviewed observed: families need time 'and we have no time'. The strain caused by the time pressure is increased by the feeling professionals have that they are not always trusted by the relatives of a potential donor. In the absence of trust, it becomes almost impossible for relatives to accept organ retrieval. Trust depends on the kind of relationship that has been established between the relatives and hospital professionals. It also depends on the pre-existing symbolic and practical relationship between the family and medical, political and health institutions. This, combined with the fact that a number of actors and variables intervene in the procurement process, gives procurement specialists the feeling of not being fully in control of these situations.

Professionals describing their encounters with relatives depict an extreme situation of social breakdown, a moment in a world of codified social interactions in which all the basic assumptions that relatives have brought with them fall apart (Chapter 6). A person who was in good health is suddenly said to be gone, yet the so-called 'dead' person does not look completely dead. The hospital staff, whose function it was to try to save this person, have failed and are now also asking the families concerned to accept a sacrifice: the opening up of the body of their loved one and the extraction of body parts in order to save others' lives. In a state of affective and cognitive shock, the reactions of the relatives are not only difficult to predict but can also be extreme. The level of pathos that can be reached in an intensive care unit is at its highest in these situations.

In the situation described and analysed in Chapters 4, 5 and 6 the presumption of consent is in practice not mobilized by hospital professionals and no retrieval decision is made against the families' will. Chapters 7 and 8 take a broader view and deal with the relationship between law and practice and bring broad social relations and policy to the centre of the discussion. The law of presumed consent goes against a number of basic assumptions about social life that the actors involved share (Chapter 7). A fundamental social assumption which the law seems to violate is that a gift is something that cannot be presumed. The basis for this idea is that a gift must be an active and personal gesture. Therefore, a presumed gift is not really a gift. Physicians' and nurses' discourse and practice reveal that in order to feel justified in taking the organs, they need to believe that a gift has *really* been made by someone in a legitimate position to do so. If not, their involvement in organ procurement takes them too far from their ideal self-representation as health professionals and their conception of their social role. The magic of the gift of life needs to be maintained to enable these professionals to participate in a process from which they gain little – as opposed to, for example, transplantation surgeons – and that provokes feelings that are difficult to deal with.

Despite all these reservations, however, the health professionals encountered in this study did not argue in favour of a modification of the law. Quite the contrary, they want the situation to remain unchanged (Chapter 8). In fact, contrary to French legal scholars who express concern about the discrepancies between law and practice, hospital professionals do not think that this is an issue. First, they see it as part of normal life that a law may not be followed in practice; second, in principle and symbolically they think the law is a good one that delivers a republican message about the state enhancing solidarity and progress; third, the existing situation is seen as one in which, after years of searching and exploring, a routine has been established, a 'decent' donation rate has been reached and the public scandals that tarnished the image of public health institutions in the 1980s have not been repeated; finally, intensivists and nurses would prefer to see the situation unchanged, so that even if the common rule is to let families veto organ retrieval under circumstances in which they do not appear to be able to cope, professionals have the law on their side if they decide to mobilize the presumption of consent in a particular case.

The findings about France presented in this book have been the point of departure for a comparative project that I am currently conducting at the University of Groningen, a study that extends to Spain, Italy and the Netherlands. The findings of this comparison study will be referred to from time to time, and in more detail in the Conclusion.

In undertaking this study I have endeavoured to describe the process of organ procurement in all its complexity because it appears that this is the only way to understand organ donation decisions and the relationship between the legal and the non-legal regulation of this area of social life. Each chapter (with the exception of Chapter 1) attempts to describe a specific aspect of the general picture, each of which makes sense in relation to the whole. For that reason, some topics and arguments are addressed in more than one chapter. Consequently, it is possible to read each chapter individually, but the clearest picture of organ procurement in French hospitals comes from reading all the chapters in order.

PART I
Law as Policy

This section presents the main features of the international context in which transplantation medicine emerged in the second half of the twentieth century, and the regulatory responses that followed (Chapter 1). From the beginning, organ transplantation has been surrounded by an aura of enchantment: it seemed to be a biomedical miracle rendered possible by a new and supreme form of generosity or solidarity – the gift of life. After the first period of enthusiasm, and as transplantation activity increased, human organs became a scarce resource and their shortage a problem to be managed, with laws being enacted and policies implemented. Comparisons of procurement rates are regularly made, showing that national and regional differences are very high. Such differences have been endlessly discussed in an international arena mainly composed of medical, legal and ethical actors. The discussions often appear detached from practice, focusing on formal – mostly legal – factors. Some authors examining the situation closer to practice stress the importance of organizational factors for understanding variations in procurement rates; however, both approaches tend to pay little or no attention to relational and cultural factors. It is these neglected factors that are central to this book, and in addressing these factors we will look in detail at the French situation, the presentation of which will begin in Chapter 2, with the legislative history of presumed consent legislation and of the public discussions that have surrounded it since the 1970s.

Chapter 1
Organ Transplantation: From 'an Eternally Hopeless Dream'[1] to the Management of Scarce Resources

From Myth to Practice

A Fantasy

A significant number of myths and fictional works present transplantation historically as a source of fantasy and anguish. The Christian history of saints is full of references to the restoration of body parts by reattachment and transplantation. A story from the thirteenth century tells of the miracle performed by Cosmas and Damian – who later became the patron saints of doctors (and especially of surgeons) – who, at the end of the third century, were reputed to have cut off the diseased leg of a rich merchant and replaced it with that of a North African slave who had recently been buried:

> … one night as he slept, the saints appeared to him, bringing salves and instruments, and one said to the other: 'Where shall we find new flesh, to replace the rotted flesh which we are to cut away?' The other replied: 'This day an Ethiop was buried in the cemetery of Saint Peter in Chains; do thou fetch his leg, and we shall put it in place of the sick one!' Thereupon he hastened to the cemetery and brought back the Moor's leg, and they cut off the leg of the sick man and put the other in its stead. (de Voragine 1941: 577–8)

Other Christian myths include Saint Peter's reconstruction of Saint Agatha's breast, which had been cut off after she refused to submit to a Roman consul, Saint Anthony's replacement of the foot of a man who had mutilated himself, and the replacement of the arm of a soldier by Saint Mark (Küss and Bourget 1992). This Christian history of transplantation miracles reveals the divine power behind an activity that, even in the words of a transplantation pioneer, seemed until the 1950s to be a fantasy and out of the reach of humanity. Joseph Murray, a member of the team which performed the first successful kidney transplant, and later Nobel

1 This expression is from the French pioneer in kidney transplants Jean Hamburger (Hamburger 1981: 41).

laureate, observed that until his team performed the feat in 1954: 'the dogma was that it would never be possible and we were told we were playing God.'[2]

Transplantation also awakened the imagination of writers, and the history of literature provides many references to this activity. In these works, the 'miracles' of religious stories become the results of human hands and minds. The scientific interest in body parts is portrayed either as a promise of progress or a threat to humanity. In the fifteenth century, François Rabelais wrote in *Gargantua and Pantagruel* about Epistemon, who had lost his head while fighting giants but had it very methodically reattached by a surgeon. Contrary to de Voragine's account of the miracle of Cosmas and Damian, Rabelais' story refers to meticulous technical work and not to miraculous acts guided by divine power. Nevertheless, the idea of playing with the boundaries of life and death remains, for the intervention brings the patient back from the world of the dead:

> … [Panurge] cleansed he his neck very well with pure white wine, and, after that, took his head, and into it synapised some powder of diamerdis, which he always carried about him in one of his bags. Afterwards he anointed it with I know not what ointment, and set it on very just, vein against vein, sinew against sinew, and spondyle against spondyle, that he might not be wry-necked – for such people he mortally hated. This done, he gave it round about some fifteen or sixteen stitches with a needle that it might not fall off again; then, on all sides and everywhere, he put a little ointment on it, which he called resuscitative.
>
> Suddenly Epistemon began to breathe, then opened his eyes, yawned, sneezed, and afterwards let a great household fart. Whereupon Panurge said, Now, certainly, he is healed, – and therefore gave him to drink a large full glass of strong white wine, with a sugared toast. In this fashion was Epistemon finely healed, only that he was somewhat hoarse for above three weeks together, and had a dry cough of which he could not be rid but by the force of continual drinking. And now he began to speak, and said that he had seen the devil, had spoken with Lucifer familiarly, and had been very merry in hell and in the Elysian fields, affirming very seriously before them all that the devils were boon companions and merry fellows.[3]

Frankenstein or the Modern Prometheus, written by Mary Shelley in 1818, is probably the most popular account among literary works dealing with this kind of scientific exploit. Contrary to Rabelais' fantasy, it is dominated by a frightening vision of humanity, science and progress: in the imagination of the writer, the construction of a being using organs, members and tissues gathered from different

2 Quoted in Landers (2004). Available at: http://www.ama-assn.org/amednews/2004/02/16/hll20216.htm (accessed: May 2010).

3 Rabelais (2007 [1653]). Available at: http://ebooks.adelaide.edu.au/r/rabelais/francois/r11g/book2.30.html (accessed: May 2010).

human corpses leads to the birth of a physically horrifying and mentally disturbed monster. Maurice Renard's *Les mains d'Orlac* from 1921 also introduces a tale fed by the fear of the consequences of a reckless transfer of body parts. In this story, the transplantation of the hands of an executed murderer onto the body of a piano player is suspected to be the vehicle through which the criminal's evil penetrates the body of the artist, whose hands seem to move autonomously to commit murder.

John Irving's novel *The Fourth Hand* tells with humour and tenderness the story of Patrick Wallendorf, a television journalist whose left hand is eaten by a lion and replaced by that of a dead man. The story describes the psychological changes that the journalist experiences because of his new hand, a limb that is his, yet not part of himself. He falls in love with the widow of the original owner of the hand, a woman who had only agreed to donate her husband's hand on the condition that she had the right to visit it, as she considered it to remain that of her husband. These old and more recent expressions of fascination for transplantation all seem to be fed by fear and hope at the same time, offering us projections that combine a fascination for biomedical knowledge with thoughts about the (im)possibility of dissociating body and personhood.[4]

From Research to Therapeutics

Küss and Bourget wrote in their history of organ transplantation that the first reports of grafts can be found in an Indian text from 800 BCE, which describes the re-implantations of noses cut off following judicial decisions. The history of Western medicine thereafter offers a long list of experiments with autografts (the grafted part comes from the body of the patient who receives it) and allografts (the grafted part comes from a different body). Yet it was not until well into the twentieth century that transplantation became more than the subject of frustrated experiments, fantasies and fears (Küss and Bourget 1992). The first phase of the history of transplantation resembles a long and hopeless medical obstacle race featuring surgical *savoir-faire* and medical knowledge encompassing the domains of haematology and immunology (Randle 2008). Immunological problems have proved to be the most difficult to master, rejection by the host organism of the foreign tissue implanted remaining the main difficulty the field faces (Carvais and Sasportes 2000: 31–48).

A major advance in the understanding of the rejection barrier was made in the mid-1950s thanks to the work of the future French Nobel Prize winner Dausset on the HLA (human leukocyte antigen) system. HLAs are used by the immune system to distinguish self from non-self cells. Dausset's findings lead to the first models for matching between organ recipients and donors, and to the development of the first immunosuppressive

4 Filmmakers have also taken organ transplantation as a source of contradictory feelings and behaviour. Among them we find Almodóvar with *All about My Mother*, Frears with *Dirty Pretty Things*, Gonzalez Iñárritu with *21 Grams* and *Monty Python's The Meaning of Life*.

drugs and treatments aimed at inhibiting the natural immunological reaction of the host organism to the foreign tissue (Müller-Ruchholtz 1999). Although there was still a great deal to be discovered, these developments marked the beginning of the normalization of transplantation medicine, namely its transition from a hazardous research activity into a standardized therapeutic technique.

The new turn was manifested in a series of achievements in the late 1950s and 1960s, reported worldwide as historic events. In 1954, Joseph Murray's team performed the first *successful* living-related kidney transplant between twins in Boston.[5] The recipient lived for seven years and died of coronary artery disease (Merrill 1981). In 1959 the same team performed another living kidney transplant between twins and the recipient lived for 25 years. In 1962 the first survival for over a year of a recipient of a cadaveric kidney was announced. Looking back, Murray writes that with this event 'the modern clinical era began' for kidney transplantation, opening a period of 'boundless optimism', with new immunosuppressive combinations and the improvement of organ preservation techniques prolonging the survival period of recipients (Murray 1981). The story of kidney transplantation is the oldest and from the beginning the most successful. Other organs produced less encouraging results.

The first attempts to transplant cadaveric livers were conducted in 1963 in the United States by Thomas Starzl's team. As he wrote years later, 'Our first recipient bled to death during the operation; the other four first Denver patients survived operation but died from 6.5 to 23 days later.' And further: 'The series of consecutive early failures caused a moratorium of 3 years to be declared on further cases' (Starzl 1981: 52). About ten years later, improved surgical techniques and immunosuppressive treatments had increased survival rates, but not to the point that liver transplantation was no longer considered experimental (Starzl 1981; Fox and Swazey 2002: 317).

The first human heart transplant was a symbolic high point in the history of transplantation. It was performed in December 1967 at Cape Town by heart surgeon Christiaan Barnard. The patient died 18 days later from pneumonia, apparently contracted as a consequence of the radiation given to fight rejection. The event was reported worldwide. Barnard renewed the attempt a month later, in January 1968, with a lightened immunosuppressive treatment. The patient survived for 20 months. During 1968 105 hearts were transplanted worldwide with poor results: Randle reports for that year a three month survival rate of 35 per cent of patients; the first European transplant was performed by a team lead by Christian Cabrol and the patient died after three days (Fox and Swazey 2002: 108–9; Küss and

5 It is not always clear what the epithet 'successful' refers to when used in the medical literature. According to Fox and Swazey (2002: 67) whether a case qualified as a success or a failure in the 1970s depended on life expectancy without transplantation and with or without other treatments, as well as assessments of quality of life. This seems still to be the general approach. The judgment of success is thus always related to the state of biomedical knowledge.

Bourget 1992: 118–19; Randle 2008). The great enthusiasm generated by the first spectacular feats lead to disillusionment among cardiac specialists to the point that many of them suspended their trials. As Frist, one of the protagonists, writes about this early phase of heart transplantation:

> By 1970, only 23 of the 166 people who had received heart transplants were still alive. … Denis Cooley, the conspicuous leader of the worldwide transplant frenzy, had for years claimed the surgeon's motto should be 'cut well, tie well, get well.' His credo, however, had not worked with transplants. Within a year, he had lost almost all of his transplanted patients. …
>
> Most surgeons who had jumped on the transplant bandwagon abandoned the procedure. Cooley, in a news conference, announced that he would no longer perform the procedure. He explained what was by then obvious, 'I have done all I can do as a surgeon. It remains for the immunologists and biologists to unravel the mysteries that have limited our work.' Teaching hospitals and research centers declared heart transplants too experimental. (Frist 1989: 65–6)

Attempts continued to be made by some teams such as Shumway's and Lower's, but at a much slower pace (Frist 1989: 66). The reduction of activity and the uncertainty that surrounded it were at any rate important enough for Fox and Swazey to write about a 'clinical moratorium' in heart transplantation that started about a year after Barnard's première. In 1970 a number of cardiac teams showed renewed interest in the activity, among other reasons due to the comparatively good results obtained by Shumway's team at Stanford (Fox and Swazey 2002: 108–34). Heart transplantation increased slowly in a context of cautious optimism. In the meantime, kidney history had been moving at a faster pace, especially in the United States, with an increasing number of kidneys coming from related living donors, which in most cases limited the scope of the immunological hazard (Fox and Swazey 2002: 305–44).

In fact, after the initial enthusiasm that accompanied the first transplants, Randle writes that these 'early times were referred to as the "dark days" or the "black years" of transplantation because most patients died' (Randle 2008: 9). But rejection would prove not to be the only obstacle that transplantation medicine had to deal with in these early times. Once transplantation medicine seemed technically ready to take over, a major finding threatened nevertheless to frustrate further progress. It became clear that organs taken from living bodies produce better results than those from cadavers, the latter being exposed to a much longer period of non-oxygenation before being grafted. While kidneys can be taken from a living donor without ending her live, this is not the case for other transplantable organs – except nowadays for part of the liver and the lungs. This problem was overcome with a legal and medical conceptual revolution, whereby death was identified with the death of the brain. Let us rapidly sketch the connection between the changing definition of death and the history of transplantation.

A New Definition of Death

The early part of the twentieth century saw an acceleration of the development of research on organ transplantation and resuscitation that led to discussions about the possibility of a modification of the definition of death (Pernick 1999). The improvement of transplantation techniques challenged the idea that death was a one-way path by showing that body parts from dead bodies could recover life when grafted onto living organisms. At the same time, the development of resuscitation techniques was moving in the same direction, blurring the frontier between life and death by making it possible to go back and forth between the two.[6]

Until the beginning of the twentieth century death was seen as the simultaneous arrest of cardiac, respiratory and neurological functions (Cranford 1995). With the development of intensive care medicine it became possible to restore lost cardiac function and to substitute for respiratory failure. As a consequence the connection between the failure of the three functions disappeared. At this point a new type of comatose patient appeared in hospitals: a patient whose brain had stopped functioning but whose heart was still beating and whose body was oxygenated thanks to an external respiratory device. This state was called 'beyond coma' and systematically described for the first time by two French neurologists in 1959 (Mollaret and Goulon 1959). It was defined by the irreversible loss of neurological functions of a patient while cardiovascular and respiratory functions could be respectively maintained and substituted for some time.[7] In their presentation of the 'beyond coma' state, Mollaret and Goulon added that heart arrest would unavoidably occur a few days at most following the irreversible loss of brain functions. All these developments led to the question of whether such bodies were already dead or still alive.

The hearts that Barnard used to perform the world's first two heart transplants came from bodies in this state. Legally speaking these were hopelessly comatose patients, hence they were alive before the retrieval intervention. Actually Gordon and Brink write that 'Because of the absence of a definition of brain death, the transplant team responsible for the explantation of the donor heart waited for the heart to arrest (and death to be certified) before they opened the donor's chest' (Gordon and Brink 2008: 137; see also Settergren 2003 and Ozinsky 1967). Although no member of Barnard's team was prosecuted, the view was shared by most physicians interested in developing transplantation medicine around the world that in most countries the activity could not safely take place without legal change. Such change could go in two directions: legislators could authorize organ

6 'Three generations of Russian and Soviet scientists from Bachmetieff in 1910 to Negovskii in the 1950s discovered that animals and people with no heart, lung, or brain activity could be revived after prolonged hypothermia, exsanguination, drug overdose, or other cause of suspended animation' (Pernick 1999: 5).

7 Timmermans writes that, still today, '… the next frontier in resuscitation research is brain resuscitation …' (Timmermans 1999: 82).

retrieval from 'beyond coma' patients, in effect decriminalizing their killing; or the border between life and death could be shifted by providing that 'beyond coma' patients were actually dead.[8] The second solution had the advantage of leaving intact – at least formally – the taboo of killing. It was the choice made around the world.

In 1968, the *Journal of the American Medical Association* published what can be qualified as the act of baptism for 'brain death' (Ad Hoc Committee of the Harvard Medical School to Examine the Definition of Brain Death 1968). The article, 'The Definition of Irreversible Coma: Report of the Ad Hoc Committee of the Harvard Medical School to Examine the Definition of Brain Death', contained the description of the neurological criterion for such a diagnosis. In the months and years that followed the first transplantation feats, most countries where transplantation technology was developing adopted legislation whereby, following the so-called Harvard criteria, beyond coma patients were decreed dead, *brain* dead. Since the dead cannot be killed, transplantation surgeons could legally remove their organs. A telling illustration of the connection between brain death and heart transplantation is the first such transplantation in France, which was performed on 27 April 1968, only three days after a legal instrument was issued by the Minister of Health assimilating brain death to death.[9]

Most authors agree that the emergence of a brain based definition of death in the 1960s was in the first place a response to the needs of transplantation medicine. Wijdicks appears to be an exception when he writes about the Harvard committee:

> Clearly there were major pressures on transplant surgeons, but I am uncertain after reading the documents whether an alleged agenda of facilitating transplantation through a new construct of death existed. The interviewed members of the committee denied that transplantation was implicit in their deliberations. (Wijdicks 2003: 976)

Singer (1994) has convincingly established such connection for the Harvard Committee. Moreover, the connection was overtly present in the discussions during the 1960s that prepared the terrain for a new definition of death based on brain criteria. To give but one example, during a workshop in 1966 about the legal and ethical questions raised by transplantation medicine attended by eminent

8 As is argued in Chapter 4, brain death cannot be understood from the usual binary perspective where the question is thought to be 'Is a brain-dead body already dead or is it still alive?' The brain-dead body has traits that are usually identified with the realm of death and traits which are seen as belonging to that of life. As a concept it is fundamentally ambiguous, and as a state it is a hybrid one (Truog 1997; Lock 2002; Hennette-Vauchez and Nowenstein 2009).

9 Circulaire n°67 du 24 avril 1968. See, for a detailed study about the past and present of brain death in France, Hennette-Vauchez and Nowenstein (2009).

physicians and legal scholars, the re-definition of the moment of death was discussed repeatedly and at length. The connection between transplantation and brain death was constantly made by participants, as in the following statement by David Louisell, professor of law at Harvard:

> The problem of redefinition of the moment of death, in the light of current medical realities and the medical need for prompt removal of organs for transplantation, requires the collaborative and precise thinking of physicians, lawyers, theologians and philosophers. (Wolstenholme and O'Connor 1968: 94)[10]

More Effective Immunosuppression

In the late 1970s a radical change took place, one which opened the door to the therapeutic normalization of the activity: the discovery of a new anti-rejection drug called cyclosporine. The new substance was much more effective than the immunosuppressive methods, such as radiation or drug combinations, used so far. With its use survival rates increased dramatically and living conditions of transplanted patients improved considerably. For example, Randle writes that 'the chance of survival was 18% in patients with liver transplant who did not receive cyclosporine and 68% in those who did' (Randle 2008: 10). Although it did not solve the entire problem of rejection, cyclosporine was in Calne's words 'a watershed in the development of transplantation'. Indeed, while today 'the biology of graft rejection is still only partly understood' (Calne 2006) and 'the large majority of organ transplant recipients … continue to require lifelong immunosuppression' (Hirose and Griffin 2008: 13), life expectancy and the quality of life have grown to the point that transplantation has become a normal medical activity in many countries.[11]

But while it made possible the treatment of patients who were suffering from desperate conditions, the passage of transplantation from the stage of research to that of therapy had as a consequence a new problem: the so-called *shortage* of human organs. Immediately after the conceptual and immunological revolutions of the 1960s and 1970s, the mismatch between the demand for organs and the supply of organs became the principal obstacle the field had to overcome. Waiting lists and waiting time grew longer, which for some patients meant the prolongation of their suffering, for others death.[12] Transplantation medicine remains dependent on donation rates and procurement policies. The alternatives to human organs that are currently being explored remain for the time being theoretical. The most

10 For a presentation of the historical and current discussions see Youngner et al. (1999) and Hennette-Vauchez and Nowenstein (2009).

11 For instance, 3,632 transplants of organs were performed in France in 2002 (Etablissement français des Greffes 2003).

12 In France 98 patients in the liver waiting list and 109 in the kidney list died in 2002 (Etablissement français des Greffes 2003).

promising of these is said to be stem cell research. However, beyond the ethical issues it is said to raise, stem cell research remains exploratory. For the processes and signals that make a stem cell become a specialized cell – and thus a group of cells become an organ – are not yet fully understood (Matesanz 2006).

Organ Procurement as a Policy Matter

Systems of Consent to Organ Donation

While the brain death revolution had made the retrieval of organs from the heart-beating-dead possible, it did not answer the question under what conditions organs could be extracted from such bodies. Legislators everywhere rejected the idea that the state could dispose of organs after death as well as the establishment of markets for organs. Instead, legislation was built around the idea that the availability of this new therapeutic material had to originate in an act of generosity (Machado 1998; Price 2000).[13] Thus 'the *miracle* of transplantation'[14] could only be fed by gifts.

Who was to consent to the *gift of life*? What form should the expression of consent take? While all living individuals are potentially cadaveric donors, it is only after having been declared (brain) dead that the possibility of donation becomes real. But a dead person can no longer give consent to anything.[15] If consent is to be given by the person whose organs will be taken, it has to be consent *ex ante*, when the person is still alive. If not, can someone else consent on the behalf of the deceased, or can the deceased's consent be inferred for or presumed?

Under the donation paradigm, legislators in different countries have chosen between systems of presumed and express consent, also known as opting-out and opting-in systems. In a sense both systems presume the wishes of the deceased, for each has a default position. Presumed consent systems consider that those who have not explicitly withheld consent are willing to donate their organs; express consent systems consider that those who have not explicitly given consent do not

13 The donation paradigm is breaking down nowadays in the face of the problem of *shortage* (Healy 2006: 3–17). The legitimacy and number of voices making a claim for the introduction of economic incentives or for a switch to the market paradigm have significantly increased (Becker 1997; Radcliffe-Richards et al. 1998; Erin and Harris 2003). For a critical view of this approach by an economist see (Frey 1997).

14 This expression is taken from the title of a recent book about transplantation by Rafael Matesanz, head of the Spanish transplantation authority and 'father' of the Spanish success in organ procurement (Matesanz 2006). But the theme of transplantation as an enchanted field is not new and as early as in 1972 Parsons, Fox and Lidz wrote an article about the aura of enchantment that surrounded the activity (Parsons et al. 1972). See also Fox and Swazey (1992: 197–210).

15 Sociologist Paterson nicely grasps this idea in the title of an article about organ donation in France: 'Solliciter l'inconcevable ou le consentement des morts' (Paterson 1997).

wish to do so (Schneider 1999). Nevertheless opting-out systems are generally thought to involve a presumption about the wishes of the deceased while opting-in systems do not. Lying behind this asymmetric interpretation of silence is the idea that the default or natural option for most individuals is not to donate. However all this may be, both systems are today accepted as ethical by most official health organizations.[16]

The Existing Debate about Systems of Consent

Although the two consent systems are more or less equally distributed around the countries that have legally regulated organ procurement, a rather strong consensus exists in the literature and in policy discussions to the effect that opting-out systems are more efficient in generating organs for transplantation (Nowenstein 2004). This is the reason why, for several decades, the main criticism of presumed consent systems has been ethical, with authors arguing that it is not just to infer consent to organ donation from silence (Kluge 2000; Calabresi 1991). Underlying the discourse in favour of opting-out legislation we usually find the belief in the possibility of producing social change via legal innovation (Moore 1978: 54). In turn this belief rests on an 'instrumentalist' theory about the relationship between law and practice (Griffiths 1979) and a 'rational-central rule approach in public affairs' (van Gunsteren 1976), involving the assumption that there is a causal and direct link between law and practice.[17]

Although consensus about the superiority of opting-out systems remains dominant, the tone since the 1990s has become less certain (Roels et al. 1990; Roels et al. 1991; Michielsen 1996; Nowenstein 2004). Interestingly, it is in countries with a long history of presumed consent legislation and medium or high donation

16 The World Health Organisation published a report in 1991 which stated, 'Organs may be removed from the bodies of deceased persons for the purpose of transplantation if: (a) any consents required by law are obtained; and (b) there is no reason to believe that the deceased person objected to such removal, in the absence of any formal consent given during the person's lifetime' (WHO 1991). See also the Council of Europe 'Additional Protocol to the Convention on Human Rights and Biomedicine, on Transplantation of Organs and Tissues of Human Origin', article 17: 'The removal shall not be carried out if the deceased person had objected to it' (Council of Europe 2002. Available at: http://conventions.coe.int/Treaty/EN/Treaties/Html/186.htm [accessed: May 2010]).

17 Van Gunsteren (1976: iii) defines the 'rational-central-rule approach in public affairs' as follows: 'Rulers try to cope with public problems by searching for general and rational solutions that are based on the findings and methods of modern science. For the implementation of their policies they rely on regulations, obedient organizations and people, and if necessary on force. The generation and implementation of rational policies are managed by one or a few centres of decision-making and steering.' Interestingly, the author concludes that this mode of regulation cannot work in practice for it departs from assumptions about a simplified and easily controllable social life. In that sense, this approach actually 'tries to circumvent politics' (van Gusteren 1976: 151).

rates such as France or Spain that one finds the more sceptical discourse and where policy discussions focus on other non-legal factors. By contrast, in countries such as the Netherlands and the UK, with opting-in systems and low donation rates, discussions in the public arena still frequently focus on the desirability of adopting this type of legislation, such as in a 2005 public statement by the British Medical Association advocating the adoption of presumed consent legislation by the British government:

> Despite the acknowledged difficulties of obtaining meaningful data about the success of presumed consent in other countries, the BMA [British Medical Association] believes that, as one part of a broader strategy, a shift to presumed consent is likely to have a positive effect on donation rates. (British Medical Association 2007)[18]

Faith in presumed consent legislation has weakened in the sense that it is now often accepted that focusing just on the law is not enough, and non-legal factors have hence gained importance in the discussions of the factors that influence variations in procurement rates. The well engrained belief nonetheless remains, in the form of a sort of intuition, that presumed consent legislation is a better option and thus, that legislators and policymakers should opt for or confirm this option. The following quotation from an article, published in *The Lancet* in 1998 by a prestigious multidisciplinary team of physicians and researchers in social sciences and law, illustrates how support for opting-out systems ultimately rests on an assumed and unverified connection between procurement rates and consent legislation. The authors, after having acknowledged that a set of non-legal variables – mainly organizational and informational – influence organ procurement rates, assert the superiority of presumed consent systems, and back their statement with the observation that the world's top procurement rates come from countries with

18 In November 2008 the UK Organ Donation Taskforce published a report entitled *The Potential Impact of an Opt Out System for Organ Donation in the UK*. As far as I am aware, it was the first time that a state institution issued an opinion so clearly sceptical about the effects that a change of legislation would entail in the UK. For that reason this report marks a turning point in the official discourse in the country. It reads: '… the more the Taskforce examined the evidence, the less obvious the benefit, and the more multifaceted and multidimensional the issue of increasing donor numbers was revealed to be. It became clear that what appears to be a simple idea to increase numbers may not in fact generate additional donors in sufficient numbers to justify the significant investment needed to put a new system in place' (Organ Donation Taskforce 2008: 34). The report caused an unusually strong negative reaction among institutional actors such as the Prime Minister, the Chief Medical Officer and the British Medical Association. See for instance in *The Guardian*, 'Taskforce opposes "presumed consent" for organ donors', available at: http://www.guardian.co.uk/society/2008/nov/18/organ-donation-health1, and 'Chief Medical Officer condemns organ donor decision', available at: http://www.guardian.co.uk/society/2008/nov/16/organ-donation-reforms (both accessed: December 2008).

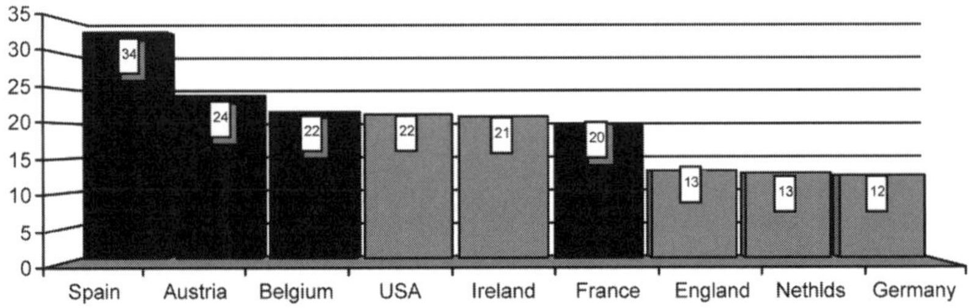

Figure 1.1 Donors per million population in 2002: Presumed and express consent systems

Note: Countries with presumed consent systems appear in black, countries with express consent systems in grey.

opting-out legislation: 'In three western countries there is evidence that changing to a contracting out system resulted in an increase in organs – Spain, Austria, and Belgium …' (Kennedy et al. 1998).

Figure 1.1, in which the number of donors per million population and systems of consent are put together, shows how obvious the idea that consent legislation is a fundamental independent variable in explaining differences in procurement rates can appear at first sight.[19]

However obvious the interpretation of such a graph has often seemed, the fact is that there is no empirical basis for the conclusion that there is a causal relationship between a legal donation regime and organ donation rates. As soon as one starts paying attention to the specificities of each country, it becomes difficult to establish any general pattern proving the superiority of presumed consent systems. We can illustrate this by taking the first three countries in the figure, Austria, Belgium and Spain, which are countries generally evoked in the literature as proof of the superiority of opting-out systems.

Austria has for a long time been hailed as the country with the strictest application of opting-out legislation, and its good procurement rates as the proof of its efficiency.[20] But as early as 1990 two prominent figures in the Austrian transplantation and procurement fields wrote in the *The Lancet* that the importance of opting-out legislation in their country had been overstated, and that Austria's good results do not coincide chronologically with the passing of presumed consent legislation.[21] Paul Michielsen, one of the few authors who has regularly

19 From Nowenstein (2004).

20 Machado (1998) and Price (2000) give accounts of this iterative reference to Austria.

21 'The "presumed consent" law and the high rate of fatal accidents in Austria are not the only explanations for this success because both conditions have been present since 1982 while the current trend did not set in until 1986. Furthermore … our rates are much higher than those reported from other countries with an opting-out law' (Gnant and Muhlbacher 1990: 479).

tried to figure out whether a relation between procurement rates and consent legislation can be established, has also noted the chronological non-coincidence in Austria between law and results. He attributes greater importance to a process of decentralization that took place in the early 1980s (Michielsen 1996).

Another case often referred to in the literature as evidence of the superiority of presumed consent systems is Belgium. It is interesting to follow the writings about the Belgian case diachronically, as one finds a clear evolution between the first attempts to evaluate the relation between opting-out legislation and procurement rates and the more recent ones. After rather naïve views based on the assumption that there was a clear link between increasing procurement rates in Belgium and the opting-out law passed in 1988, more complex analyses emerged in the 1990s (Roels et al. 1990; Roels et al. 1991).

In 1996 Michielsen noted a parallelism between the Austrian and the Belgian successes, and questioned also for Belgium the centrality he had himself attributed to the legislative variable in his previous work (Michielsen 1996). As in Austria, he wrote, decentralization played a key role in increasing organ procurement rates in Belgium in that it strongly motivated the hospital professionals in charge of organ retrieval decisions by enhancing their feelings of responsibility and autonomy. This lead him to displace the legislative variable in his analysis from a central position to being one among a set of conditions that make good procurement results possible. He argued that presumed consent legislation contributed to the creation of a normative context favourable to the procurement of organs. More precisely, together with a policy of decentralization, it contributed to enhance the feelings of legitimacy among professionals in charge of procurement, who regard the various changes as signals of the import of their action for medicine, public health and society as a whole. Michielsen's argument seems plausible, yet, as often with arguments about the symbolic effects of legislation, the absence of empirical evidence makes it difficult to confirm or reject the idea.

It seems, from the small amount of literature available about Austria and Belgium, that in neither country is the legislation of presumed consent applied, or at least not in a systematic way. However, the fact that other variables explain the good Austrian and Belgian rates does not invalidate the hypothesis that, if applied, presumed consent legislation would result in good donation rates. Spain seems to be the ultimate exemplar case to turn to. This country has a history of three decades of presumed consent legislation and has by far the highest procurement rates in the world, with the lowest refusal rates ever registered. Indeed, the number of donors per million population in Spain has moved from 14.3 in 1989 to 34.3 in 2007 (Matesanz 2008: 23). Most countries considered to be doing quite well register much lower rates, like France (25 donors pmp) or Ireland (21 donors pmp) (Newsletter Transplant 2008). If it were proved that the Spanish opting-out law has had a positive influence on procurement rates, the hypothetical superiority of opting-out systems would receive empirical support.

In the Spanish case, as in the Belgian and Austrian cases, a diachronic approach shows that there is no automatic connection between the enactment of presumed consent legislation and an increasing procurement rate. Indeed, while the Spanish legislation goes back to 1979,[22] the Spanish success story only starts in 1989, after patient associations attempted to call the attention of the general population and of health authorities to the dramatic situation of dialysed patients awaiting transplantation (Matesanz 2006: 40–45; Matesanz 1997). After years of stability with low rates, the number of donors per million population started regularly to grow: 14.3 in 1989, 20.2 in 1991, 27.0 in 1995, 34.3 in 2007.[23] This impressive record became visible more than ten years after the presumed consent legislation was enacted, at the time when the Organización Nacional de Trasplantes (ONT) (National Transplantation Agency) came into operation.[24] But one could still argue that it is likely that it was only then that the presumed consent law started being applied, thus launching the Spanish success story.

The writings of Spanish physicians and transplantation authorities emphasize that that law has never been applied in Spanish hospitals. Already in 1995, when the Spanish success was well under way but had not yet attracted international attention, the general director of the Organización Nacional de Trasplantes, Rafael Matesanz, wrote that, as a rule, relatives of potential donors were consulted in Spain and asked to give consent: 'All organs for transplantation are obtained after informed consent has been obtained from the relatives' (Matesanz et al. 1995: 1404). He developed the argument a few years later in a Spanish nephrology journal:

> There are many countries trying to increase organ donation … and [there] are many discussions about 'presumed consent' or 'opting out' laws.
>
> In 1989, when the ONT was created, there were many people in Spain who believed that the main solution to solving the problem of organ shortage was to … apply a strict presumed consent law. However, we found little evidence to suggest that the style of legislation influences the organ donor because regardless of how the donor might become available, relatives are always consulted, as in most European countries, and their wishes are always respected. (Matesanz 2001: 59)

Again in 2002 two important actors in the Spanish procurement and transplantation spheres insisted on the erroneous interpretation of the Spanish case dominant in international discussions. They wrote that the 'universal' belief that legislation is the key factor when it comes to evaluate organ procurement rates is simply wrong. This is proved, they argued, by the Spanish situation, where the existing legal

---

22 Ley 30/1979, de 27 de octubre, sobre extracción y trasplante de órganos, art. 5.

23 See: http://www.ont.es/estadisticas/graficas/Donantes20072.JPG (accessed: October 2008).

24 The ONT was created on paper in 1980 but was not endowed with a physical infrastructure and personnel until 1989.

presumption of consent is not applied and relatives have always been asked to participate in decisions of organ retrieval (López Navidad and Caballero 2002: 10). In a more recent book published in 2006 Matesanz refers to the request for organ donation as a request for 'family consent' and as a 'request for permission' made to the family to take the organs. He adds, concerning the role of relatives in these decisions, that it is illusory to believe that 'social reality' can be changed 'by legislative *coup*' [a golpe de ley] (Matesanz 2006: 40, 43–4).[25]

After rejecting the notion that consent legislation explains the Spanish success, the Spanish authors point to a set of organizational, structural and communicational factors. Credit is given to the first two for one of the main successes of the system, namely, that the number of unreported cases of potential donors is very limited, by contrast with the situation in most other countries. In this sense, the Spanish donor pool can be said to have been pretty close to its maximum for a long time. However, this does not explain why the rate of opposition to organ retrieval is, by far, the lowest in the world, which has been roughly 20 per cent for years (and dropped to 16.8 per cent in 2007).[26] In comparison, France's refusal rate has been stable for decades at roughly 30 per cent.

These authors attribute the low rate of refusals in Spain to the way in which the professionals in charge of the donation decision, known as transplant coordinators, deal with the relatives of potential donors. They put at the core of the so-called Spanish model their training and action and not legislation on consent (López Navidad and Caballero 2002; Matesanz 2001; 2006; 2008). Empirical research I am currently conducting in Spain confirms that presumed consent is not and has never been applied in practice and that the family is treated in effect as the active donor. For example, discussion with family members often develops around the idea that by agreeing to organ donation they enter a solidarity network from which they may benefit in the future.

The Spanish case being taken internationally as a model, how should we interpret the fact that the law is not mobilized in practice? Does the non-application of presumed consent legislation in Spain mean that it would not work elsewhere? If, on the other hand, it had successfully been applied, could we conclude that it would also work elsewhere? Posing these questions in such a way rests on

25 In a recent interview with the author, Matesanz confirmed that written authorization by the relatives was very early on integrated in Spanish protocols, among other reasons because some judges who were asked to authorize organ extraction conditioned authorization on the presentation of a document signed by the family agreeing to organ retrieval, notwithstanding the law of presumed consent (a judge must authorize organ retrieval in cases when there is a judicial investigation about the death of the potential donor) (see Ley 30/1979, de 27 de octubre, sobre extracción y trasplante de órganos, art. 5-3, and Real Decreto 2070/1999, de 30 de diciembre, por el que se regulan las actividades de obtención y utilización clínica de órganos humanos y la coordinación territorial en materia de donación y trasplante de órganos y tejidos, art. 10-5).

26 See: http://www.ont.es/Estadistica?accion=3&id_estadistica=78&posicion=10 (accessed: May 2009).

assumptions that are theoretically wrong and empirically unfounded. First, it treats the legal variable as crucial for the success of procurement systems.[27] The problem with this approach is that the route from law to practice is, generally speaking, all but straightforward and depends on a complex set of factors which may have very little to do with the law (Goodin and Tilly 2006: 3–32). The second wrong assumption is that the variables that explain procurement levels in one country will explain it in others, ignoring the importance of *ceteris paribus*.

Such approaches ignore the importance of normative pluralism (Griffiths 2003): the specific situation that a given law aims to regulate is usually already subject to pre-existing (non-legal) rules and structured around relations of power that are not necessarily based on legal legitimacy. Which rules become dominant depends on the social organization of a specific situation. This is why, in order to answer the question whether consent legislation influences donation rates, one needs to understand the specific characteristics of the 'social field' that is the object of regulation (Moore 1973). In the field of organ donation for transplantation, this implies paying attention both to the characteristics of transplantation and intensive care medicine (many of which can be said to be transnational within wealthy Western countries), and to the degree of autonomy of hospital professionals *vis-à-vis* state authorities and of authority *vis-à-vis* patients and relatives of patients. An important theoretical consequence of this approach is that, because different social fields have different relationships to the state and state authorities on the one hand, and to other social institutions and actors that may impose non-legal normative requirements on the other, one and the same law will not necessarily produce the same results in different social fields.

To say that the relationship between law and practice is neither simple nor straightforward does not imply rejecting the project of producing some general conclusions. The point is that such general conclusions can only be reached from a bottom-up, detailed study of the shop-floor, namely 'that concrete social situation where the social action and interaction that are the subject of regulation take place' (Griffiths 2003: 19). With regard to the international comparisons about organ procurement, general conclusions can certainly be drawn, but only after a sound model has been constructed on the basis of what happens in hospital practice and on how the participants react to situations where decisions to retrieve organs from deceased potential donors are taken.

France as a Case Study

When I began my research for this book, no data allowing the design of a sound comparative project existed. Thus the study presented in this book is a one-case study conducted with an inductive, explorative and qualitative approach (Becker

---

27 It is this assumption that leads some authors either to stress the superiority of opting-out systems or to conclude that they have failed and to call for legal change (i.e. establishing market systems or systems of compensation for donors or their relatives).

1996). However, the historical depth of the study covering the French case since the 1970s is itself a way of producing a comparison (Ragin 2000), for it allows exploring the aims and fate of presumed consent legislation in historically different socio-political contexts.

The general hypothesis that inspired the beginning of this study is that the legal regulation of consent cannot be assumed to be an independent variable when it comes to understanding regional and historical variations in procurement rates. This implies that the analysis needs to go beyond the legal frame to encompass macro and micro contexts that include the general discussions in the public arena, health policy and the specific situation where organ retrieval decisions are taken in hospitals. I chose France for this study because it has the oldest presumed consent legislation in Europe and because – by contrast with Spain, which has an almost equally long history of opting-out legislation – its effectiveness has been an issue of public and legislative discussion over the last few decades.

Enacted for the first time in 1976, presumed consent began in the 1990s to be presented in the media as a failed attempt by legislators and health authorities to modify donation behaviour by law; in other words, as a failure in socio-legal engineering. Such failure was said to cause the death of hundreds of patients every year.[28] Although non-application of the law was presented in the media as an established fact, no research had in fact been done to establish it.[29] The first empirical aim of this study, therefore, was to verify the assumption.

The second and most important aim was to understand what had happened and was happening to presumed consent legislation, from its drafting in parliament to its (non)application in hospitals. From the start the more 'mundane'[30] hypotheses that might explain the failure of presumed consent legislation in France were quickly discarded. The first of these hypotheses is the lack of means, both material and human, to proceed with organ retrieval operations. If this were the case, the problem would be anterior to that of the application of presumed consent legislation and would concern the very possibility of the French health system affording organ procurement activities. The fact is that the scarcity of means explains only occasional decisions not to proceed with organ retrieval and is not a structural bridle to procurement activities either for the past or for the present.

---

28 In 2000 more than 300 patients died in France on the waiting lists for transplantation (Benoît 2000: 265).

29 The written press was the media that was evoking the issue in more depth and with more regularity (Nowenstein 1999).

30 Becker (1996) writes about the need for the sociologist not to neglect 'mundane' reasons of social actors when it comes to understanding social practice. He mentions the example of a student who studied the reasons why Kansas City letter carriers preferred to work on certain roots and neighbourhoods rather than on others. A series of theoretically loaded hypotheses centred on class and race were elaborated to answer this question. Yet the student found that the most important factor for letter carriers was that in a hilly city such as Kansas City they preferred to work in flat neighbourhoods.

The second mundane hypothesis is professionals' misinformation or lack of information about the law presuming the consent of the dead with regard to organ donation. Theoretically relevant (Aubert 1967; Griffiths 2003; van Tol 2005), this hypothesis is also logically deduced from surveys conducted since the 1980s that have regularly shown that the population was mostly ignorant of the existence of the law. According to polls a significant part of the general population indeed believes that the law is one of express consent; and/or one that leaves the donation decision to relatives, especially when the wishes of the deceased are not known. A question included in a survey in 1997 illustrates this point (see Table 1.1) (Carvais and Hermitte 2000: 845).[31]

Table 1.1 Question from a 1997 survey

If the deceased has not expressed his will before her death…	
The law understands that he has agreed to the removal	14.0%
The law understands that he objects to the removal	15.1%
The law understands that the relatives decide	67.2%
Does not know	3.7%

Could it be that medical professionals were misinformed or wrong about their role as set out in the law? Information gathered during the research for this book invalidates this hypothesis and shows that professionals in charge of these situations were in the past most of the time knowledgeable about the law, and are today very precisely informed about its existence and content – many informants actually quoted the text by heart.

The most obvious and simple hypotheses having been discarded, research about the fate of the law presuming the consent of the dead in France requires that one looks at various levels of discourse and practice: the level of discussion, elaboration and adoption of legal regulations, and the level of practice in the social situation where organ retrieval takes place. Furthermore, the methodology to be followed requires looking at the spheres of the production of legal regulation and of social practice in a diachronic and dynamic way, not as two parallel spheres or from a linear – top-down or bottom-up – perspective.

31 Previous surveys had shown the same absence of knowledge about the legal frame given by French lawmakers to cadaveric organ donation. Paterson (1997: 55) refers to two surveys, one from 1987, the other from 1993, where the great majority of respondents were ignorant of the existence of the presumed consent device and thought retrieval was only possible if authorization had been expressed by the donor while alive and/or given by her family after her death. See also the survey conducted by the Conseil Économique et Social, *Les droits de la personne malade*, 1996 (quoted in Hennette-Vauchez 2004: 291).

This book also seeks to change the character of the question that is now central in the literature about consent systems and procurement rates. It intends to show that organ donation decisions are not usefully analysed as straightforward answers to the questions: 'Was the deceased an organ donor?' or 'Do you wish to donate the organs of your relative?' or 'Are people more or less generous?' Decisions to donate and retrieve, as this study will demonstrate, are the result of interaction between hospital personnel and a group of persons confronted with the unexpected and tragic loss of someone they loved and with the failures and limits of biomedicine. In this setting, the relatives' family history, and their pre-existing relation to the state, to public health institutions and to health professionals will play a crucial role. Sometimes, the views of the deceased about organ donation will be brought into the picture and lead to a decision that reflects these views. But usually it is a family's views concerning donation, how each member of the family responds to the announcement of death and how the members of a family relate to each other, that are really important.

Note on Methods and Data

The material gathered for this research includes:

- *Contextual, legal and policy data*: a search of the most important French newspapers between 1986 and 2005; parliamentary reports and debates and legal regulations concerning organ donation for transplantation between 1975 and 2004; directives of the Etablissement français des Greffes (French Transplantation Agency); interviews and meetings with members of the management team of Etablissement français des Greffes.
- *Data from and about the shop-floor*: research on the shop-floor was conducted in the Parisian Region, which encompasses Paris and its surroundings. This region is characterized by a high concentration of easily accessible hospitals. It included 30 centres registered by the Etablissement français des Greffes as 'retrieval centres' [centres préleveurs].

Exploratory semi-directive interviews were conducted in the autumn of 2000 with hospital directors of ten of these centres, in order to see whether hospital management teams (i) were aware of the legislation concerning presumed consent, (ii) expected hospital professionals to apply it, and (iii) exhibited an interventionist approach toward controlling physicians' and nurses' retrieval decisions at the local level. It quickly became clear that hospital directors knew about the presumed consent legislation but had little insight into actual practice in their institutions. Their role seemed to be limited generally to encouraging or discouraging retrieval and donation activity in their centres. They did not expect that professionals would make use of the presumption of consent and seemed to think that physicians and nurses in charge of the process were likely to know how best to manage specific situations. Although these interviews are not analysed in this book, they were useful in terms of triangulation of information and confirmed that the most interesting actors to focus on are the nurses and physicians directly involved with procurement activities.

Ethnographic observation seemed at the beginning to be a good way of obtaining information relevant to the questions raised in this research, especially taking into account the insufficiency of existing data as a point of departure for a survey by questionnaire. Ultimately, however, the possibility of direct observation was rejected. Although 30 centres were registered by the Etablissement français des Greffes as retrieval centres in the Parisian Region, when these centres were contacted it appeared that only 14 were actively retrieving organs. Most of these did not have more than five or ten cases per year. One of the centres visited regularly during the research period had about 40–50 cases per year. On average this means about 3–4 situations per month, but the arrival of patients who become potential donors is very irregular. At the end of December 2003, for example, the centre stated that there had not been a single case for weeks; two months later, things had changed and they had received several cases in a few weeks. The irregularity and infrequency of relevant situations made the observation of cases essentially impossible within a reasonable time.

Another potential obstacle to observing encounters with relatives of brain-dead potential donors was related to the particular features of the situation. Some professionals within the selected units would refuse to allow a researcher to be present in their encounters with relatives. There was also the possibility that families would object to my presence. Furthermore, was it actually ethically acceptable to impose the presence of an outsider on families going through such a process of intense grief? Was it justifiable to disturb them before the meeting and ask them to let me in as a 'scientific' witness of their sorrow? One of the physicians interviewed suggested that I should simply put on a white coat and introduce myself as a member of the staff in meetings I wanted to observe. Apart from the fact that no other professionals suggested this, the ethics of such an approach are questionable.

Such considerations led me to reject ethnographic observation. While the choice may have been wise and justified, there may have been another reason for taking it that was not apparent at the time: I probably just did not feel like being present. A combination of diffidence and a fear of not being able to cope emotionally with such situations may explain the decision. While it may be true that a sociologist should go everywhere and look at everything related to her research topic, the fact is that at this stage of the research I may have run up against personal limitations. However all this may be, even if observation would have rendered the study more complete, it was not indispensable. The data presented in this book made it possible to get to the points that were to be explored and much further.

Having rejected direct observation the options were a survey and/or interviews. Because of the absence of data mentioned above, a questionnaire or structured interviews were not feasible without first conducting more in-depth interviews. The decision was made to conduct semi-structured interviews and to limit them to hospital professionals because some research had already been conducted with relatives and very little was known about those in charge of procurement and who formally have the power of imposing the presumption of consent upon relatives. Last but not least, this group of professionals was limited in size, which made it feasible to contact a substantial part of the relevant population.

Thus interviews were conducted with nurses and physicians of the Parisian Region. The physicians contacted were those registered with the Etablissement français des Greffes as 'referent physicians' [médecins référents] of their units. They were all 'anesthésistes-réanimateurs' (French hospital specialists in resuscitation and anaesthesiology), working in units of 'anesthésie-réanimation'. This specialization is very close to the one generally known in English as 'intensive care', with the addition that in France most 'réanimateurs' are also anaesthesiologists. To facilitate reading, units of 'anesthésie-réanimation' will henceforth be referred to as 'intensive care units' and physicians working there as 'intensivists'. Each hospital authorized to retrieve organs must have one referent physician. Referent physicians are in charge of the activity of donation and retrieval in collaboration with one or several hospital coordinators. Hospital coordinators are most often intensive care nurses.

The referent physicians and hospital coordinators of the 30 hospitals registered by the Etablissement français des Greffes as having received authorization to retrieve in the Parisian Region were contacted by letter in the autumn of 2000. Sixteen replied noting that their activity was either nonexistent or very limited – one or two cases per year, sometimes none. Amongst the remaining 14 centres, only one did not reply. Thus 13 centres of different sizes were visited, both academic and non-academic hospitals, with big and small intensive care units. The main difference among them was the number of cases of potential donors they received per year. Two had less than five cases per year, four between six and ten, four between 11 and 20, two had 30 cases, and one 55 cases. The rates of refusal of donation oscillated around the national average of 30 per cent. Twenty-five interviews were conducted, 13 with hospital coordinators and 12 with referent physicians; 12 of the interviewees were female and 13 male. Because the field of hospital coordinators and referent physicians in the Parisian Region is quite small, in order to preserve anonymity all will be referred to as *she*. The average length of interviews was 75 minutes (from 54 to 110 minutes). Among the 25 interviewees there were 10 'tandems', namely a hospital coordinator and a referent physician who worked together in the same hospital. Because the interviews were conducted separately, this was very useful for verifying the information each of them was giving.

For the interviews, a guide was used covering the topics upon which interviewees were requested to elaborate. Only the first three questions were pre-formulated, and they generally served to launch a fluid discourse on the part of interviewees. Apart from these initial questions, interviewees were given a free rein to touch upon the different topics covered by the guide. This they generally did, with of course some variations of order.

Occasionally I adopted a less passive role in order to encourage interviewees to elaborate upon points of special interest. Generally my approach was not directive until about three quarters of the way through an interview, when I had the impression that the most substantial part of the interviewees' 'natural' way of presenting the situation had emerged. At that stage I steered the discussion onto issues which had not yet been dealt with sufficiently or apparent contradictions in what had been said. Confronting interviewees in this way with some contradictions or logical knots in their discourse and gently challenging them can be fruitful and not necessarily artificial. Interviews in general stimulate self-reflexion (Attias-Donfut et al. 2002: 18–19). In particular, being interviewed about their role in organ procurement proved a strong stimulus to self-reflexivity for those involved. Moreover, such situations are exceptional enough, both in quantity and in content, to imply the breaking of routine in intensive care units (Machado 1998). Breaks of routine produce cognitive disruption and are enhancers of self-reflection for those confronted by them. Last but not least, it should be noted that, the professionals interviewed are under considerable external pressure and criticism, since health authorities, the media and transplantation surgeons regularly reiterate the need to improve the efficiency of the system in order to collect more organs.

Although interviews constitute the main source of information about the shop-floor of organ donation decision making, attempts have been made to overcome the limitations inherent in this choice by engaging with more diverse sources of information and initiating broader contact with the actors in the field. After all the interviews had been conducted and codified, a national questionnaire survey was conducted in 2002 with French hospital coordinators (Nowenstein and Podyma 2003). All hospital coordinators registered with the Association Française des Coordinateurs Hospitaliers (450 nurses) received a questionnaire, to which 28 per cent responded. The questionnaire included closed and open-ended questions about years of experience, working conditions, motivation, training; about the reasons to decide or not to retrieve; and about the role of the law in these decisions. The results of the survey are only occasionally invoked in what follows because the interview material is usually more telling. Nevertheless, the survey results are present in the background, confirming and thus giving more weight to the conclusions drawn from the interviews. It is not only that the content of the answers given to the questionnaire coincide with what was learnt from the interviewees, but that the way these answers are expressed echoes the way those interviewed expressed themselves.

All the information thus generated has been complemented with the published results of other research, regular contact with other researchers about their work in progress, mail and phone exchanges with privileged informants, visits to intensive care units, conversations *in situ* with professionals, and attendance at several professional and informative events: the Journées annuelles de l'Etablissement français des Greffes in Paris in November 2000; the Journées annuelles de l'Etablissement français des Greffes and the European Transplantation Coordinators annual meeting in Lyons in November 2002; the Journées de formation de l'Association Française des Coordonnateurs Hospitaliers in June 2004; the National Donation Day (21 June) in 2002 and 2004, in two hospitals.

Like the survey, these contacts and observations confirm the validity of the information obtained from the interviews. They also enriched and stimulated reflections upon the research as a whole. During the course of the project (2000–2005) informants have often surprised me, above all because their beliefs and opinions were not fixed but evolved with increased experience, as a response to the evolution of the public debate or to policy changes, or in light of personal experiences with the practice of organ donation and retrieval.

What about the *general* value of data thus produced? They inform us about the views of those in charge of the processes of donation and retrieval, those who have the formal possibility of applying the legal presumption of consent. Theirs is but a partial view of the situation, which could only be complete if complemented with information from the other actors involved, mainly the relatives of potential donors. It can be argued that the partiality of such an approach is not necessarily problematic. It is even argued that, for a researcher to understand and transmit the reasons for the action of a group of actors properly, it is necessary to look at the situation under study from their partial perspective (Goffman 1961: 8). Furthermore, whereas an ideal study would have included the views of relatives confronted by the situations of brain death and organ donation, in order to answer the specific questions posed in this research, professionals are the key actors on which to focus. It is their (non)application of the presumed consent law that largely determines the effectiveness in practice. And while relatives will hopefully be confronted only once in their lifetime with such a situation, professionals prepare for it in advance and confront it as a regular part of their work. Thus they are, in the area of organ procurement, the agents of continuity, and of accumulation of knowledge and experience.

This book is thus the result of the exploration and analysis of diverse data about a specific topic: the regulation of organ donation in France since the 1970s. Each type of data used has its limitations. All together, however, they afford a rich picture of organ procurement in France, one that can take its place in the wider mosaic of sociological research.[32]

32 On qualitative research as an accumulative mosaic see Becker (1958).

Chapter 2
Law as a Tool for Enhancing Social Change: From Faith to Disenchantment

This chapter traces the legislative history of presumed consent legislation in France and presents the main topics around which discussion of the relation between law and organ procurement was structured in the public sphere. It thus confronts the uneasy question of the motivations and intentions of the legislators who drafted, discussed, modified and eventually enacted the various pieces of legislation that regulate organ procurement in France. This is a difficult and uncertain task, for some it may even be irrelevant. Griffiths writes that 'In the theory of the social working of law it is not the intention of the legislator but the shop floor of social life that is at stage center' (Griffiths 2003: 18). However, if like Griffiths one is interested in understanding rule-following behaviour, the (supposed) intentions of legislators can be an important part of the complex process that gives shape to practice on the shop-floor. Thus, informants for this study often refer to the motivations and expectations of legislators in their description and explanation of everyday practice.[1] Actually, Griffiths acknowledges that the values or principles reflected in a given law are part of the set of factors that might shape the effect that a law may have in practice (Griffiths 2005: 152). These values and principles are usually not given by the letter of the law but are the result of interpretation in the light of parliamentary debates and reports as well as contemporaneous and subsequent public discussion of the legislation. If only for this reason it is important to begin this study with some legislative history of presumed consent in France.

The process by which a legal rule is enacted can also be relevant for understanding its degree of legitimacy within its field of application: is the law the result of a process in which actors in the social field concerned were involved or do they see it as an external imposition (Hertogh 2005)? Another reason for not neglecting the legislative process of elaboration of a law and the intentions of the legislators involved is that these can be useful in understanding the statutory or policy measures taken by authorities after the enactment of the law. For example, the fact that a law is not enacted with the expectation that it will be applied in practice may explain the later absence of consistent implementation policy and hence the absence of direct effects of the law on shop-floor practice.[2]

1 These are also a reference in the discourse of French legal scholars and judges who write about or judge cases regarding organ procurement.

2 Castel (1988) nicely illustrates this possibility in his study about the regulation of madness in France in the nineteenth century.

Legislation is a complex social fact: it is both law in the books as well as the result of social and political practice (Foucault 1979). Each new law results from formal and informal processes of which only some aspects leave traces in texts or otherwise. The world of the motivations and expectations of those involved will always remain at least partly impenetrable (Commaille 1994). But the *true* motivations of each legislator are only of secondary importance for the type of research presented here. What counts, instead, are the intentions of legislators as they exist in documents, in the public arena or in the minds of the participants on the shop-floor, here of those who participate in organ retrieval situations.

The French case is particularly rich in such data. This is true not only because of France's long history of presumed consent legislation but because French legislators have drafted, discussed and enacted legislation on the subject three times over a period of 30 years. The following sections present first the reasons that were used to justify the drafting and enactment of the first version of the law in 1976, before moving to those that surrounded the two legislative confirmations in 1994 and 2004.

1976–Early 1990s: The Law as a Tool for Social Change

The 'Need' for Legislation

In 1976 Senator Caillavet, with the support of the Minister of Health, presented a bill in parliament concerning the regulation of organ donation for transplantation.[3] The bill contained five articles of which number two presumed the consent of the dead to organ donation. A general opinion that the development of transplantation medicine would become important for individual well-being and the public good appears clearly in parliamentary material from the 1970s. This development was presented as blocked by the mismatch between the demand for and the availability of organs. In other words, a 'shortage' [pénurie] of raw material was preventing the revolutionary new practice from bringing progress to French society. The shortage was principally attributed to opposition from the relatives of brain-dead potential donors (BDPDs hereafter) to organ retrieval, with an opposition rate estimated at 30 per cent of potential cases.[4] It was argued that although physicians were not obliged by law to consult the relatives of potential donors, many of them in fact

3 The French parliament includes the National Assembly [Assemblée Nationale] and the Senate [Sénat]. Bills pass from one to the other, where they are examined and discussed in parliamentary committees [commissions] and/or in open sessions in the chambers. The text about organ donation was discussed in committees in both chambers.

4 Sénat, Rapport n° 58, Annexe au procès-verbal de la séance du 16 novembre 1976, fait par M. Auburtin. This estimation was completely unreliable if one considers the high heterogeneity of behaviour in hospitals at the time: there were units where relatives were not even informed that organ retrieval had taken place (see Chapter 3).

did so. In fact, a decree dating from 1947 could be interpreted as allowing the retrieval of organs for transplantation without the authorization of the deceased or her relatives:

> … in hospitals included in a list drawn up by the Ministry of Public Health … if the chief doctor of the unit considers necessary for scientific or medical reasons, the autopsy or the removal may be carried out at once, even without the authorization of the relatives ….[5]

However, it was argued that a decree was too weak a legal basis to give physicians the necessary reassurance.[6] As Senator Auburtin, author of one of the reports that played an important role in the discussion, observed: 'some doctors have become used to asking for the consent of the relatives and today it is difficult for them to be able to abandon this practice, which they adopted *probably because they felt insufficiently protected by a legal instrument that is merely regulatory*.'[7] A law, he concluded, would reduce physicians' hesitations in their dealings with relatives. Moreover, the applicability of the 1947 decree to the situation of transplantation medicine was questioned, since it had been issued to facilitate the practice of post-mortem examination, not transplantation (Thouvenin 1997). A law specifically made for organ transplantation would clarify the situation and thereby contribute to the development of transplantation medicine.

The belief that an opting-out law would increase the number of organs available for transplantation is made clear in the following quotation from a speech by Senator Auburtin (note his use of the future tense):

> It is true that this domain, more than any other, must be legally regulated. This is precisely the purpose of article 2 [about presumed consent] that is before you and that will make it possible to overcome a real obstacle to the increasing number of renal transplantations ….[8]

A few days after Senator Auburtin is even more explicit and concrete about what he expected the law to achieve:

5 Décret n° 47-2057 du 20 octobre 1947.

6 The hierarchy of legal texts in France is, in growing importance: *circulaire*, *arrêté*, *décret*, *loi*. The government publishes *décrets* to explain how it expects a law to be applied. In an *arrêté*, a minister gives more precise information about a *décret*; and in a *circulaire* instructions about the application of a *décret* or *arrêté*.

7 Sénat, Rapport n° 58, Annexe au procès-verbal de la séance du 16 novembre 1976, fait par M. Auburtin: 9. Italics added.

8 Sénat, Rapport n° 58, Annexe au procès-verbal de la séance du 16 novembre 1976, fait par M. Auburtin: 9.

> If, as we expect, this law is approved, we will have at our disposal the necessary number of organs, and that's not simply 330, it will probably be possible to carry out between 1,000 and 1,100 transplantations every year.[9]

The same certainty is present in the concluding remarks of a report signed by deputy Delaneau:

> … we ought to consider the positive contribution of this law, which is certain to make it possible during the next years to give back a real quality of life to thousands of people who currently survive miserably and in anguish.[10]

The bill drafted by senator Caillavet was examined in parliamentary committees with the strong and enthusiastic support of the participants to the discussions. Parliamentary enthusiasm was based on the supposed promise of transplantation medicine coupled with the general belief in the effects the law would have in practice.[11] Eventually the text that would become known as the 'Caillavet law' was enacted. Article 2 reads:

> Organs may be removed for medical or scientific [autopsy] purposes from the corpse of a person who has not objected to the removal during his lifetime.
>
> However, if the corpse is of a minor or an incapacitated person, removal for transplant may not be carried out without prior authorization of his legal representative.[12]

---

9 Sénat, séance du 18 novembre 1976, Journal Officiel: 3316.

10 Assemblée Nationale, Rapport n° 2654 fait au nom de la commission des affaires culturelles, familiales et sociales sur la proposition de loi, adoptée par le Sénat, relative aux greffes d'organes. Par M. Delaneau, député, Distribué le 7 décembre 1976 pour la séance du 8.

11 Sénat, Rapport n° 58, Annexe au procès-verbal de la séance du 16 novembre 1976, fait par M. Auburtin: 3. The tone of these quotes seems in retrospect astonishingly enthusiastic, when one bears in mind that transplantation was, at the time, still very much a research activity: a promising technique which had so far produced encouraging but very uncertain results (see Chapter 1).

12 Loi n° 76-1181 du 22 décembre 1976, article 2. The law contained four other articles: articles 1 and 4 regulated consent to living donation; article 3 forbade the remuneration of donation; article 4 stipulated that a decree by the Conseil d'Etat should determine the formalities for living donation, the modalities for the expression of refusal or consent to cadaveric donation, the conditions hospitals must meet to be allowed to retrieve organs for transplantation and the procedure for establishing a diagnosis of brain death; article 5 stated that the new law did not modify the formalities or the donation and retrieval of corneas regulated by a law of 1949 (Loi n° 49-480 du 7 juillet 1949) specifying that a written authorization was required for the retrieval of corneas from cadavers. This specific provision for corneas was removed from the law in 1994.

The Power of the Law

Support for the bill was not completely uncritical with respect to the implications of the presumption of consent for the relationship of the individual to the community and to the state. It was thus admitted that the community had no indisputable 'right' over corpses, that express individual consent was the best way to protect individual dignity against a possible violation of physical integrity and that presuming the consent of the dead to organ donation conflicted with this idea.[13] But since no one doubted that the law would have the effect of increasing the number of organs available for transplantation, the device of presumed consent was thought to be justified by the triple contribution to progress it was expected to make: improving public health, enhancing medical and scientific development, putting solidarity and reason at the core of the relationship among French citizens.

The contribution of this law to progress was thus assumed to go beyond medical and scientific development. Because of its *rational* inspiration the law itself was a contribution to socio-political progress. *Rational* thinking appears in the parliamentary material as opposed to remnants of obscurantism, depicted as the combination of popular resistance to scientific progress and an attachment to old and irrational conceptions of the body–personhood relationship. These *irrational* representations were presented as a source of the shortage of organs. Senator Caillavet expressly based his law on a dualistic perception of the body–personhood relationship. Such a dualistic view was justified, it was argued, not only by a rational and materialistic approach, but also by the Christian tradition where body and soul are distinct entities. Both approaches were said to share a view of the corpse as meaningless and valueless for the dead person and the next of kin.[14] Caillavet combined such dualism with a utilitarian approach to the contribution that individuals can make to the well-being of their fellow citizens after their death, and with a belief in policy/law as a tool to enhance scientific, medical and social progress.

Sharing his approach, deputies and senators supporting the initiative argued that refusing to donate organs after death was not only *irrational*, it was also morally wrong, for it meant denying to others whose life depended on it something that was useless for oneself. Senator Caillavet returned before a parliamentary committee in 2001 to the ideas that had inspired him in 1976. He qualified the connection between organs and personhood as a 'stupidity' unfortunately still widespread among the general population and added that this was precisely what he had tried to fight with

13 Sénat, Documents, 1975–76, proposition de loi n° 436, enregistrée à la présidence du Sénat le 18 juillet 1976. None of the previous law drafts on organ donation submitted to the French parliament (in 1967, 1974 and 1975) included presumed consent proposals. They required express consent and/or empowered families of potential donors to decide. For instance, article 9 of the Proposition de loi n° 2080 (1975), 'De la liberté', stated that 'no element from the human body could be retrieved without the agreement of the person or, if the person has deceased, without the authorization of the family'.

14 Sénat, proposition de loi n° 436; Sénat, séance du 18 novembre 1976.

his opting-out law. In 1976 Caillavet stressed that the law 'constitutes a testimony of fraternity towards the rest of mankind'.[15] Enacting the law was therefore a gesture of 'moral value'. Or, as a member of the Senate put it: 'If this text is necessary from the perspective of human life, it is even more so for the dignity of parliament.'[16]

Concluding the session where the final draft was adopted, Simone Veil, Minister of Health, praised the legislators for their consensus behind such a 'delicate' issue:

> Before this debate closes, I would like to underline that, in relation to such a delicate subject, which has philosophical, moral or for some even religious implications, no opposition has been raised during the discussions. Indeed, it is with unanimity that this bill has been approved by the National Assembly … [as it] previously had been by the Senate ….[17]

It is true that the law had elicited little discussion or modification when examined by parliamentary committees.[18] More specifically, article 2 about presumed consent remained unmodified from the beginning to the end of the parliamentary process, and its form and content were barely discussed. Legal scholar Hennette-Vauchez finds this absence of substantial discussion 'astonishing' since, she notes, the presumption of consent at the core of the Caillavet law implied the subversion of principles that had traditionally regulated the fate of corpses in France (Hennette-Vauchez 2001: 212–13). It is true that there was no consistent discussion about the legal principles at stake and only a few shy attempts to raise the matter at all. When this occurred, discussion was cut short by reference to the pragmatic necessity of solving the problem of organ shortage and the *fact* that presumed consent was the means to reach that end. Senator Caillavet, for example, acknowledged that the presumption of consent is not consistent with the principles of autonomy and integrity of the person – extended to the corpse – but in one breath dismissed the problem by invoking the possibility of drastically reducing the shortage of organs. He saw a:

> [dilemma between] the protection of the physical integrity of the corpse of the deceased and the possibility of saving one or several other individuals through the transplantations of organs removed from his corpse. [The] argument [based on the right of individuals to decide on the fate of their corpses] – which would result in a considerable reduction of the scope of available transplants, since such organs could not legally be used – is today rejected almost unanimously by all those who have objectively looked into the problem ….[19]

15 Sénat, séance du 18 novembre 1976, Journal Officiel: 3321.

16 Sénat, séance du 18 novembre 1976, Journal Officiel: 3318.

17 Sénat, séance du 14 décembre 1976, Journal Officiel: 4474.

18 Modifications concerned donation among living persons. Sénat, séance du 14 décembre 1976, Journal Officiel: 4474.

19 Sénat, Documents, 1975–76, proposition de loi n° 436.

Thus he concluded, 'It is the right of the living that must prevail over that of the dead.'[20]

Another illustration of the weight of the utilitarian argument of public health against the argument of respect for individual autonomy can be found in the discussion about the convenience of including autopsies under the umbrella of the principle of presumed consent.[21] Deputy Foyer suggested for example that such an extension was going too far and could be misunderstood by public opinion. While in his view the public could be expected to understand and accept the necessity of presuming the consent of the dead for therapeutic aims, the case for autopsies was less obvious. Indeed, he stressed, the adoption of an opting-out system implied an almost 'revolutionary' shift in French law with regard to the protection of the integrity of the dead body, only acceptable as a direct means to save lives.[22] His reasoning was at once rejected by the Minister of Health, who argued that the extension of the presumption of consent to autopsies was justified because these were indispensable for increasing epidemiological knowledge and thereby for the improvement of public health. This ended the discussion and the article remained unchanged.

In the same session another deputy observed that presumed consent infringed on the right of relatives to decide on the fate of the corpse of a loved one. Yet he did not ask for a modification of the text and added that he would actually vote in favour of the bill because it was bringing a solution to the problem of organ shortage:

> In spite of the violation of the liberty of the relatives to dispose as they wish of the remains of a loved one, and despite regrets that the idea of free donation should be abandoned, I shall vote in favour of this bill since it offers a solution to the problem of organ transplantation.[23]

In short, legislative consensus on the suitability of an opting-out system flowed from the combination of two beliefs: further development of the practice of organ transplantation was socially important and a law presuming the generosity of the dead would have the effect of increasing the number of organs available for transplantation. Thus it was not in the first place the presumption of consent as such that was defended in the French parliament but the promise it brought of the development of organ transplantation. Presumed consent being the best means to enhance transplantation, opposition to it was not rationally justified. French legislators also denied any legitimacy to religious or 'spiritual' opposition to organ donation – and *thus* to opting-out legislation:

---

20 Sénat, Documents, 1975–76, proposition de loi n° 436.

21 Article 2 read: 'Organs may be removed for medical or *scientific* [autopsy] purposes from the corpse of a person who has not objected to the removal during his lifetime.'

22 Assemblée nationale, séance du 8 décembre 1976, Journal Officiel: 9095.

23 Assemblée nationale, séance du 8 décembre 1976, Journal Officiel: 9091.

> After looking at the problem from a technical point of view, let us consider the moral perspective, the religious perspective … Why should it matter to the materialists, who believe that along with their human existence concludes once and for all their earthly transit, who do not have the refuge of an afterlife, that after their death their organs should be removed to bring life to someone else? …
>
> For the spiritualists, only the soul is immortal and, on Ash Wednesday, every year the Christian is reminded that, being dust unto dust he shall return.[24]

To reassure the Catholic who might have had doubts about the presumption of consent, reference was made to a text from 1956 by Pope Pius XII on cornea transplantation, which was quoted: 'to consent expressly or tacitly to serious violations of the integrity of the corpse in the interest of those who suffer does not contravene the respect owed to the deceased, if there are valuable reasons for doing so.' Caillavet referred to Pius XII's use of the adverb 'tacitly' to justify the presumption of consent: 'The word "tacitly", employed by the Sovereign Pontiff, clearly demonstrates his intention not to require an express declaration of consent of the deceased or of his family for the organ transplantation to be possible.'[25]

The Minister of Health for her part concluded that the bill had a high moral legitimacy since 'prominent persons in the medical and religious worlds' had concluded that it departed from 'no moral rule'.[26] The ethics of organ donation was thus seen as an 'objective' matter that could be settled by 'authoritative' pronouncements.[27]

Having thus dealt with the 'moral' and 'rational' opposition to presumed consent, the remaining arguments against it were said to be a matter of psychology and sensitivity. Such subjective considerations could not stand against another ideological pillar of the presumed consent law: a duty of solidarity. As Caillavet recalled in an interview in 1992, the law was based on the principle that individuals have duties towards their fellow citizens: 'The human being has, indisputably, a moral dimension. Consequently, he may not shirk his responsibility when the time comes to help his neighbour.'[28]

Nevertheless, the French legislator did not carry this idea to its perhaps logical conclusion and dispense altogether with the idea of consent. Philosopher Dagognet, for whom the duty of solidarity in this area was more important than the right to individual autonomy, reproached senator Caillavet for not having gone far enough

---

24 Sénat, séance du 18 novembre 1976, Journal Officiel: 3316.

25 Sénat, Documents, 1975–76, proposition de loi n° 436.

26 Sénat, séance du 18 novembre 1976, Journal Officiel: 3320.

27 Sénat, Documents, 1975–76, proposition de loi n° 436.

28 'Présomption de consentement. La loi Caillavet. Un entretien avec son auteur', *Revue de la mutualité*, septembre, 148 (1992): 12–14: 12.

in that respect, namely not to have supported a right of disposal of corpses by the state (Dagognet 1990: 84–6).[29]

The system remained expressedly one of 'generosity' from which citizens could opt out. The implementation decree pursuant to the law, issued in 1978, specified: 'A person who intends to object to the removal [of organs] from his dead body may express his objection by any means.'[30] Hospitals authorized to retrieve organs were required to have a registry where opposition to donation could be made. But no centralized system for collating the information collected by these local registries was made. Thus a registered opposition could only be effective if an individual became a BDPD in the same hospital where she had registered her opposition. The decree also stated that information about an opposition to donation could be found among the personal belongings of the BDPD or from her relatives. In the *circulaire* of 3 April 1978 further developing on the decree of 31 March, although the relatives are referred to as 'usually' familiar with the wishes of the deceased and 'best placed' to 'discover' such wishes if these are not known, physicians are not encouraged, let alone obligated, to consult with them.[31] In effect, the burden was on relatives to take the initiative of informing hospital professionals about the BDPD's objection to removal and to prove the truthfulness of their contention.[32] It seems rather unlikely that relatives would realize from the announcement of the brain death of a loved one that her body had become a source of organs and that they should report her opposition to organ donation.

Thouvenin, a legal scholar, argues that contrary to the repeated statements by legislators and health authorities, the Caillavet law did not establish a donation system in which citizens would have been given the opportunity to decide whether to donate or not. In reality, she argues, it merely provided the conditions under which the retrieval of organs could legally take place in hospitals (Thouvenin 1997). It is true that both in the letter of the law and in parliamentary debates one finds more statements and discussions about refusals to donate than about organ donation as a positive act. The more the stress is put upon oppositions to donation and how irrational, un-generous or even immoral they are, the less the act of donation seems a virtuous, fully generous gesture.

---

29 Harris (1986) goes even further in a thought experiment based on the idea of 'compulsory sanctity'. He describes a system where according to transplantation needs a citizen would be chosen through a lottery to be a donor in order to save the lives of several patients awaiting transplantation.

30 Décret n° 78-501 du 31 mars 1978, article 8.

31 Circulaire du 3 avril 1978 concernant le décret n° 78-501 du 31 mars 1978 pris pour l'application de la loi n° 76-1181 du 22 décembre relative aux prélèvements d'organes.

32 'Toutes les personnes pouvant témoigner qu'une personne hospitalisée a fait connaître qu'elle s'opposait à un prélèvement sur son cadavre, en particulier les membres de sa famille et ses proches, consignent leurs témoignages assortis des justifications nécessaires dans le registre mentionné à l'alinéa précédent. Elles doivent notamment préciser le mode d'expression du refus, les circonstances dans lesquelles il a été exprimé et, le cas échéant, sa portée.' Décret n° 78-501 du 31 mars 1978 (article 9).

Thouvenin's argument corresponds with the anthropological theory of the gift and, as we will see in coming chapters, with hospital professionals' concept of a gift. From the anthropological Maussian perspective, while there is a moral-social obligation to give, receive and reciprocate, for a gift to be a gift, individuals or groups must have the feeling that they have the freedom to give or refuse to give, and to accept or refuse to receive. In other words, even though generosity is a social obligation, it must be perceived as free (Mauss 1985). The gift thus entails the acknowledgement in some form of the value of the act. The way in which the act of donation of organs after death was deemphasized in the French parliamentary discussion made of 'consent' to organ retrieval, at best, a morally obligatory rational renouncement of something valueless.

Last but not least, legislators' restrictive approach to organ donation was reinforced by a very limited conception of autonomy enjoyed by patients or relatives as against the sphere of discretion of the medical profession. The idea of autonomy in medical settings implies that the person concerned has the right to be informed about decisions regarding her body or that of an incapable relative, and not to be put under pressure by an expert or any other person in a position of authority. No such idea is to be found in the parliamentary discussions of the Caillavet law. The lack of a robust conception of autonomy may have contributed to the fact that no substantial critical analysis of the bill emerged. This, added to the argument that there is no good reason to oppose organ donation (Calabresi 1991: 17–18) and to the instrumentalist belief on the power of the law, left little space for counter-argument. The argument in favour of presumed consent legislation was also strengthened by the idea that emerges from parliamentary data that one of the legislators' functions in French society was to impose the right behaviours and beliefs upon the general population.

The Complementary Roles of Legislators and the General Population

Evoking the urgent need to solve the problem of organ shortage, the Minister of Health emphasized the importance of a parliamentary decision, since:

> It [is] the responsibility of parliament, as the qualified representative of the consciousness and opinion of the nation, to undertake such an initiative [passing the Caillavet bill] and to contribute in this way to this new form of generous solidarity.[33]

The idea of qualified representation belongs – it seems naturally – together with that of an unqualified general population. In spite of the apparently well-spread instrumental faith in the law, there was a shadow over the expected effectiveness of the legal mechanism of presumed consent: a fear of negative reactions from the population in general and from the relatives of potential donors in particular.

33 Assemblée Nationale, séance du 8 décembre 1976, Journal Officiel: 9091.

This fear rested upon a representation of the general population as irrational and morally disoriented. Actually, according to the Minister of Health, the delay of parliamentary consideration of a law on organ retrieval until 1976 was attributable to the idea that public opinion was not yet prepared to face the issue.[34] Attitudes towards corpses are not just dependent on the development of scientific and medical knowledge, she noted, but also on social factors that can adversely affect the reception of such a law by the general population:

> History and sociology show us that views regarding the body of the deceased have changed significantly over the ages and that they differ just as much depending on the country or even the religion.
>
> The question is therefore the following: is public opinion currently prepared to receive, with the appropriate serenity, the bill that is proposed to you and whose stance seems the only one compatible with the purpose that is sought, that is, to guarantee the treatment and often even the survival of the critically ill?[35]

By 1976, she observed, the needs of transplantation activity had increased to a point that enactment of such a law could no longer be postponed. Her warning was thus not intended to question whether the bill was opportune, but rather to identify a need to disseminate information about the benefits of 'this new form of generous solidarity'.[36] If the general population was probably not yet fully ready for presumed consent, she was of the view that it was now better prepared to accept this type of legislation than it could have been in the past, in particular thanks to the work that had been done by the media:

> Today the situation seems a little different. ... the broadcasting done by television, newspaper and radio of the technical progress accomplished by transplantation teams has allowed everyone to develop an awareness of the nature of the problem and of the solidarity that binds people together, even beyond death.[37]

The Minister's assumption – shared by most participants in the debate – is that social acceptance of the practice of transplantation is simply a matter of information and reflection, and that it leads automatically to the choice for an opting-out system. Nevertheless, the proposal by one deputy that the enactment of the new law should be accompanied by a large public information campaign was received with scepticism.[38] As another deputy argued: '... Many long years were

34 Assemblée Nationale, séance du 8 décembre 1976, Journal Officiel: 9091.

35 Simone Veil, Sénat, Séance du 18 novembre 1976, Journal Officiel: 3320.

36 Simone Veil, Sénat, Séance du 18 novembre 1976, Journal Officiel: 3320.

37 Assemblée Nationale, séance du 8 décembre 1976, Journal Officiel: 9091.

38 Deputy Honnet, in Assemblée nationale, Rapport n° 2654 fait par M. Delaneau, Annexe au procès verbal de la séance du 1 décembre 1976.

necessary for the campaigns in favour of blood donation to yield any substantial results ...'[39] Another deputy feared that such a campaign could have 'an opposite effect from that intended'.[40] This idea that a campaign informing the public about the existence of the presumed consent mechanism might lead to an increase in the level of formal or informal statements of opposition to donation has, in fact, been a constant concern expressed by legislators and transplantation authorities in France since 1976 (for the current discussion see Chapter 8).[41]

The general population, referred to as 'public opinion', 'the population' or 'the public', was depicted as archaically attached to traditional (that is, primitive and irrational) beliefs, as well as ignorant and hence afraid of science and progress. Although no data was invoked to illustrate or justify these ideas, these traits were presented as making it necessary for the legislative to give guidance on the relevant values and behaviour. The absence of data did not seem to trouble legislators involved in the legislative process, who appear to have assumed they *knew* the beliefs, fears and needs of the general population. This vision of political representation is reminiscent of that of political journalists in a semiological study conducted by Landowski in the late 1970s (Landowski 1980). According to this author journalists claimed to speak in the name of the public, even when revealing facts of which members of the public were said to be unaware, or which they were supposedly unable to articulate. Like members of parliament in the debate on organ procurement, journalists in the same period were so confident of their direct knowledge of public opinion, Landowski observes, that their assertions on its behalf were not shaken even by surveys that produced contradictory data.

'Public opinion' appears in parliamentary discourse as the 'phantom entity' described by Memmi in her analysis of public discussions about artificial reproduction in France in the 1980s (Memmi 1992). It was something to which constant references were made but that did not seem to exist as an active participant in public discussions; something fantasized as: 'a ghost population, ceaselessly evoked and forever absent, phantasmagorically seen as unhealthy and "dangerous" in its innocence ...' (Memmi 1992: 123).

39 Deputy Bolo, in Assemblée nationale, Rapport n° 2654 fait par M. Delaneau, Annexe au procès verbal de la séance du 1 décembre 1976.

40 Deputy Gau, in Assemblée nationale, Rapport n° 2654 fait par M. Delaneau, Annexe au procès verbal de la séance du 1 décembre 1976. Both arguments recall Hirschmann's classification of types of rhetoric arguments against reform: futility and jeopardy (Hirschmann 1991).

41 Paterson confirms that no information campaigns were organized by public authorities about organ donation or about the legal system of consent in the 1970s or 1980s (Paterson 1997). Public campaigns organized by health authorities became a reality only in the 1990s, after it appeared that the media could not only convey positive information about organ donation and transplantation, but were also a key vector in the spread of scandals that would for years soil the image of French public health institutions in general, and of transplantation and organ retrieval activities in particular.

Statements about the behaviour, fears and beliefs of the relatives of BDPDs and physicians appear to have been very much based on the views of professor Jean Hamburger, a pioneer kidney transplantation surgeon. He spoke as an expert with members of parliament about his experience with relatives and physicians involved in donation decisions. In the absence of surveys or any other type of systematic data about the beliefs and behaviour of the general population, this physician's personal – and quantitatively limited – experience with the relatives of potential donors was treated in parliament as general knowledge.

Hamburger's statements were invoked as the justification for not affording to the relatives of the BDPDs any active role in organ retrieval decisions. A potential donor's relatives, he claimed, are in such a deep state of emotional shock that they might recklessly refuse organ donation, and even regret their refusal later on. It was his advice to the legislators that for the good of the community, and that of the families concerned, this was to be avoided.[42] The best solution being hence to presume the consent of BDPDs. Actually, Hamburger's role in the legislative process went beyond that of expert witness. As Senator Caillavet recalled in 2001, Hamburger had asked him to write a law that would allow transplantation activity to take off by producing the necessary organs: 'He had told me: "Mister Caillavet, you are a brave man. Make us a law. We need organs to graft."'[43]

The fact that Hamburger was himself a transplantation pioneer with a special interest in obtaining organs seems not to have troubled legislators who relied heavily on his assertions. Similarly to the 'physician-investigator' or the 'research physician' described by Fox and Swazey in the United States, his image was that of a detached and objective professional (Fox and Swazey 2002: 87). In the eyes of legislators, he also appeared as knowledgeable and reasonable. All qualities required for channelling the beliefs and behaviour of ordinary citizens.

The law eventually enacted in 1976 would remain unchanged until 1994, when the presumption of consent was reconfirmed with some additions and modifications. What happened in practice between the late 1970s and the early 1990s will be described in the next chapter. Let us, for the time being, focus on the public and legislative discussions leading up to the 1994 law.

---

42 Sénat, Rapport n° 58 fait par M. Jean Auburtin, annexe au procès verbal de la séance du 16 novembre 1976: 10.

43 Senator Caillavet recalled this conversation in 2001 in front of a parliamentary commission. In Assemblée Nationale, Rapport n° 3208 du 10 juillet 2001, Audition de Henri Caillavet.

Losing Instrumental Faith

The Need for New Legislative Intervention

In the early 1990s the regulation of biomedical activities was a lively topic in the French public and parliamentary arenas. An ambitious legislative draft was discussed whose aim, it was said, was to produce a coherent regulatory scheme applicable to all biomedical activities. The so-called 'Bioethics Laws' were eventually enacted in 1994, at the end of a legislative process that had been partly inspired and partly accompanied by several scandals that exposed some cases of serious negligence within public health institutions.

The most important scandal broke out in 1991 and became known as the contaminated blood affair.[44] The government was accused of having delayed the systematic testing of blood donors for HIV in 1985 and of being thereby responsible for the infection of haemophilic patients. A minister and a secretary of state were accused of not having stopped the transfusions even though they knew that some patients had been infected and that others were being exposed to risk. Public authorities and physicians were accused of a complete lack of concern for the risks to which haemophilic patients had been exposed (Beaud 1999).

It was in such a political context that four other scandals specifically related to transplantation and procurement activities shed a negative light on the organization and regulation of this branch of biomedicine. The first of these was the so-called Amiens affair, which came to public attention in May 1992, and where the parents of a young man denounced what they thought had been abusive retrieval of their son's eyes after his death. The second and third concerned irregularities in procurement, allocation and transplantation of organs and were revealed by the press in 1992 and 1993. The fourth was known by the title of a TV documentary broadcast for the first time in 1993, 'Voleurs d'yeux' [Eye Thieves], which revealed the apparent existence of a system of criminal extraction and traffic of eyes in Colombia.

The Amiens affair The Amiens scandal broke out in May 1992, just a year after the blood scandal. A 19-year-old young man, hit by a car while cycling, was diagnosed brain dead soon after his arrival at the hospital. His parents claimed that they had had a meeting with a physician where they eventually agreed on the retrieval of the heart, the kidneys and the liver. Four months later they discovered that veins, arteries and eyes had also been taken from their son. They only learned of this accidentally in the course of the criminal proceedings against the driver who had fatally injured their son. They also learned that the incision in his chest made to retrieve the organs had been closed carelessly and with wire.

44 The scandal emerged in April 1991 when the weekly journal *L'Evénement du Jeudi* revealed the irregularities that had led, in the mid 1980s, to the infection of patients who had received blood transfusions contaminated with HIV (see Hermitte 1996).

The media reported the affair in an emotional and accusatory tone, the doctors being presented as having abused two generous and trustful parents.[45] The parents brought criminal charges for theft and 'violation de sépulture' [desecration of a grave]. In 1996 a court in Amiens held that there could be no theft of the human body because this cannot be the object of appropriation, and that desecration of the grave could not have occurred since the organs were taken before any funeral proceedings were undertaken (Hennette-Vauchez 2004: 294).[46] In December 2000 the administrative court of Amiens held that, since the person from whom the organs had been taken was an adult, the presumption of consent was applicable and the retrieval of organs thus licit. Yet, the court continued, this did not exempt the hospital from its 'duty to inform' the parents about the acts to which the body of their son had been submitted. As Hennette-Vauchez observes, it is on the basis of basic principles of medical ethics that the hospital was condemned by an administrative court, not on the enforcement of presumed consent legislation (Hennette-Vauchez 2004: 287).

Irregularities in organ procurement and allocation Two weeks after the Amiens affair came to public attention the press discovered a report from the General Inspectorate of Social Affairs [Inspection Générale des Affaires Sociales] (hereafter IGAS), responsible among other things for the control of health institutions with regard to legal regulations and the management of funds. The report accused surgical units in Paris of having given priority for transplantation to non-resident patients sent by colleagues from Italy. Not only did this entail bypassing the regular system of waiting lists, the report also revealed that the costly interventions had not been reimbursed by the Italian patients or their health insurance.[47]

45 *Le Monde*, 17–18/05/1992, 'La mort violée'; *Le Parisien*, 18/05/1992, 'Vol d'organes: Une famille accuse'; *Le Figaro*, 18/05/1992, 'Le respect des morts face à la médecine'; *L'Evénement du Jeudi*, 20/05/1992, 'Plus jamais ça!'; *Le Canard Enchaîné*, 20/05/1992, 'Dernières nouvelles du cannibalisme'; *L'Express*, 28/05/1992, 'Les voleurs de regard', etc. See also the book written by the father of the boy (Tesnière 1993), as well as his article (Tesnière 1996). The parents also had a website: http://www.geocities.com/alain_tesniere (no longer available).

46 Hennette-Vauchez (2004) notes that a new offence included in the new Criminal Code (of 1994) would perhaps have strengthened the charges, namely that of 'invasion of bodily integrity' [atteinte à l'intégrité corporelle].

47 See, for instance, *Libération*, 04/06/1992, 'Les greffes d'organe sous le scalpel de l'IGAS'; *Le Parisien*, 04/06/1992, 'Transparence pour la transplantation d'organes'; *Le Figaro*, 04/06/1992, 'Les critères ambigus des greffes d'organe'; *Le Monde*, 04/06/1992, 'Evoquant l'existence de "filières de recrutement" un rapport de l'IGAS dénonce la proportion élevée de greffes d'organes réalisées en France sur des malades étrangers'; *Le Monde*, 06/06/1992, 'Après le rapport de l'IGAS sur les transplantations, le débat est relancé sur la nationalité des greffés'; *Le Figaro*, 12/06/1992, 'La satisfaction de France-Transplant'.

A year later, in July 1993, the media discovered a new report by IGAS, which revealed new irregularities, particularly concerning the lack of control upon the diagnosis of brain death, kidney procurement and distribution systems in some Parisian hospitals.[48] This time the inspectors found that, in violation of the law, brain death certificates had been signed by physicians from a nephrology unit, directly interested in the organs of the person diagnosed as brain dead. The report also accused some kidney surgeons of having bent the rules of the waiting lists for reasons of favouritism. Moreover, it appeared that hospitals which did not have legal authorization were part of an informal network where kidneys were being transplanted. Last but not least, reminiscent of a key feature of the blood affair, the report accused France-Transplant,[49] hospital authorities and the Minister of Health of having had knowledge of all or some of these facts and of having closed their eyes to it.

The two reports exposed the lack of respect of renowned physicians and officials of the public health system for the law. Physicians in the transplantation field were seen to be acting to further personal interests rather than the public interest. Last but not least, France-Transplant appeared, at best, to be incapable of regulating an activity that had grown too big to be left to a private organization and, at worst, as a non-transparent group whose members had forgotten that they were meant to be at the service of the public. Publication of the contents of the two reports was the occasion for the government and most newspapers to call for a reform of the organ procurement and distribution system.

---

48 See for instance, *Le Canard Enchaîné*, 28/07/1993, 'La bataille du rein empoisonne le marché de la greffe d'organes'; *Le Parisien*, 29/07/1993, 'Greffes: pratiques édifiantes à Tenon'; *France Soir*, 29/07/1993, '30 reins greffés dans des services non agréés'; *Libération*, 29/07/1993, 'Les greffes peu conformes de l'hôpital Tenon'; *Le Figaro*, 29/07/1993, 'Pratiques "interdites"pour des greffes de rein'; *Le Monde*, 29/07/1993, 'Un spécialiste de néphrologie de l'hôpital Tenon est accusé de ne pas avoir respecté la loi sur les prélèvements d'organes'; *La Croix*, 30/07/1993, 'L'hôpital Tenon fait les frais d'un contrôle'; *L'Humanité*, 30/07/1993, 'Des greffes d'organes loin d'être au-dessus de tout soupçon'; *Le Figaro*, 30/07/1993, 'Greffes de rein à Tenon: l'Assistance publique s'explique'; *Le Monde*, 30/07/1993, 'Des mesures ont été prises à l'hôpital Tenon de Paris'.

49 France-Transplant was a non-profit organization created in 1969 by transplantation surgeons and to which the state had delegated the power to organize and control procurement and transplantation activities. Until these scandals broke out, France-Transplant seems to have enjoyed a positive image due both to the prestige of the new transplantation activity and to that of its founders, Professors Jean Dassuet, Christian and Jean Hamburger. Dassuet's research on immunology played a major role in the history of transplantation. He was awarded the Nobel Prize for medicine in 1980. Cabrol performed the first heart transplant in France. Hamburger was a world pioneer in nephrology and kidney transplantation. France-Transplant was in charge of the distribution and allocation of organs and tissues until 1996 when an official body, the Etablissement français des Greffes, assumed authority.

In this context transplantation appeared to be at a turning point marked by the end of the era of 'pioneers', where transplantation surgeons had exerted exclusive control over the just born activity of transplantation, and the beginning of a time where transplantation would become normalized medical practice.[50] The approval of a new law was presented as a way of accompanying a crisis of the growth of an activity that needed a transparent and fair legal and organizational frame. In the words of a journalist in *Le Figaro*:

> Just as some politician considered war too serious a matter to leave it to the military, one may also wonder whether transplantation is not too delicate a thing to remain within the exclusive control of doctors.[51]

Eye thieves While the topic of (international) organ traffic had been present in the media for some time, a new and particularly shocking case made organ transplantation seem a frightening source of evil behaviour. In 1993 a TV documentary told the story of a poor Colombian boy whose eyes were said to have been removed to be transplanted into wealthy patients. According to the documentary the boy had been taken to a Colombian hospital for intestinal troubles and had left the hospital eyeless. It was said that no information had been given to his mother, whose consent had not been sought and, above all, there was apparently no medical indication to justify the removal of the boy's eyes. Press articles were often illustrated with a shocking picture of the eyeless face of the boy. The documentary won a prestigious journalism prize (Prix Albert Londres).[52] Here is how an article from *Libération* reports on the beginning of the documentary:

> Put into hospital with acute diarrhoea, the child comes out blind. Enucleated. That happened to Jenson, a young Colombian from a shantytown, a few years ago. In the Bogota school where Marie-Monique Robin [name of the journalist] found him, the other children proclaim, almost with pride: 'Jenson, a doctor tore out his eyes. Maliciously.' They go look for the kid …. A local curiosity. The eyelids open up over two cavities, and at that precise moment we believe his story. The impossible becomes evident, the rumour is confirmed: this child's eyeballs have been removed to be sold to the 'rich' in need of corneas. Maybe even in France …?[53]

---

50 *Libération*, 04/08/1993, 'Les greffes d'organes victimes de la suspicion'.

51 *Le Figaro*, 21–22/08/1993, 'La crise de croissance des transplantations'.

52 See for instance *Le Monde*, 30/10/1993, 'Trafic d'organes et adoption'; *Le Monde*, 08/12/1993, 'L'Europe contre le marché des organes'. About the spread in France of rumours on organ traffic in the early 1990s see the report written by the sociologist Véronique Campion-Vincent (1996).

53 *Libération*, 08/12/1993, 'Trafic d'organes en Amérique latine'. See also *Le Monde*, 05/12/1993, 'Télévision Documentaire: Voleurs d'organes'.

About one and a half years after the release of the documentary, the press reported doubts about the veracity of the story.[54] The main question raised was whether the child had actually lost his eyes as the result of an infection. At this point, the boy and the specifics of his story faded into the background and the focus enlarged to organ traffic generally. It was presented as a general and scandalous problem and the tone remained tragic and outraged, with journalists elaborating on this ultramodern and cannibalistic form of exploitation practised on the bodies of the most vulnerable populations of the world. These closing remarks from an article in *Le Monde* are typical:

> Nobody seriously denies the existence of a horrifying underground market whose victims are the destitute populations of the underdeveloped countries. After gold, silver and precious stones; after petrol, coffee and cotton, will the search for organs become a modern variant of the pillage of the South by the North? Why should the children be spared, now that the lack of organs is so great?[55]

Consequences of scandals and rumours The scandal of little Jenson's eyes burst onto the scene at a time when other stories about organ retrieval and allocation were increasingly in the media, and rumours about organ traffic were flourishing. The sociologist Campion-Vincent and anthropologists Shepherd-Hughes and Cohen have done research into the actual existence of organ markets and rumours about them in France, South America and India (Campion-Vincent 1996; 2000; Shepherd-Hughes 1996; Cohen 1999). The two anthropologists tried to test the veracity of rumours, concluding that some of the Asian stories can be verified with more certainty than the South American ones. The existence of organ selling by living individuals in India appears to be proved (Das 2000), as well as the public organization of the use of executed Chinese prisoners as sources of organs (Human Rights Watch 1994; 1996; 2008; Amnesty International 2002; Charatan 2001).[56]

In France, social scientists, political actors and hospital professionals refer to such scandals and rumours as having considerably soiled the image of transplantation activities and health institutions, thereby causing an increase in

54 See for instance in *Libération*, 07/01/1995, 'Quand les yeux ont le prix des yeux'; *Le Monde*, 17/08/1995, 'Un reportage sur les greffes de cornée en Colombie suscite la polémique'; *Libération*, 26/09/1995, 'Suspension du prix Albert-Londres. La mesure vise le reportage "Voleurs d'organes", lauréat 1995'; *L'Humanité*, 20/08/1996, 'Les yeux des enfants d'Amérique'.

55 *Le Monde*, ??/04/1993, 'Un nouveau pillage du tiers-monde'.

56 French surgeon Jean-Michel Dubernard – head of the surgical team that performed the world's first hand-forehand transplantation – stated at the European Transplant Coordinators Organisation's annual conference in 2002 that Chinese surgeons had performed hand transplantation with limbs taken from executed prisoners. Jean-Michel Dubernard, presentation, 'Composite tissue procurement and graft: hand allograft: current situation', European Transplant Coordinators Organisation Annual Conference, Lyon, November 2002. Notes from fieldwork.

oppositions to donate among the general population and a lowering in donation rates. The idea seems plausible, since a decline in organ donation and procurement rates is noticeable immediately after the scandals became public during the first half of the 1990s, as Figure 2.1 shows.[57]

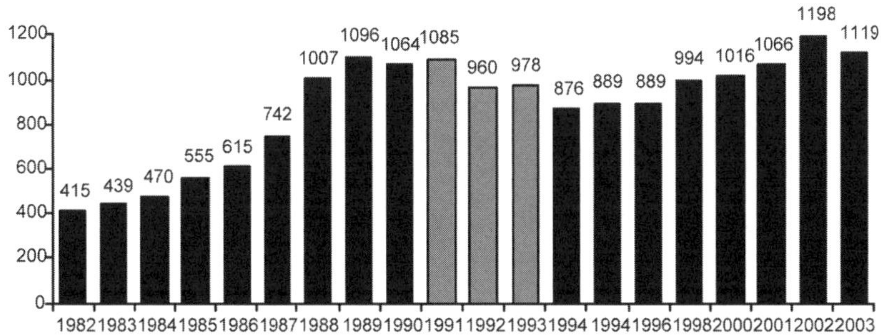

Figure 2.1 Organs extracted in France per year

Note: The years of the scandals are shown in grey.

Yet, as we will see in the next chapter, a deeper and more long-term process of normalization of procurement practice was taking place during these years, with relatives of potential donors being more systematically consulted about organ donation decisions. It therefore cannot be concluded that the general level of opposition to organ donation had increased (perhaps due to the scandals) since it may simply be that a broader space was being offered to relatives to express oppositions that had existed before but had basically not been heard. However, the increased inclusion of relatives in the decision process was certainly a response to the scandals and in that sense the lower level of retrieval may well be connected to the scandals (this point is discussed more fully in Chapter 3).

Neither the truthfulness of rumours about organ retrieval and traffic nor the effects these may have had on donation and procurement rates are of central importance here. What is for us important is that those having access to the public and legal arenas treated the relationship between scandals and increasing refusals to organ donation as a fact, and that belief in the existence of such a relationship seems to have influenced the modification of the mechanism of presumed consent that was ultimately included in the new law in 1994. An illustration of this influence is found in a report written by deputy Jean-François Mattei, author of one of the two parliamentary reports produced to inform the political and legislative discussion on the proposed legislation. He attributed the increase of the refusal rate between 1991 and 1992 to scandals and rumours, and stated that the

57 From Etablissement français des Greffes (2003; 2004).

parliament needed to address the situation with a legislative response.[58] He wrote in his report that the first aim of the law should be to 'restore confidence' among the French population. This required, he argued, increased transparency, a more precise and strict organization of transplantation practice and the development of a policy of public information. What Mattei was in fact proposing was to reduce the scope of self-regulation of procurement practice by the medical field in favour of increased state control.

The general impression that the discourse among public and elected authorities during this period leaves on the observer is one of a feeling of tragedy mixed with pragmatism: justifiably or not, mistrust had grown among the population, leading to a decrease in organ procurement rates that was causing the death of more patients. This view was at the core of many articles in the press during 1992 and 1993, with journalists depicting the situation in tragic terms.[59] The presumption of consent itself was not called into question, but it was conceded that the decision-making power of professionals and the right of potential donors and their relatives to refuse organ donation should be adjusted in favour of the latter. A journalist in *Le Figaro* writes:

> … the parliamentarians are aware of the urgency to 'clean up' ['toiletter'] the Caillavet Law, while maintaining the principle of presumed consent. The reduction of 10 to 12 per cent of donations, sometimes more in certain regions, is proof of the disquiet in public opinion, which demands greater transparency.[60]

The main objective of the legislative, as this appears in newspapers and parliamentary material, was, by making some adjustments in the law, to deal with the so-called 'reticence' of public opinion concerning organ donation, transplantation and hospital professionals. While the law of 1976 had been enacted with the explicit aim of changing beliefs and behaviour among the general population, the aim in the early 1990s was to deal with what had been feared in the 1970s: the power of resistance of the general population. A switch in the perception of the general population in public discourse is thus evident. From a passive entity upon which legislators thought they could act more or less at will, the general population comes to be seen as needing to be handled with caution, if only because of its power to endanger the optimal functioning of transplantation activities.

---

58 Rapport à Monsieur le Premier Ministre sur l'éthique biomédicale, 15 novembre 1993.

59 *Le Figaro*, 07/02/1992, 'Greffe et don d'organes, comment obtenir les greffons indispensables? Comment expliquer les "refus familiaux"?'; *Le Figaro*, 10/01/92, 'Greffes: ces enfants qui meurent de trop attendre'; *La Croix*, 14/01/92, 'Les limites du don de soi'.

60 *Le Figaro*, 23/04/1993, 'Bioéthique: la loi en panne. Elle ne sera pas examinée avant l'automne'.

1994–2004: Towards a Softer Approach

The 1994 Bioethics Laws

In 1994 the French parliament confirmed the presumption of consent in the Bioethics Laws. This is a set of three laws, one about the treatment of medical data;[61] one about the respect due to the human body;[62] and one about the donation and use of human body products and parts, medical assistance in procreation and prenatal diagnosis.[63] The stated aim of this set of laws was regulation that, integrated under a common set of principles, would constitute a coherent answer to the different issues raised by the use of biotechnologies in the medical sphere.

The third law, regulating organ donation for transplantation, included the principle of presumed consent. Leaving aside the modifications made to the device in the new law, to which we will come later, the most noticeable difference between the 1970s and 1990s is to be found in the tone of the discussions about law as an instrument of social change: where the tone had been assertive in the 1970s, voices had become shyer in the 1990s. Compared with the self-assurance of Caillavet and his fellow legislators, faith in the effectiveness of presumed consent has disappeared. Indeed the Minister of Social Affairs Jean Louis Bianco concluded his presentation of the bill in 1992 with a rather tepid statement in favour of maintaining the presumption:

> Concerning the removal of an organ from the deceased, it is proposed to maintain the system of presumed consent. This may give rise to discussion: for some, it does not allow enough space to the liberty to choose of the deceased, while others emphasise that its scope is, in reality, limited, in as much as the relatives and close friends can freely attest to the objection of the deceased.
>
> These remarks do not seem to require reconsideration of the 'Caillavet' Law, which, as it is, achieves a good balance.[64]

As this quote illustrates, while no real debate took place about the legitimacy of the principle of presumed consent, it was admitted more clearly than in 1976 that it could be opposed on moral grounds. Pragmatically, it was acknowledged

61 Loi n° 94-548 du 1 juillet 1994 relative au traitement des données nominatives ayant pour fin la recherche dans le domaine de la santé et modifiant la loi n° 78-17 du 6 janvier 1978 relative à l'informatique, aux fichiers et aux libertés.

62 Loi n° 94-653 du 29 juillet 1994 relative au respect du corps humain.

63 Loi n° 94-654 du 29 juillet 1994 relative au don et à l'utilisation des éléments et produits du corps humain, à l'assistance médicale à la procréation et au diagnostique prénatal.

64 Assemblée nationale, Rapport n° 2600 présenté le 25 mars 1992 par Jean Louis Bianco, Projet de loi relatif au don et à l'utilisation des éléments et produits du corps humain et à la procréation médicalement assistée, et modifiant le code de la santé publique.

that the state had failed at imposing it in practice. Reflecting this evolution of political judgement, the drafts around which discussions took place introduced two significant modifications: the creation of a centralized registry for refusals in order to facilitate the expression of individual choice and thereby to legitimate the use of the presumption of consent in non-registered cases; and the increased importance of relatives, who were made the most legitimate source of information after the potential donor herself (Thouvenin 1999; 2000; Carvais and Hermitte 2000).[65] These modifications were presented as a way of softening an otherwise too authoritarian approach to organ donation:

> Allowing … the relatives or close persons to attest to the opposition of the deceased is an appropriate measure to guarantee both the respect for the memory of the deceased and the acceptance by the public of the practice of removal.[66]

This approach was said to echo the orientation sketched in the decree and *circulaire* implementing the Caillavet law more than the strict letter of the law itself. Indeed, noted the Minister of Health Jacques Toubon, the decree, mentioning relatives as a source of information, 'says more than the law'. In order to strengthen the practice of systematic consultation of persons close to a potential donor, the substance of the decree must be included in the law.[67] Discussion about these points led to the bill being sent back and forth between the National Assembly and the Senate several times, as senators were reluctant to create a registry for refusals while several amendments to that effect were passed in the National Assembly.

As to the effect that the presumption of consent would have, expectations in the early 1990s had become more modest and legislators no longer seemed to believe the principle would be applied in hospitals. This disenchanted view was mainly justified by the necessity – rejected in the 1970s – to take the affective difficulties of relatives into consideration.

In the end, the legislators in 1994 enacted a longer and more complex text than in 1976. The presumption of consent was confirmed while at the same time being qualified by the addition of three elements (a fourth would come in 1997 with the publication of the decree of implementation of the law):

---

65 Assemblée nationale, Rapport n° 2600 présenté le 25 mars 1992 par Jean Louis Bianco, Projet de loi relatif au don et à l'utilisation des éléments et produits du corps humain et à la procréation médicalement assistée, et modifiant le code de la santé publique; Rapport fait au nom de la commission mixte paritaire chargée de proposer un texte sur les dispositions restant en discussion du projet de loi relatif au don et à l'utilisation des éléments et produits du corps humain, à l'assistance médicale à la procréation et au diagnostic prénatal, Jean-François Mattei, député, Jean Chérioux, sénateur, annexe au procès verbal de la séance du 9 juin 1994.

66 Assemblée nationale, Rapport n° 2600 présenté le 25 mars 1992 par Jean Louis Bianco, Projet de loi relatif au don et à l'utilisation des éléments et produits du corps humain et à la procréation médicalement assistée, et modifiant le code de la santé publique.

67 Assemblée Nationale, Débats, 1992, Séance du 24 novembre, intervention de M Jacques Toubon: 5947. Quoted in Hennette-Vauchez (2004: 290).

1. A registry of refusals (Registre National des Refus) intended to facilitate the use by citizens of their right to express their opposition to organ donation and, at the same time, to strengthen the donor status of those who have not explicitly opted out.
2. Explicit recognition of relatives as a vector of information about the wishes of BDPDs: in the absence of information about the wishes of a BDPD, physicians were obliged to 'seek' to consult family members about this.
   Article L. 671-7 thus reads:

   > The removal of organs from the deceased … may be carried out if the person concerned has not objected to removal during his lifetime.
   >
   > The objection may be recorded by registering it in the appropriate automated national register ….
   >
   > If the physician is not directly aware of the will of the deceased, he must seek to obtain the evidence [témoignage] from the family.

   The obligation to try to consult with the relatives requires that reasonable efforts be made but not that these are successful.[68] Once hospital professionals have obtained confirmation that the BDPD had not registered in the registry of refusals, and if relatives are not reachable, they can legally proceed with organ retrieval. While the 1997 decree implementing the law and an *arrêté* of 1998 remain rather vague about the meaning of the verb to seek [s'efforcer de], they include the following procedural requirements: professionals must establish a written procedure in order to gather the following elements: name, kin link, telephone number of the person or persons contacted as well as the time and the number of calls. This procedure should include the countersignature of a witness who may be a staff member of the health centre. Once all necessary measures have been taken, even if it has not been possible to contact any family members, the removal may legally take place.[69]
3. The decree of promulgation of the law published in 1997 required all hospitals involved in organ procurement to have a physician (referent physician) and at least one nurse (hospital coordinator) responsible for the control and coordination of all related activities. The new function of hospital coordinator was modelled on the practice in some centres where one professional (often a nurse) coordinated the retrieval process and was the person primarily responsible for the relatives. Today, most hospital coordinators participate

68 See Thouvenin's intervention in front of the parliamentary commission of re-evaluation of the 1994 law (Claeys and Huriet 1999).

69 Arrêté du 27 février 1998 portant homologation des règles de bonnes pratiques relatives au prélèvement d'organes à finalité thérapeutique sur personne décédée.

with physicians in the meeting with the family, and it is not uncommon that they are left alone with the relatives to raise the question of donation after the physician has announced and explained brain death.[70]

Actually, the first time the figure of the coordinator appeared in a legal text was in 1986, when a *circulaire*[71] recommended that every transplantation centre had a 'local coordinator' in charge of the administrative aspects of transplantation and of its promotion. At the end of the 1980s, there were little more than 20 such coordinators in France (Etablissement français des Greffes 2001: 19). In 1997, an *arrêté* from the Minister of Health gave a more detailed definition of the function of hospital coordinator:

> [Hospital coordination] refers to duties assigned to specific persons or groups in the hospital facility. These duties include in particular guaranteeing the proper support for family members and facilitating that removals be carried out in an appropriate manner.[72]

Hospital coordinators are responsible for organizing the process of organ retrieval from beginning to end. This includes the management of the arrival and departure of the transplantation teams, the control of the security procedures, verification that the last surgeon closes up the body of the donor in a 'decent' manner (art. L. 671-11)[73] and ensuring that surgeons do not take more organs or tissues than those donated by the BDPD.[74] Their most important task is to accompany relatives during the whole process and even thereafter: they are supposed to remain available to the family after the body has been returned.[75] Their role also includes the dissemination of information about donation, retrieval and transplantation both within and outside the hospital.[76]

70 In the national survey I conducted in 2002 with French hospital coordinators 49.6 per cent of respondents answered that they often did the interview with the families without a physician.

71 Circulaire du 14 mars 1986.

72 Arrêté du 1 avril 1997 portant homologation des règles de bonnes pratiques relatives au prélèvement des tissus et au recueil des résidus opératoires issus du corps humain utilisés à des fins thérapeutiques.

73 'Les médecins ayant procédé à un prélèvement sur une personne décédée sont tenus de s'assurer de la restauration décente de son corps.'

74 As the rest of this book shows, although there is no legal basis for this, hospital coordinators also check that any restrictions imposed by the relatives of a BDPD over the specific organs to be taken are respected (see Chapter 7 in particular).

75 Arrêté du 27 Février 1998 portant homologation des règles de bonnes pratiques relatives au prélèvement d'organes à finalité thérapeutique sur personne décédée.

76 Décret n° 97-306 du 1 Avril 1997 relatif aux conditions d'autorisation des établissements de santé effectuant des prélèvements d'organes et de tissus à des fins thérapeutiques et modifiant le code de la santé publique.

4. Transplantation teams must be excluded from retrieval decisions and have no contact with the relatives of BDPDs. This modification was a response to some cases that had been brought to the public sphere by the media, in which transplantation surgeons were accused by some relatives of BDPDs of having been disrespectfully insistent about obtaining organs (see for cases of these kind Waissmann 1996).[77]

Thus, unlike the law of 1976, which consisted of a short statement presuming the consent of BDPDs to organ donation, the law of 1994 was longer and more complex. It gave people the possibility of registering their opposition to organ donation in a national registry; it introduced the family, if not as an active participant in donation decisions, at least as a source of information whom hospital staff were required to try to contact; it made the relatives of BDPDs persons deserving special consideration and care; and it excluded transplantation surgeons from the decision processes concerning donation and retrieval.

Renewed Criticisms from the Legal Field

The 1994 modifications to the mechanism of presumed consent appeared in the press and in parliamentary discussions to be a response to public scandals and not to the criticisms voiced by some legal scholars of the 1976 law. Nevertheless, the new law does seem to have addressed some of this criticism. The presumption of consent had, for instance, been described as a 'nationalization of corpses', an 'expropriation of the human body', a 'collectivization of the human body', a 'kidnapping of organs'.[78] Some legal authors continued after 1994 to argue that the presumption of consent was an attempt to put corpses at the disposal of the state. The presumption of consent, it was argued, subverts the French legal tradition that since 1887 holds that an individual has the right to decide on the treatment her body will receive after death.[79] Another criticism was that while presumptions in French law traditionally benefit the person whose wishes are presumed, the presumption of consent to organ donation reverses this rule (Hennette-Vauchez 2004; Thouvenin 1997).[80]

77 Arrêté du 27 février 1998 portant homologation des règles de bonnes pratiques relatives au prélèvement d'organes à finalité thérapeutique sur personne décédée.

78 For a review of the legal criticism made of the presumption of consent see Hennette-Vauchez (2004).

79 See Hermitte (1993). This trend of legal criticism was prolonged after the vote of 1994 by Thouvenin (1997), Iacub (1998) and Hennette-Vauchez (2004). All these authors refer to the so-called 'Loi des funérailles' from 1887, insisting on the contradiction between the logic sustaining it and the presumption of consent to organ donation.

80 This criticism is based on the shared assumption that the opening of a corpse, the extraction of some of its parts and their spread in different bodies are not socially perceived as acts done in favour of the person who is presumed to be a donor. It would lose validity if the assumption were reverted. In other words, if it were assumed that citizens could

Last but not least, although the new law did give more room to individuals to have their wishes respected – by creating a clearer, and more secure, means to refuse organ donation – the idea that a donation can only be legally valid if based on the express will of the person concerned remains at the core of legal criticism. It is argued that while the vocabulary of the law is that of donation, what the law does is establish the conditions that allow the circulation of human organs and not the possibilities for individuals to donate their organs. For Thouvenin the ambiguity in the letter of the law is not the result of clumsy drafting but of the inability of legislators openly to accept the consequences of attempting to enhance organ procurement by limiting the sphere of individual autonomy. She concludes that a coherent text would either have established a community right to dispose of corpses in the general interest, or have protected individual autonomy by allowing people to give their consent to organ retrieval. The in-between solution of 1994 exposes, she argues, the fundamental difficulty of the presumed consent device, namely that it seems culturally impossible for the French 'society' to dissociate the body of a newly dead person from the person that has just died.[81] Thouvenin seems uncritically to assimilate French legislators to French society, but if one replaces *society* with *legislators*, her observation seems well taken.

The legal critics are not alone in noting the tension at the core of the law. Its supporters have occasionally observed that a rigorous application of the law would be socially disruptive. Even Caillavet, the father of the law of 1976 and a faithful supporter of the idea of presumed consent, conceded in 1992 in an interview that there would be something 'brutal' in the literal application of presumed consent legislation:

> There is …, in practice, a discrepancy between the will of the legislator and the practice of doctors … who, in the name of a certain morality, have shown themselves to be a little reluctant to apply [the law] in its entirety, I was about to say in all its brutality. (*Revue de la Mutualité* 1992)

2004: Disenchanted Continuity

Parliament confirmed the presumption of consent again in 2004. Article 21 of the law of 1994 regulating (among other things) organ donation provided that, because of the changing nature of biomedical technology, it should be re-examined within

consider it a waste that their organs were not taken just because they had not thought of notifying they wished to donate them while they were alive.

81 '… l'impossibilité pour notre société de se représenter le défunt comme un cadavre sans lien avec la personne qui l'avait jusqu'alors abritée' (Thouvenin 1997: 91–2). It is arguable that this ambiguity also derives from the difficulty of integrating the relatives of the BDPD into the equation, thus from the difficulty of thinking of the donor not as an isolated individual but as a member of a network of affective relations. This will be explored in the coming chapters.

five years. The process of re-examination began with the production of several reports and drafts of bills both within parliament and by other public institutions (Claeys and Huriet 1999; Conseil d'Etat 1999; Comité Consultatif National d'Ethique 2000; Commission Nationale Consultative des Droits de l'Homme 2000; 2001). Although the fact that the presumption of consent was not being applied in practice was acknowledged, the new law left the opting-out device of 1994 almost untouched. Two modifications were made that confirmed the turn taken in 1994 that consisted of maintaining the presumption of consent while facilitating the participation of close relatives of BDPDs as informants concerning the wishes of the latter. First, the group of people who are accepted as legitimate informants about the wishes of the deceased was broadened from 'family' members to 'close persons' [proches].[82] Second, the 2004 law obliges hospital professionals, whenever possible, to inform close persons about the purpose of organ retrieval and their right to be informed about the organs and tissues removed.[83]

The 2004 law is also innovative concerning information policy, including public acknowledgement of the value of acts of donation. The focus of this is on late teenagers and young adults, with general practitioners being expected to check that their patients between the age of 16 and 25 have received such information.[84] Citizens doing their 'national service' must also be given information about the practical details concerning consent to organ donation and about the registry of

82 The term 'proches' is difficult to translate. It refers to the group of persons who were the closest to the deceased. Most often it is used as a synonym for 'close relatives', but, legally speaking, it encompasses a broader group of persons than those related to the deceased by blood or marriage.

83 Loi n° 2004-800 du 6 août 2004 relative à la bioéthique, article 1232-1. The whole text reads:

> Le prélèvement d'organes sur une personne dont la mort a été dûment constatée ne peut être effectué qu'à des fins thérapeutiques ou scientifiques.
>
> Ce prélèvement peut être pratiqué dès lors que la personne n'a pas fait connaître, de son vivant, son refus d'un tel prélèvement. Ce refus peut-être exprimé par tout moyen, notamment par l'inscription sur un registre national automatisé prévu à cet effet. Il est révocable à tout moment.
>
> Si le médecin n'a pas directement connaissance de la volonté du défunt, il doit s'efforcer de recueillir auprès des proches l'opposition au don d'organes éventuellement exprimée de son vivant par le défunt, par tout moyen, et il les informe de la finalité des prélèvements.
>
> Les proches sont informés de leur droit à connaître les prélèvements effectués.

84 Loi n° 2004-800 du 6 août 2004 relative à la bioéthique, article 1211-3: '… Les médecins s'assurent que leurs patients âgés de seize à vingt-cinq ans sont informés des modalités de consentement au don d'organes à fins de greffe et, à défaut, leur délivrent individuellement cette information dès que possible.'

refusals.[85] The law also provides for the creation of special memorial areas in hospitals devoted to acknowledging and honouring the generosity of donors.[86]

The legislators involved in the process of re-examination of the law of 1994 could hardly close their eyes to the renewed criticism by legal scholars of the legal inconsistencies of the presumption of consent, as well as that of social scientists about its 'brutality' (Le Breton 1993; Waissmann 1996). Some participants in the discussions observed that the widespread non-application of the law was problematic, especially in connection with the (paralegal) role played in practice by relatives (Charles and Claeys 2001, tome II, auditions, vol. 3; Conseil d'Etat 1999; Commission Nationale Consultative des Droits de l'Homme 2000; 2001). Although this led some to call for the application of the law, such calls were systematically followed by the pragmatic acknowledgement that this would in practice be difficult, if not impossible. Actually, the fact that the law cannot be applied as written and that relatives play a central role in decisions to retrieve is accepted in parliamentary and other institutional reports as inevitable. For instance, a parliamentary report observes that opposition by the relatives explains two thirds of decisions not to proceed with organ retrieval in hospitals in the 1990s, the remaining third being due to opting out by the deceased or objections by a public prosecutor (Claeys and Huriet 1999).

*****

The history of French opting-out legislation given in this chapter is, despite the significant additions and modifications in 1994 and 2004, one of continuity. Such continuity is also apparent in the top-down approach to legislative processes and in the understanding of the situation to be regulated adopted by legislators. Indeed, although the legislators were better informed about practice than in the 1970s, the legislative process in 1994 and 2004 remained based on elitist assumptions about the relevant sources of information about practice in hospitals. This is particularly visible in the status of those who were called for hearings and provided the information in the various reports. Indeed, while it is true that compared to the 1970s, later legislative processes were somewhat more open to divergent views and sources of information,[87] the hospital coordination nurse, probably the most

85 Loi n° 2004-800 du 6 août 2004 relative à la bioéthique, article 10: 'Le deuxième alinéa de l'article L. 114-3 du code du service national est complété par une phrase ainsi rédigée: "Il est délivré une information sur les modalités de consentement au don d'organes à fins de greffe et sur la possibilité pour une personne d'inscrire son refus sur le registre national automatisé prévu à l'article L. 1232-1 du code de la santé publique."'

86 Loi n° 2004-800 du 6 août 2004 relative à la bioéthique, article 1233-3: 'Dans les établissements de santé titulaires de l'autorisation mentionnée à l'article 1233-1 [authorization to retrieve], il est créé un lieu de mémoire destiné à l'expression de la reconnaissance aux donneurs d'éléments de leur corps en vue de greffe.'

87 Dominique Thouvenin, one of the most critical legal scholars, was for instance heard in the 1990s and 2000s. Similarly, while only a transplantation surgeon was heard in the 1970s in order to inform the chambers about hospital practice, in the 1990s and 2000s

knowledgeable professional about the situation on the shop-floor of organ retrieval practice, remains out of the picture. As we will see later on in this book, these nurses are central to procurement practice. Neither legislators nor political authorities or their advisors appear aware of, or willing to consider, the wealth of knowledge and experience possessed by these professionals who, more than most intensivists involved in organ procurement, follow the process from beginning to end and have a longer and closer contact with relatives.

Such assumption about a hierarchy among types of professional knowledge was shared by many of the hospital coordinators encountered in the course of this study. One of them, encountered several times, had been a member of the ethics committee of the Etablissement français des Greffes. She was the only nurse in a group composed mostly of physicians; she was also younger than most of them. Although she seemed to be a strong character, she recalled her participation in the meetings of the committee with some unease, noting that she was not necessarily always listened to, and that she did not always feel like expressing or pushing her views. Another hospital coordinator who was a regular informant and who was highly respected in the community of hospital coordinators because of her experience and her professional and affective strength, when asked why she would not actively participate at organ procurement conferences where only the point of view of physicians was being presented, answered: 'we nurses' do not know how to speak in public: 'not like you' she added, referring to the fact that I had been to university.

In sum, what we find over time in French law regulating consent to organ donation results from the combination of the views, interests and compromises among physicians, legal scholars, legislators and health and political authorities with access to the public and political arena where organ procurement policies were discussed and decided. Thus the history of the development of legislation concerning consent to organ donation in France illustrates Thompson's thesis that the content of legislation reflects a specific power structure (Thompson 1975: 219–69).

The views, interests and actors around which the regulation of hospital practice is organized are more diverse. We now move to the working of the law of presumed consent from the perspective of hospital professionals involved with organ procurement activities. Does it effectively regulate their everyday practice? If they do not follow it directly, are there ways they nevertheless take it into consideration, or is it for them an irrelevant factor? If the law is not shaping practice, what then are the norms, rules or interests that seem to do so?

---

the views of intensivists, directly involved in decisions to retrieve, were sought. For the experts called to parliament for hearings see Claeys and Huriet (1999) and Charles and Claeys (2001), the latter available at: http://www.assemblee-nationale.fr/rap-info/i3208-23.asp (accessed: September 2008).

PART II
Organ Retrieval in Hospitals: Walking on Thin Ice

This section presents the way in which hospital coordinators and referent physicians encountered during this research describe and analyse how decisions to retrieve organs for transplantation are taken. While legislators justified the enactment of a law presuming the consent of the dead with the aim of putting patients in need of an organ at the centre of such decisions, it is the views and feelings of relatives of BDPDs that appear to be central today. However, professionals observe that it has not always been that way. Chapter 3 examines the process of normalization followed by organ retrieval practice from the 1970s until the early 2000s. Until the mid-1980s, local practices varied widely. Organs from a BDPD could be retrieved without the relatives being informed about it, with them being previously informed or with relatives being asked to take part in the decision. This heterogeneity of local practices diminished during the late 1980s and, from the early 1990s onwards, decisions to retrieve have been made rather in the same way in all hospitals. However, according to hospital professionals, homogenization did not entail predictability. To the contrary, the normalization of relatives' participation makes them feel they walk on thin ice every time they must handle such situations. In fact, a double feeling of impotency and insecurity emerges from their words that develops around three themes: brain death (Chapter 4), time and trust (Chapter 5) and family dynamics and values (Chapter 6).

Chapter 3
From Heterogeneity to Normalization

1976–Early 1990s: The Time of Pioneers

Medical Discretion

In the first years following the enactment of the Caillavet law, the way in which decisions to retrieve organs for transplantation were taken varied considerably. In fact, behaviour was highly heterogeneous and little standardized. This does not mean that there was a context of anomie in the Durkheimian sense, where there is no 'moral' frame limiting individuals in their actions and where participants have no sense of what is right or wrong, just or unjust (Durkheim 1950; 1967; 1970; Isambert et al. 1978). What emerges from the media and the discourse of professionals encountered during this research is that no specific framework of rules and norms inspired practice.[1] Whether or not the relatives of the BDPDs were consulted, whether or not the presumption of consent was used to obtain organs, appears to have been highly dependent on the composition of the team in charge and even on which members were involved on a given occasion. Was the head of an intensive care unit interested in the new activities of procurement and transplantation? What were her views about the role of relatives? What was the general policy of an intensive care unit with regard to the information and care due to the relatives of deceased patients? Was the relationship with patients and their families more, or less, paternalistic? Was there in the unit a nurse or a physician particularly interested in the activity of organ procurement and with enough authority to impose common standards of practice? What was this person's attitude towards the relatives of potential donors? Were there transplantation surgeons within the hospital which put intensive care professionals under pressure? Were transplantation surgeons allowed to approach the relatives of potential donors?

In some intensive care units, the next of kin were consulted by a member of the unit who would proceed either according to directions that she had received from the head of the unit or, with no directions at all, according to her own assessment of what was to be done and to her individual personality. In other cases, especially in hospitals with transplantation units, a transplantation surgeon would directly approach the family within the walls of the intensive care unit. Depending on who was in charge and on the physical features of the unit, a discussion with the family would take place in the waiting room, in an office, in the room where the potential

1 This is also what sociologist Paterson observed in the late 1980s and early 1990s (Paterson 1997).

donor was or in a corridor.[2] The duration of the encounter with relatives and the information given to them also varied considerably. One intensivist recalls that she would usually simply announce to the relatives that the organs of the deceased would be retrieved and that the corpse would be returned to them afterwards. No discussion took place about the wishes of the BDPD or of the relatives. Other professionals would sit down with relatives in a quiet room and talk with them at length, listening to their expressions of sorrow.

One interviewee recalls that the information given to relatives in her unit depended on contextual variations and on the need for organs at a particular time. The approach, she adds, could sometimes be rather manipulative:

> I do remember, we used to tell the relatives: OK, announcing the death, explaining … brain death …; and then, it was a little, a little two-faced, there was without doubt some dishonesty there, we used to tell the relatives: 'are you aware of any wishes expressed by the person during his lifetime?'
>
> …
>
> How is it possible that the relatives, at that moment, 3 minutes, 10 minutes, 15 minutes after you tell them that the person has died, even think REQUESTING YOU TO MAKE CLEAR what you are asking them? (Hospital Coordinator 6)[3]

The intention to proceed with organ retrieval would sometimes be completely hidden from relatives. After arranging for the family to be away from the bedside of the potential donor, the body would be taken to the operating room. After extraction, the body was cleaned, dressed and sent to the morgue, where it was released to relatives.[4] One of the hospital coordinators recalls the case of a physician who used to proceed in that manner, using a strict reading of the law of presumed consent:

> … he didn't ask the families! He simply took [the organs] … because there was no opposition, nothing you could see: there was no tattoo saying 'I don't want to' [she points to her forehead], he just took [the organs]!

2 See for illustration with cases from interviews with relatives who had been exposed to such situations Waissmann (1996).

3 Capital letters are used to mark stress in the voice of an interviewee.

4 Paterson also reports this sort of behaviour, noting that it could happen that the family would be told death was inevitable – while brain death had already been diagnosed – and that someone from the intensive care unit would contact them when it would occur. The idea was to have the family out of the unit during the operation of retrieval and then call them to tell them that the patient had died once the intervention was finished (Paterson 1997: 62).

> – [GN] Without telling the relatives?
>
> Without telling the relatives! Without telling the relatives. (HC 3)

The same hospital coordinator recalls that giving the relatives a larger role in the process could give rise to problems with transplantation surgeons in her hospital. The head of her intensive care unit had delegated organ procurement to her. She had adopted the practice of talking with relatives to establish what the wishes of the deceased had been or would have been. Some transplantation surgeons in her hospital questioned this approached, sometimes in a way that she qualified as aggressive: '… at that time the transplantation staff called me an outlaw because I used to meet the relatives! They told me: "Hey! Why do you ask? What does that mean?!"' (HC 3). She did not give in to their reproaches because the head of her unit was supportive of her work and attitude. Nevertheless, she remembers it as an unpleasant experience for the young female nurse, that she then was, to be in such a situation of opposition to senior male surgeons.

Non-Standardization of Behaviour

A factor that significantly contributed to the variability in procurement practice was that protocols and other forms of standardization were largely absent. Many units had no specific guidelines and, because of the novelty of procurement situations and the low number of cases, different strategies may be tried within the same unit. An intensivist remembers the case of a 40-year-old man who was brought from a sports field and was quickly diagnosed brain dead. It took some time for the family to reach the hospital and the decision to retrieve was taken before their arrival.

> … during the removal, the family arrived. This man DID CARRY, a paper stating that he didn't want his organs to be removed, but it was in his trousers, which were in the dressing room and we didn't have them. In any case, we needed 40 policemen to protect us! (Referent Physician 8)

Although they were sure that their behaviour had been lawful, this was the last time they made so little effort to seek information about the wishes of a BDPD.

This trial and error approach was not necessarily based on any advance planning, so it was not uncommon that the nurse or physician who dealt with the relatives was absolutely unprepared, without any kind of instructions or training concerning the interaction with relatives who were at the very beginning of a profound grieving process, or about how to raise questions related to organ donation and retrieval. One physician remembers her first interview with a family of a BDPD in the early 1980s, when she was undergoing her period of specialization to be an intensivist:

> It was 20 years ago, the first time that they told me, 'hey, we've got to ask.' I was on duty, and my boss came and told me 'oh boy it's 6 o'clock I've got to go, hey, there's that family there you've got to go ask.' And there you go! And then and there my training was over! My first [meeting with a family of a BDPD], it happened LIKE THAT. And I, at that time I was much younger, I didn't know … And that was it. There was no training, wasn't anything …, nobody you could call …! That was that, completely amateurish! You got by as you could. (RP 11)

If an intensive care unit had a more standardized way of proceeding, this did not necessarily mean that it engaged with all families in the same way. For instance, the intensivist who was usually responsible for organ retrieval decisions in a university hospital near Paris had the habit of not herself talking to families she identified as Jewish. Instead, she would ask a Jewish transplantation surgeon to come over to the unit to discuss the situation with them.

Another intensivist recalled that when she was in charge there were families who would not be given any information at all; and others who would be informed before retrieval but without giving them any room for participating in the decision. When asked about the reactions of relatives to being dealt with that way, she noted that they generally accepted her approach without protest. But she added that such a way of proceeding would not be possible today, for paternalism is no longer so dominant in doctor–patient or doctor–family relations. At that time, she explained, a surgeon who thought that one of her patients needed to be operated upon would simply inform the patient that the operation would be performed, without asking for her opinion, let alone her consent. If the patient or her family asked questions about the pros and cons of the operation, the answer would be something like 'don't worry, I'm in charge'. The same approach was taken, she said, to a BDPD's relatives, who would simply be informed that the organs of their loved one were about to be taken.

Her description of the diminishing strength of paternalism is an illustration of the historical move in doctor–patient dynamics toward less hierarchical relationships. In the paternalistic or Parsonian model, the patient (or her relatives in our case) plays a passive role, her physician decides what is best for her and what should be done, and transparency on the behalf of the physician is not necessarily valued – a duty to lie is even assumed (Parsons 1964: chapter 10). The doctor–patient relationship has tended over the last few decades to allow patients and/or their relatives to take a more participatory role. Studies, particularly about chronic illness and disability, thus present portraits of patients who have acquired agency: they are knowledgeable and tend to be pro-active. In other words, they act less as patients-agents and more as clients-actors (Bury 2000; Fox 1988: 479).

The Beginning of Normalization

The Waning of the Paternalistic Model

Except for Herpin and Paterson (1992), at the time research for this book began social scientists had shown little interest in the regulatory normalization of the activity in France. These two sociologists studied organ retrieval and transplantation in the 1980s from the perspective of the discretionary power of transplantation surgeons to set the rules concerning the retrieval and distribution of organs. They conclude that rules organizing the activity in practice had usually been generated on the basis of ideas about 'local efficiency' and ethical criteria, rather than universal ones serving the general interest imposed by centralized and external structures such as France-Transplant[5] or the law. The non-mobilization of the presumption of consent was thus not uncommon, with physicians in some hospitals not showing '… any eagerness to apply, strictly, this aspect of the law' (Herpin and Paterson 1992: 50–51).

The research presented in this book shows that with time, procedures became less local and more universal: applied and applicable to all retrieval centres. The heterogeneous paths of the early years started to converge into standardized behaviour at the end of the 1980s. It is then, informants recall, that families of BDPDs started being more systematically informed and solicited. Until then – with the exception of highly paternalistic encounters – it was rather on the sly that hospital actors resorted to presumed consent. This is confirmed by research conducted by Boileau in the early 1990s. In her book about transplantation in a hospital in Bordeaux she reports that retrieval took place in the absence of the relatives, who would for instance be told that visits were not possible because the unit 'was too busy'. As one of her informants explains: 'We played hide and seek with relatives' (Boileau 2002: 55).

In the view of most of the professionals encountered during research for this book, the change in direction in relation to the participation of relatives in the decision process is strongly related to the changing pattern of doctor–patient encounters and to the scandals evoked in Chapter 2. Fear that cases in which relatives who thought they had been treated in an inconsiderate way might attract the attention of the media lead professionals to broaden the space for communication with family members. Chronologically this change of approach coincides with an increase in the frequency of opposition to organ donation in hospitals.

5 As a reminder, France-Transplant was a non-profit organization created in 1969 by transplantation surgeons, to which the state had delegated the power to organize and control procurement and transplantation activities. The Etablissement français des Greffes, a state agency, was created in the mid-1990s and took over the activities of France-Transplant.

Transparency versus Presumed Consent

As we saw in the previous chapter, many journalists and political actors argued that scandals had caused the general population to be less positive about organ donation and thus for families to object to retrieval more often than they had in the past. While most professionals encountered for this study agree that there was a connection between the scandals and the growing number of objections, they say that the most relevant factor explaining the latter is the fact that people were now being asked about their wishes or those of their relatives, and not the increase in the general level of opposition to organ donation. As one hospital coordinator who participated in the normalization process explains:

> … [Before] we didn't talk about organ retrieval [with the family] and that's no doubt the reason why THERE WERE NO OBJECTIONS!
>
> From the years '90–91 onwards … there was a certain number of affairs that were the talk of the town … All that did that … there was a kind of shock and, the doctors, ALL OF US, who until that moment DIDN'T USE TO ASK the family [about the wishes of the BDPD] … these affairs had an effect on us, the moment society started asking questions and saying: 'well, that's enough now. We want to know what you are doing, we want to know.'
>
> …
>
> So we STARTED to inform the families about the removal of organs, about the intention. And, from that moment, I LINK BOTH THINGS: from that moment, we started to get objections …. I think that there's a link between the two things. (HC 6)

From this perspective it is very likely that the observed increase in the opposition rate was related to increasing levels of transparency in hospitals *vis-à-vis* relatives of BDPDs. This is especially likely since we have seen that, with a few exceptions, application of presumed consent legislation appears to have been negatively associated with levels of transparency: the less transparency the more the law seems to have been applied. As exchanges with relatives became more open and explicit, strict application of the law of presumed consent declined, which does not mean that the real level of opposition among the general population had grown.

According to professionals, this relationship between increasing transparency and declining donation rates was not only a result of relatives, once informed, being less willing to abandon the body of their loved one to the discretion and authority of physicians. It also seems to be strongly related to reluctance, on the part of professionals, to impose the presumption of consent openly. Increasing levels of transparency meant that professionals were more closely confronted with the sorrow of relatives and more aware of the impact of organ retrieval on them. Furthermore, as the weight of paternalism decreased, professionals began to see the open imposition of the presumption of consent as an almost certain source of augmented emotional and even violent reactions on behalf of the relatives. All this led them to take more account of the needs and views of the relatives to the detriment, in a sense, of those of patients on the waiting list. This is not a matter of simply taking the course of least resistance when confronted by the opposition of the family since, for professionals, the needs of both families and patients on a waiting list are important ethically speaking. It is a matter of rebalancing the needs.

According to informants the process of normalization of the participation of relatives in the decision making was not just a defensive response to external pressure. Its source also rested among other professionals directly or indirectly involved in organ procurement – especially nurses in intensive care units, in the operating room and in the morgue. In the early years many of these had silently condemned their colleagues who were behaving in authoritarian and/or non-transparent ways with relatives. In June 2004, I gave a lecture in a Parisian hospital where I mentioned that organs had been taken in certain units during the first years without informing the relatives of BDPDs. At the end of the talk, a middle-aged nurse commented that she had worked at the intensive care unit of a university hospital where such behaviour took place; she noted that by remaining silent she had had the feeling of being an accomplice to acts of disloyalty towards these families. 'I never want to be in such a position again!' she exclaimed.

Paterson observes about nursing staff during the period before 1994 that:

> In certain cases, the psychological burden of the removal of organs and the secrecy towards the relatives was badly borne by the staff members, or by the staff that was exterior to the team, such as the morgue staff. It happened that they sparked off conflicts by deciding to inform the relatives about the operation that had been carried out. This situation led some teams to adopt a procedure of systematically asking the families. (Paterson 1997: 66)

It seems that such hospital workers found themselves in a more receptive context for the expression of their trouble, uneasiness or moral objections after the public scandals of the 1980s–1990s. The processes of 'emancipation' from medical authority and of 'humanization' of the profession of nursing under way in the same years undoubtedly also played a part in the development of organ retrieval practice.[6]

The scandals of the 1980s and 1990s were the result of information being brought to the relatives by nurses and/or by relatives to the media. They can actually be seen not only as a cause but also as a result of the redistribution of discretionary power in hospitals. Gould and Tilly argue that situations of reduced asymmetry, and in particular situations of transition from more to less asymmetry,

6 See for a summary of this process of change in the training and identity of nurses Paillet (2007: 191–201).

are especially likely to produce conflict, protest and blame, as divergent views can be made explicit (Tilly 2005: 13–21; Gould 2003). This focus on symmetry helps understanding why relatives and non-medical hospital staff started then being more openly critical about non transparent and paternalistic medical practice.

It is difficult to say why at the end of the 1980s journalists and the media started describing some of the behaviour associated with procurement activities as transgressive. After Durkheim we know that the causes for specific behaviour to raise social moral outrage are context dependent (Durkheim 1964; 1967), and the same applies to scandals (Lemieux 2007; de Bic and Lemieux 2005). This question would deserve a whole study and answering it is in any case not crucial here. What matters is to take these scandals as cause and part of the process that lead to the normalization of behaviours in hospitals. Indeed, the scandal as social phenomenon has two characteristics: it unveils or exposes existing positions of power, norms and structures; and it shakes established positions and reveals the existence of challenging forces. It thus exposes a threatened power structure and has thereby a transformative potential (de Bic and Lemieux 2005; Fillion 2005).

Professionals encountered during this research saw their behaviour become a source of public scrutiny and blame. The weakening of medical paternalism and the more critical attitude of the media were feeding each other: relatives became more inclined to question the behaviour of hospital professionals and to express their discontent, and the media became more interested in publishing critical articles on procurement practice. Professionals perceived the scope of medical discretion as shrinking, which made it seem less legitimate that decisions on the fate of a corpse should be taken without the consent of the deceased or of her relatives. In short, the reduction of asymmetry between hospital personnel and relatives of BDPDs, and between physicians and nursing staff, in the late 1980s–early 1990s deprived physicians in charge of decisions to retrieve of the legitimate monopoly of decision making with regard to a matter that started to be classified as personal – or familial – rather than as exclusively medical (in its broad meaning encompassing technical and ethical matters).

This brief overview of the early years of organ procurement in France points to two factors as central to understanding the mobilization and non-mobilization of presumed consent legislation. The first is the level of public exposure to procurement behaviour. The second is how hospital professionals in charge of organ retrieval decisions assess their own position and practice: are they willing to impose the extraction of organs upon relatives? Do they feel they can cope with the consequences – personal, professional and public – of doing so? The following chapters will show in great detail that these two factors remain to this day key to an understanding of procurement practice.

Chapter 4
The 'Living Cadaver'[1]

After some introductory chatting, the question with which all the interviews for this book began was 'Can you tell me about a typical situation from the beginning to the end? Namely from the admission of the patient to the intensive care unit until the body is returned to the relatives?' Without exception professionals answered that there is no such thing as 'a typical situation', that each encounter with relatives of BDPDs is unique and unpredictable. Nevertheless, they all convey that there is at the beginning of all such situations an obstacle that must be overcome: 'the problem of brain death'. The question of organ retrieval cannot be raised until brain death has been accepted by the relatives: 'because if they haven't understood it, we can't ask them to donate organs: it's the same thing as asking them for the organs from somebody who's alive. It's simply not possible' (Hospital Coordinator 1). This chapter will focus on this 'problem', before moving to the unpredictable aspects of the processes in the next chapters.

A Counter-Intuitive Kind of Death

'We No Longer Accept that We May Die'

Nurses and physicians note that the trouble relatives of BDPDs have with the idea of brain death must in the first place be understood as part of a general social context of denial of death. This phenomenon they see as a kind of perverted side effect of the successes of modern medicine, which has contributed to reduce the sense of the inevitability of death. When someone dies, especially in a hospital setting, relatives may suspect that a mistake or a fault has been committed. As noted by one hospital coordinator:

> … it's true too that surgery, medicine has made SUCH progress, that we can't talk any more about death. You go [to hospital] to get well and, if you don't get better it's because there's been a mistake somewhere. The surgeon or doctor could even be sued. That's just not normal! And, hey, with all that we get the extraordinary idea that it is unacceptable that we may die one day. (HC 9)

1 Label used by Starzl, transplantation pioneer, during a meeting in 1966 (Wolstenholme and O'Connor 1968: 70).

In other words, another hospital coordinator explains: 'scientific medicine' has pushed the frontiers of death back so far that, when it occurs, people tend to suspect it could have been avoided:

> Scientific medicine has EMPHASIZED this suspicion, this doubt about death: medicine today has led people to believe that we CAN push back death, [that] we may even be able to avoid it. But the idea of avoiding it at a given moment because a new possibility exists transforms this idea into a notion that is limitless. … So people reject the idea of death. (HC 5)

Anthropologist Augé writes that all human beings have such an incapacity to grasp fully the idea that each of us will eventually be dead. This is not, he adds, a matter of an individual *knowing* rationally that death is the fate of all human beings, but of not *believing* that she herself is going to die (Augé 1995: 76).[2] Historian Ariès formulates the same idea in slightly different terms: 'Technically, we admit that we might die; we take out insurance on our lives to protect our families from poverty. But really, at heart we feel we are non-mortals' (Ariès 1974: 106). Ariès extends the reach of this disbelief to those we love: neither I nor those I love can pass away.

In such a context, professionals explain, most announcements of death in hospitals cause cognitive shock among the relatives. The less troubling deaths are those that result from a sickness and dying process of an old person. In such a case the relatives have had time to get used to the idea of the death of a loved one, and they can more easily accept the death of a person who has lived a whole life. But by contrast, situations of brain death have features that aggravate the trouble of relatives: they are unexpected and *prima facie* counter-evidential. In a sense, the announcement of brain death has the characteristics of an ethnomethodological experiment where the most basic taken-for-granted assumptions about death are called into question. Garfinkel showed how the questioning of apparently unimportant assumptions can be a source of anxiety (Garfinkel 1967: 35–76; see also Giddens 1991: 34–42). If one applies such reasoning to the end of life, it is not difficult to imagine how unsettling the announcement of brain death can potentially be.

A Rather Indigestible Concept

Brain death cases most often occur suddenly and unexpectedly. In fact informants note that their interlocutors are in a state of mental 'knockout' where propositions and events are not necessarily processed in a 'logical' manner. The sequence of events is 'brutal' for relatives, as in the following example:

---

2 For a most interesting essay on the difference between *knowing* and *believing* see Pouillon (1982: 1–8).

> When it's brutal, that is, someone who has just had an accident on the road, with, who was on a motorbike, who has his head, completely, well, bashed in, and where the accident has happened at 10 o'clock in the evening and at 2 o'clock in the morning he passes over to the state of brain death, sometimes the family hasn't EVEN BEEN TOLD YET! …
>
> So: the first contact with the family, already, who arrives at the hospital … It was a, a young man 20 years old, he was on a motorbike, he was 40 kilometres away from home ….
>
> And so you see people arrive … at the hospital, who don't even know that their son was there, that he's had an accident. So, you have to announce it to them: the accident, the fact that he's been transported here, 'is it serious doctor?' and you, you know that he's already dead. So can you imagine the psychological blow of the news to tell them?! (Referent Physician 4)

Another interviewee assimilates such a completely unexpected loss to a 'catastrophe' for relatives:

> … I call this a catastrophe, it's my way of saying it, because I think that when you are fine the evening before, that you have projects underway and all that, and that in the middle of the night or the morning after there's no more sound, no more light, that must be a real catastrophe … for the person who stays alive and lives through this. (HC 12)

In such a situation relatives will not only be incapable of linking propositions to one another in a cool-headed way, they may also lose psychological and physical control, exteriorizing their sorrow, their feelings of loss, grief and revolt in more histrionic ways than would a person confronted with a death that seems more natural or less unexpected: 'people express their suffering more' (HC 2), they can be 'completely hysterical, hitting out all around the place, rolling around on the floor' (HC 12). A hospital coordinator reports the example of a young woman who had been told that her father was brain dead and who suddenly interrupted the exchange with the hospital coordinator and the intensivist: '[she] stands up shouting [runs out and] collapses on the corridor …' (HC 2).

Hospital coordinators and intensivists encountered during this research talk about relatives *digesting* rather than *rationally understanding* the idea of brain death. They thus describe the cognitive work that they see relatives go through not in terms of rational reasoning but as a process of progressive assimilation. They refer to this process with images and words such as 'digestion', 'absorption', 'integration', or 'acceptance', by which they mean: 'the fact that, the death has been understood, taken in, and that, that it is ACCEPTED' (RP 4). The same intensivist recalls a 'difficult' encounter with a group of relatives:

… I remember once … the people didn't believe me: they told me: 'It isn't true, he's not dead' … and I say, 'I am telling you. Yes, I assure you, with all of the, the medical information: I can ASSURE you that he's dead.'

They say to me: 'we don't believe you.'

[she breaths in deeply]

What do you do?

…

'No! – I tell them – Listen, in any case, it's his brain that's dead, but er, it's true that the heart continues to beat, the lungs …'

'We want to talk about it between ourselves!'

It was a family of origin, I don't know any more, from an Overseas Department. OK, we phone the father, OK. And the father on the telephone says to me: 'I don't believe it, you know that some have woken up.' Well … 'I forbid you to unplug him, I forbid you to do this or that.'

And I say to him: 'Fine! Very well' hmm … And he says 'I'm coming.' The time [for the father] to take the plane, then, the morning after, they had DIGESTED … (RP 4)

The informants consider this common initial reaction of rejection understandable and rather natural. When relatives are told that their loved one is brain dead nothing seems to have changed between before and after the announcement. There have in fact been no changes in the state of the brain-dead body. While the verification of *traditional* death consists of observing the immediately perceivable ceasing of the cardiac and respiratory functions, the diagnostic procedure for brain death extends over time.[3] The time of death is thus the time when two physicians have signed a

3 Depending on the type of test used, several hours can pass between the moment when the first and the final confirming tests are done. The following is part of the decree establishing the tests that must be done to produce a diagnosis of brain death (Décret n° 96-1041 du 2 décembre 1996 relatif au constat de la mort préalable au prélèvement d'organes, de tissus et de cellules à des fins thérapeutiques ou scientifiques et modifiant le code de la santé publique): 'Art. R. 671-7-1. – Si la personne présente un arrêt cardiaque et respiratoire persistant, le constat de la mort ne peut être établi que si les trois critères cliniques suivants sont simultanément présents: 1. Absence totale de conscience et d'activité motrice spontanée; 2. Abolition de tous les réflexes du tronc cérébral; 3. Absence totale de ventilation spontanée. Art. R. 671-7-2. – Si la personne, dont le décès est constaté cliniquement, est assistée par

certificate after having made all the necessary tests. The diagnosis of brain death is therefore the confirmation of something that has already occurred – the death of brain tissue.

It is true that this is also the case with normal death, since the official time of death is that of signature of the death certificate. Yet the lapse between the formal time of death and the moment when death occurs is cognitively less problematic with normal deaths, for relatives themselves can identify the moment of death on the basis of everyday knowledge. By contrast, a diagnosis of brain death is of a performative kind, for it is the diagnosis itself by which the person concerned becomes legally dead; and it is the doctor's announcement of the diagnosis that renders the person dead for her relatives (Hennette-Vauchez and Nowenstein 2009). If, as sometimes happens, the physicians involved do not sign the diagnosis of brain death, the patient will be left to die a *normal* death.

All this is not to say that no signs are given to relatives to prepare them for the worst before brain death is announced to them. What is more, the appearance of the brain-dead patient is not at all reassuring: she seems to be submerged in a deep state of coma and often shows visible signs of trauma to the head and face. Here is a very visual description by an intensivist of what relatives may be confronted by when they look at their loved one:

> … often … the face is badly damaged. Somebody with a cranial traumatism … he's been badly beaten. And, and he has often a very bumped up face, with large bruises, large black eyes, he may have wounds on his face …
>
> … And then in addition, you ought to know this, those with cranial traumatisms …, they are shaved almost immediately, all their hair is shaved off. It's because they put … a small optical fibre catheter, which goes into the brain parenchyma, to measure the arterial pressure within the skull.
>
> And then, er, you can see the relatives, who come in panic, as any relative, any relative who may come [following] a car accident, something serious, a cerebrovascular accident …. They come into the hospital in a panic, they come into, into, they enter into the room, and often they don't recognize [their relative] … [they will] see the face of their relative, which they will find extremely

---

ventilation mécanique et conserve une fonction hémodynamique, l'absence de ventilation spontanée est vérifiée par une épreuve d'hypercapnie. De plus, en complément des trois critères cliniques mentionnés à l'article R. 671-1, il doit être recouru pour attester du caractère irréversible de la destruction encéphalique: 1° Soit à deux électroencéphalogrammes nuls et aréactifs effectués à un intervalle minimal de quatre heures, réalisés avec amplification maximale sur une durée d'enregistrement de trente minutes et dont le résultat doit être immédiatement consigné par le médecin qui en fait l'interprétation; 2° Soit à une angiographie objectivant l'arrêt de la circulation encéphalique et dont le résultat doit être immédiatement consigné par le radiologue qui en fait l'interprétation.'

> difficult to RECOGNIZE – as, he has a head the shape of a watermelon, his eyes are completely black, he's got all sorts of intubations, he's got catheters, he's got this, this tube that comes out like this [she points to the top of her skull], the hair completely shaved off. (RP 10)

Nevertheless, all the negative signs relatives may see and hear are not enough to identify the brain-dead person as a corpse. She does not look dead, or at least not completely dead. Informants note that the relatives sometimes seem to start grasping the reality of death only in the morgue, when the body has become cold and inanimate (that is, a 'normal' corpse). It is then that some relatives may display the most devastated reactions: '… when they see the corpse it … there, it's really as if they discovered the, the dead person. People fall apart, well … worse than when, than before when they've seen him warm' (HC 12).

It is thus confrontation with a socially shared image of death that sometimes gives rise to the first signs of acceptance of death, and signs of overwhelming sorrow replace histrionic reactions of denial. For professionals the perplexity of relatives in front of BDPDs is all but surprising because of the counter-evidential nature of the assimilation of the death of the brain to death:

> Because they [the brain dead] are, they are connected to a machine, and it's true, it's true that it's difficult to be able to understand that this person is DEAD. Because he's still breathing, he's warm, he's rosy-coloured, er, you see the heart pressure and the heart beat on the monitor, it is therefore difficult to say that all of this will be finished. For them it is true that, well, it's difficult to understand. (HC 1)

It is therefore crucial to take time with such shocked families in order to combine the 'technical proofs' of brain death with simple vocabulary and repetition, to insist on the word 'death', and to pause in order for relatives to process the information that is given to them. Most of the informants encountered say that they frequently make a break between the announcement and explanation of brain death and the moment when they raise the question of organ donation. During this pause, it can be suggested to relatives that they join the BDPD and spend some time with her if they wish, so that they can look at her after having heard the diagnosis of brain death. They all note that there is a minimum lapse that needs to be respected if one does not want to risk causing the start of a pathological grieving process, and/or aggressive reactions on behalf or relatives.

Since acceptance of death must precede the question of organ donation and retrieval, the phase of explanation/acceptance of the idea of brain death can sometimes be prolonged, notes one hospital coordinator, to a point that can be draining to all those who take part to the situation:

> We have cases where it goes very well …. So the discussion is over in 10 min, 15 min. And then there are families where it can take 5 to 6 hours.

– [GN] Yes. And so there you say that the problem is often brain death?

Yes because they don't understand. (HC 1)

Professionals and Brain Death

Death as failure Informants stress that the continued presence in their unit of the BDPD is in some respects dysfunctional for the unit. In the language of Glaser and Strauss, it is 'disrupting to the sentimental order of the ward' (Glaser and Strauss 2007). The two sociologists describe how the presence of a patient who is labelled as 'hopeless' in an intensive care unit threatens the delicate sentimental balance of the unit. They note that in the units they studied in the United States in the 1960s the staff efficiently functioned around a 'strong motivation to save' ethos with all energies focused at once on a single very critical situation. The presence of a patient who is seen as hopeless, such as the BDPD, threatens this motivation by making manifest the risk of failure, and this can make it more difficult for the staff to rise to the challenge of saving the lives of those who still have a chance of survival.

Moreover, for as long as the BDPD remains in the unit, so may her relatives, with displays of behaviour that can also be highly disrupting. It is well documented that professionals working in units where death occurs frequently display escapist strategies in front of relatives making 'scenes' (Glaser and Strauss 2007: 44, 162; 2005: 178; see also Sudnow 1967; Castra 2003). In normal situations of death, where the corpse is of no use, the deceased and her relatives will be evacuated relatively quickly from the unit. The need to wait for relatives to calm down and to explain brain death to them in order then to raise the issue of organ donation delays considerably the unfolding of such strategies.

In these situations, where relatives of BDPDs are said often to be unable to deal 'rationally' with the information they receive, and where time is short (the problem of time is discussed more fully in Chapter 5), professionals stress that their own attitude is a key factor in the outcome of the encounter. But the responsibility is not felt to be exclusively theirs, for it is the attitude of all the professionals relatives meet during their hospital trajectory that counts, especially in relation to possible attitudes of suspicion about the treatment their BDPD received. They explain that relatives must not have perceived the hospital as a hostile environment but as a reliable institution whose members are competent professionals and trustable persons. In that sense, although the attitude of the nurse and physician who will be the relatives' last interlocutors is central, relatives will judge them in continuity with their whole experience in the hospital. If their feelings about what occurred previously are negative, it is likely that brain death will not be easily accepted.

Informants stress the import of what they call a 'professional attitude'. The term 'professional' is used in the sense of being able to explain and repeat, and to show enough concern yet not too much empathy. A professional attitude is in that sense one that finds the right balance between affective distance and proximity;

between communicating scientific knowledge[4] and giving affective support; between keeping a certain distance in order to be in a position to inform and guide relatives, and being sensitive to their state of psychological shock and sorrow. It is not easy, they note, to find this balance when dealing with people who are under shock and intense affective pain. Concerning their own psychological balance they stress that becoming too involved implies that they may not be fully functional as physicians or nurses in the following hours or even days. It also entails bringing home from work their psychological malaise. As to the relatives, professionals believe they can be irritated by too much proximity. Many recall situations where relatives have 'taught' them what the limits of empathy must be, as in the following example related by a hospital coordinator:

> I did it once … with a mom who had a son of my age, I mean, the age of my son and, I tell her 'I know how you feel' and she tells me: 'no madam, you don't, and I hope you'll never do.' She was right. … and I told myself that, I'll never do it again. That, I would NEVER EVER say it again. We, we get involved, we say that we understand their distress. It's true that we, that we understand it, but we are not in their shoes. (HC 3)

Nevertheless, even if their position is not that of the relatives, professionals are affected by such situations. A number of studies in the social sciences and humanities have shown how difficult the relationship is that modern medicine maintains with death, and how problematic – both socially and cognitively – it is for physicians and caregivers to be confronted by death and grief (Sudnow 1967; Glaser and Strauss 2007; 2005; Castra 2003). Interviewees do talk about their own personal difficulties in facing death, but more often illustrate the point by describing what they perceive among other members of staff. Such difficulties can be due to specific cases or to personal situations but often they reflect a more general uneasiness with death. On one occasion, while walking around an intensive care unit, a hospital coordinator, who also happened to be the head nurse of the unit, related the difficulties that some physicians and nurses experience when confronted with death. Passing a physician she said:

> That one is an intensivist and her partner is very sick. It is difficult for her to deal right now with death in general. Her colleagues try to replace her in terminal situations and especially when death has to be announced to families, and even more so in cases of brain death. (HC 3)

---

4 Scientific knowledge is here taken in the sociological sense. It refers to systems of classification that, although based on observation, cannot be definitely or neatly separated from interpretation and practice. Scientific knowledge can thus not be understood as dissociated from culture and social relations (Durkheim 1995; Bloor 2002; Barnes et al. 1996: 46–80; Yearley 2005). For an illustration of this approach applied to the history of brain death as biomedical knowledge see Hennette-Vauchez and Nowenstein (2009).

Another hospital coordinator illustrates the uneasiness of some of her nurse colleagues by referring to their escape strategies from death and corpses: 'I have nurse colleagues …: [if a patient has died] they don't go into the room' (HC 7). Examples like these were cited in all interviews as threats to the outcome of encounters with relatives, for the uneasiness of professionals is inevitably reflected in the attention and care given to grieving families: '… even in hospital circles, there's a lot of people death frightens them. So, well, how can you have the right attitude towards the relatives when even you, you haven't worked, worked out your own problems regarding death?' (HC 7).

The informants depict intensive care professionals as sharing with the relatives of deceased patients the notion that modern medicine has rendered death unthinkable, hence the idea that every death is a failure of the medical team. Referent Physician 3 gives the example of students in their fourth year of medical training who do internships in her unit, and who seem to assume that patients cannot die: '… for a 4th-year student whose, whose foremost idea is that EVERYBODY survives treatment. It's not at all, it's not at all a given [that patients can die]. It's really difficult.'

Moreover, physicians are depicted as sharing an ethos of intervention, thus, acknowledging that nothing can be done for the patient in terms of treatment can be a source of trouble (see also Castra 2003). One hospital coordinator explains:

> … for a doctor, it's also realizing a failure. … They teach them to face everything but death.
>
> – [GN] Doctors?
>
> Yes. And this, this poses an enormous amount of problems for us, an enormous number. Because, for them it's a failure. Death is a failure. …
>
> … people who are pre-mortem, who are at the end of their lives, but who stay in intensive care for a month …, they stay sometimes for weeks without seeing a doctor! BECAUSE, BECAUSE THEY [doctors], BECAUSE FOR THEM TO HAVE SOMEONE ILL AND NOT TO BE ABLE TO DO ANYTHING AND TO WAIT FOR DEATH, THAT'S, THAT'S INCONCEIVABLE, IT'S A TOTAL FAILURE FOR THEM. … for them it's so difficult to experience! … And no matter how much we try to explain to them that … well, EVERYBODY MUST DIE, be it passing in the care of a doctor or not, but, I'd like to say, everyone will, will go through it one day. But they have a lot of trouble with this … (HC 11)

A supplementary source of discomfort and frustration derives from the feeling of being incapable of soothing and consoling the pain of the family members. Indeed, not only do professionals feel uncomfortable, they also stress that their lack of training in responding to and managing grief makes things worse. As noted by one head of unit:

> … for me it's an enormous problem since no one is ever exposed, during his training … to any instruction about [dealing with] death … The exchange with the relatives in that connection is not easy: to confront them with the fact that the patient has died, and that in addition we are going to proceed to remove the organs … The medical staff are not well trained for it …. (RP 11)

Hospital coordinators and intensivists paint quite a pessimistic picture of the continuity of this problem since they see no significant improvement in the training received by new generations of physicians and nurses. One of the heads of unit interviewed notes that young physicians finish medical school with solid technical knowledge but no communication skills. She adds that the best students are frequently the worst in relational terms: they may know all possible *technical* answers to *technical* problems, but are lost in the face of emotional distress. They also stress that the high technicality of their specialization in intensive care contributes to the inability of the medical staff to handle affects and feelings:

> It's even more difficult for us intensivists, because we have a bit, we have the job of a mechanic and of a plumber. We are not psychiatrists, we don't have, we don't always have the words … That's it, we are, somehow, plumbers, we are mechanics, we take care a lot more of the pipes, a lot more of the mechanics than of the emotional …. (RP 10)

This lack of preparation for death is said to be shared by nurses.[5] One hospital coordinator recalls that something that particularly puzzled her at the beginning of her activity as a hospital coordinator – she had ten years of experience at the time of the interview – was that the relatives of some BDPDs would remain apparently unaffected by the announcement of death, not showing the rather histrionic behaviour she had learned to expect. For years she interpreted this absence of reaction as heartless indifference, until she attended a conference about reactions to the announcement of the death of a loved one. Here she was introduced to the phenomenon of 'petrification', in which relatives remain wordless and affectively paralysed. She regretted having only learned after so many years that petrified relatives are as much in shock and in pain as others who display their feelings more visibly.

Interviewees stress that they consider themselves a little different *vis-à-vis* their nurse and physician colleagues in this respect. They depict themselves as

5 Although Paillet (2007: 193–4) notes in her book about end of life decisions in neonatology in France that, over the last two decades the ideology of nursing as a profession has taken a more humanistic turn – so the relational and palliative aspects of practice have become, considered together with the mastering of techniques, professional skills – she observes that their practice and training remain mainly technical. This is particularly true of intensive care nurses who, together with nurses working in operating rooms, are among the most technically specialized – and prestigious – nurses.

feeling less uneasy and thus less clumsy in situations of death and in encounters with relatives of a newly deceased patient. Most of them have had some training besides that of the Etablissement français des Greffes, and above all, they add, their interest in these situations and their experience have helped them develop stronger coping capabilities. If their colleagues could learn to accept death more easily, the uneasiness of most of them would decrease. This would in turn facilitate contact with relatives and contribute to preserving the fragile sentimental order of intensive care units in situations of brain death. Indeed, the more disoriented the staff feels the more uncontrolled the reactions of relatives may become: the disorientation of professionals and the uncontrolled reactions of relatives are said to feed each other in a negative dynamic.

'A healthy dead man' In this general context where professionals are said to be poorly equipped to deal with the death of patients, and in particular with the family of the deceased, brain death situations exacerbate the difficulties staff experience. Together with the relatives of BDPDs (obviously at a minor level), professionals see situations as 'catastrophes' that strike persons whose age, way of life and general state of health should have *protected* them from dying.[6] One intensivist interviewed describes the typical BDPD as follows:

> … in order to be a suitable donor, [it] is necessary to be a healthy dead man. That's in any case a bit of a paradox, that is! A healthy dead man! Who's a healthy dead man? It's someone who, prior to his accident, is someone young, someone who didn't use to booze much, who didn't use to smoke much, who had no chronic illnesses and who finds himself brutally, brutally confronted by, by a bad joke …. (RP 10)

One of the hospital coordinators describes how upsetting the situation of a BDPD is for the nurses:

> On one occasion the girls said to me 'it scares us seeing how young men arrive with aneurysm rupture.'
>
> … there are times when one can't bear the context, the context in which, in which it has taken place: everybody is shocked. It only takes a young man run over for whatever reason, say FOR NO REASON! … a young man who arrives … you try a complete resuscitation … the staff will fall apart!

6 In 2001 the mean age of brain-dead donors was 42.5 years (Etablissement français des Greffes 2005: 37). The etiology of the causes of brain death has evolved in the recent years, with the proportion of traffic accidents decreasing and that of cardio-vascular accidents increasing. Thus the mean age is also increasing (50 in 2007) (Agence de la Biomédecine 2008: 17).

> … And then the question that the girls ask me is: '… do you realize?! A brain haemorrhage at 25?!' (HC 12)

With such cases the feeling of failure is stronger for the staff and thus the level of self-questioning. Hospital Coordinator 12 adds that, following cases of brain death, her colleagues ask 'always the same question: "have I done the right thing? Have I, have I, have I, have I ?"' By contrast with death after a long illness, or death due to drug-addiction or in a criminal context, these unexpected deaths of rather healthy and *normal* persons are perceived as reversing the normal and natural course of life. Brain-dead persons leave behind un-ended projects, bereaved parents, widows with young children, orphans, and brain death occurrences are particularly disruptive for those who have not managed to prevent them from happening.

When the BD becomes a potential donor Another reason why brain death is emotionally difficult for the staff is because this condition transforms a body into a potential source of healing material. As a consequence, the corpse will remain under treatment in the intensive care unit for some time. This transformation of the patient into a potential donor requires a practical and a cognitive transition. When a patient arrives in the unit, one of the hospital coordinators notes, the whole team is involved in trying to save her and is motivated by a shared stress. When death occurs, she continues, there is a sort of vacuum, as if a balloon full of air had been deflated. This is always a difficult moment, when the whole team has to shift from total concentration on saving life to an acceptance of and preparation for death. When the patient who is diagnosed as brain dead is a potential donor, the shift towards treating the body as a *normal* corpse and preparing it to be moved to the morgue cannot take place, for the body needs to be monitored and treated – it may even be subjected to resuscitative efforts. In fact, it enters a practical and emotional limbo that is hard for everyone involved to adjust to.

A further consequence of having a BDPD in the unit is that those who have not managed to save the patient not only have to expose their failure to the relatives but also must confront them with the fact that the hospital now intends to deal with their loved one as a potential source of healing material for third persons:

> IT'S VERY DIFFICULT. That's to say that … when we have been in charge of someone ill … that, to the relatives we've told them 'we are going to do this to try to have him pull through, we are going to give ourselves a few days, we treat the pressure, the heart, the infection …' and that, finally, we'll have to pass to, to brain death and to tell them: 'he's still there, as you've seen him, but he's dead, and now his organs could be taken.' There, it's very very hard. (RP 5)

All these emotionally negative consequences attached to a diagnosis of brain death sometimes lead professionals simply not to treat a brain-dead body as a potential source of organs or even as a brain-dead body at all. This can happen, for instance, if brain death occurs at a very busy time on an intensive care unit, or in the middle of the night when there are few intensivists on shift, when nurses are very busy, when intensivists or the hospital coordinator feel physically and/or psychologically exhausted. In a nutshell, the professionals in charge must feel they will be able to cope with the situation. As one intensivist notes:

> It's very hard psychologically … and it's the part that's most, most awful of, of our job! Oh, because to announce a recovery you expect handshakes, thanks, photos, and so forth … anyway anything, anything that you want, all things that please you. But for a death … er, whew, you never thank a doctor when someone has died!
>
> Well, for certain chronic illnesses one can say: 'you've been very caring, you've done the best you could' because the reaction of mourning has been able to start to develop, with chronic conditions. But in intensive care … mourning comes as a sudden shock: in 12 hours it's very difficult … (RP 4)

Apart from the situations in which the professionals lack the time or energy to engage in an organ procurement procedure, there are two other situations where a brain-dead body will not be treated as a potential donor. First, if death is thought to be of suspicious origin, the public prosecutor can veto the extraction of organs in order to preserve the body for judicial investigation. Second, a medical contraindication can render the organs of the BDPD unsuitable for transplantation. For whatever reason, when the decision is taken not to proceed with the retrieval of organs, the policy of most intensive care units is to stop all drug treatment and to switch off the artificial respirator. In some others, the drug treatment is withdrawn but the body is left connected to the artificial respirator until the heart stops functioning. Whichever option is followed, the brain-dead body will soon become a normal corpse, will be sent to the morgue and eventually returned to the family.

However, since most of the time a brain-dead body is treated as a potential source of organs, both the corpse and the family will fill the unit with their presence and needs, demanding from the staff a supplementary effort of care and of sentimental work. Indeed, in general terms relatives of BDPDs receive more care than those of other *normally*-dead persons and there is a higher degree of tolerance of the externalization of their suffering: '… we allow the family of a donor to express themselves much more than the family of someone else' (HC 2). Hospital Coordinator 2 also recalls the case of an old lady who expressed her surprise at the support she received as a relative of a BDPD compared to her experience when her husband had died in the same hospital three years earlier: 'It's good this service now, it's good …, at least you are given support [when there is a death], because it's big, you get lost. I remember when my husband died three years ago there wasn't this and I got lost.' The hospital coordinator remembers her embarrassment. She did not dare explain to the lady that nothing had changed except that, this time, her relative was a potential source of organs.

The job of the hospital coordinator as defined by French law, and as more specifically described in the directives of the Etablissement français des Greffes, is not only to ask relatives about organ donation and to organize procurement. It is also to take care of them, whatever the decision about organ retrieval may be. With *normal* deaths, the care received by the relatives is much less standardized and varies considerably depending on the policy of the head of the unit, on the attitudes and training of individual physicians and of the head nurse of the unit:

> … depending on the personality of the various people, and [there] are some who are going to hide in a corner who are not going to see the family, who are going to announce the death and are going to run off because DEEP DOWN, they personally have problems, or someone ill in their families … (HC 2)

Glaser and Strauss wrote in their studies on American intensive care units in the 1960s that the communication capabilities of medical professionals, especially when it comes to bad news, were not seen by their peers as part of what makes a good doctor. The situation informants for this book depict paints a similar picture. If a physician is good at talking to grieving relatives, it is a positive, yet personal, quality. A physician who, on the other hand, runs away or is particularly non-communicative with families, will not be considered a bad professional. Among the functions of hospital coordinators it is explicitly part of the professional skills of these specialized nurses to be able to communicate in a soft and sympathetic way with relatives. This also applies to the physicians who, in each unit, are in charge of the activity.

Keeping a corpse alive There are two more factors that contribute to the discomfort professionals may feel in cases of brain death. The first is that some of them share with families a sort of uneasiness about the concept of brain death. One afternoon, when I was visiting a coordination team composed of three intensive care nurses, two of them told the third about an incident that had recently occurred in the unit. After a diagnosis of brain death had been established, a contraindication to transplantation was discovered. The intensivist in charge decided to disconnect the body from the respirator, as was normal practice in the unit. A nurse who was also in the room started to shout, telling the physician to stop what she was doing. In the nurse's view the physician was killing a patient.

The anecdote illustrates a major difficulty for professionals: the necessity to intervene on the brain-dead body, either to allow it to reach a state of *normal* death, or to keep it functioning until it reaches the operating room so that the extraction of organs can take place. Both situations require that professionals do things that can be felt to be in contradiction with their professional identity as nurses and physicians. When professionals withdraw life support because there is a contraindication for transplantation or because there is an objection to donation, they cause the last signs of life to disappear. When a brain-dead body is treated as a donor, professionals must monitor bodily functions and perform interventions normally carried out on living patients in the expectation or hope of some benefit. When the brain-dead donor is in the operating room for retrieval, the professionals involved must perform a highly disturbing operation: after having opened the thorax and before extracting the heart, the aorta vein is clamped so that blood circulation ceases. The process of extracting several organs and sometimes bones and tissues from a body which until minutes before showed signs of life is itself distressing.

Although in a rational and scientific mode the professionals involved say that they assimilate brain-dead persons to corpses, the concrete acts of stopping medical treatment, of treating a body with no hope of recovery, of extracting a beating heart from a warm body, these operations in fact make them feel uncomfortable with regard to their professional identity. One of the hospital coordinators sums up this feeling: 'The management of death is not really my profession. It's for other reasons that I'm a nurse.' This is why, she adds, 'I am only a part time hospital coordinator' (HC 3).

All these elements make informants say that brain death situations are a potentially serious source of tension in a hospital. Doubts can arise about the accuracy or validity of a diagnosis, or about the whole idea of the assimilation of the death of the brain to death itself; rumours about malpractice can circulate within hospital walls and beyond. For this reason most hospital coordinators are involved in efforts to spread information about the concept of brain death and the security of such a diagnosis in practice:

> … the number of times where I have to, to, to, to explain, with, with as much effort as possible, this thing about brain death! Saying: 'but he really is dead! I promise you that he's dead! No way round it.' And well, I ASSURE you that even my nurse colleagues they hesitate! …
>
> [They tell me] 'Don't you realize?! What if you are mistaken?' 'But we can't be mistaken! We can't be mistaken!' (HC 9)

With an eye toward the situation inside the hospital, hospital coordinators and intensivists say that it is important that they behave transparently and carefully when involved with BDPDs and procurement activities. Precautions need to be taken that are not strictly necessary from a technical or medical point of view, they say, but that are important if they want to avoid tension with other nurses and physicians. One of the most sensitive of situations concerns the nurses in the operating room who take part in the difficult phase of organ extraction that transforms a body with a beating heart into a normal (and empty) corpse. A most striking precaution is the so-called 'curarization' of the BDPD. Curare is a muscle relaxant and is injected into the brain-dead body in order to avoid movements during the organ extraction. Informants explain that the brain-dead body can produce medullar reflex movements, such as back arching, vomiting and the so-called 'Lazarus' sign' – 'the arms rise above the body and the body and head also may flex into a semisitting position for a matter of several seconds to minutes' (Plum 1999: 52; see also Jain and DeGeorgia 2005). According to the literature and to the professionals interviewed, such movements should not be interpreted as invalidating the diagnosis of brain death. They are nonetheless potentially quite shocking and are said by informants in some centres to be at the origin of rumours about organs having been taken from living patients:

> … everybody will tell you that, when a removal is carried out, the patient sometimes moves …. It's because of this that we, it's absolutely necessary that the anaesthetist curarizes the patient and gives some products so that those movements do not take place, which have nothing to do with normal movements. But, everyone is, is wary, saying 'you see I told you, yesterday they removed organs from a living person, he was moving.' (RP 1)[7]

Informants sometimes qualify the behaviour and attitudes of their colleagues as 'non professional', meaning that they do not act *rationally* and according to medical knowledge. Yet, they add, nobody should be surprised if, just like anyone among the general population, physicians and nurses hold widely shared fears or beliefs about life and death. Indeed, except for those directly involved with organ procurement, health professionals are not that different from the general population: '… the lack of confidence of the public … well in the end, the public, it's even the people wearing white shirts in the unit next door' (HC 2).

Although informants tend to distinguish between the difficulties of their colleagues and their own beliefs and attitudes, the line appears to be less neatly defined than they tend to assume. The vocabulary they sometimes use shows that they too make a conceptual distinction between brain death and *normal* death. The clearest illustration of this is the way they refer to the brain-dead body. While *traditionally* dead bodies are generally referred to as 'cadavers', a body in a state of brain death is only referred to in this way when the warm body with a beating heart becomes cold, silent and breathless. A quote from a hospital coordinator with several decades of experience in the field nicely illustrates this difference in the way brain-dead and *just plain* dead bodies are referred to. She recalls the case of a BDPD whose organs eventually could not be retrieved because his heart stopped beating before he reached the operating room: 'The young man, we didn't, we didn't retrieve [his organs] because he died before, OK? He had a cardiac arrest'(HC 6).

Another illustration of the conceptual difference made between the brain-dead body and the traditional corpse is given by another hospital coordinator who describes the difficulties intensive care nurses experience until the very end of the process. Nurses give care and treatment to the patient when she arrives at

7 In her book about organ donation and transplantation Boileau (2002) reports the case of a transplantation surgeon who ceased his activity after he witnessed these kinds of movements in a BDPD in an operating room.

the intensive care unit as a person to save; when the diagnosis of brain death is delivered they take care of the potential donor until she is taken to the operating room; after the retrieval of organs has taken place, an 'empty' corpse with big and visible scars is taken back to them to clean and dress before finally sending it to the morgue. During this process they follow the transformation of a 'person' into a 'dead' patient:

> … It's not always easy in intensive care: they [intensive care nurses] have received a patient, the resuscitation fails, it's not easy to live for them either, and the person goes to the operating room, comes back, the patient is dead huh! The patient is dead … so it's not obvious either. (HC 10)

It is only when the brain-dead person becomes *just* dead, that the professionals involved feel that they are dealing with a *real* corpse. The end of the process in the operating room is said to be particularly difficult to cope with. It consists of closing up what has become 'a body without life' (RP 10), whereas the one that entered the operating room was still in some sense *living*. At that moment all the surgeons have left and the level of stress in the room is said to decline. It is only then that the professional(s) who have been there from the beginning, who have announced brain death to the relatives and who had until that moment been caught up in the flurry generated by the process of organ retrieval, become really aware of the death of the donor: 'And for those who have put most into it, I mean those who are there since the beginning …. If you want, one becomes conscious of death at that moment' (RP 10).

Anthropologist Lock refers to the brain-dead entity as a 'brain-dead patient-cadaver' and describes it as 'a particularly complex hybrid, constituted from culture and nature while in transition from life to death; both person and nonperson, entirely dependent on a machine for existence' (Lock 2002: 40). The in-betweenness of the BDPD is at the core of the discourse of professionals. While the death of the brain may well have been put by medical and legal taxonomies into the death box, the ambiguity of this state remains in the words and the experiences of hospital coordinators and intensivists and in their exchanges with relatives. Indeed, notes one head of unit, the fact that the brain dead are legally dead does not mean that they are perceived as such:

> … when can it be said that someone is dead? Well, even, even us intensivists well, there are the legal criteria for brain death but do those criteria define death? …
>
> And so I think that the, the good sense of the parents, perceives this very well.
>
> It's: 'you are telling me that [my son] is dead but are you sure?' 'Yes because the' to tell them 'yes because the law says so and the tests prove it', it's not enough as an answer. (RP 6)

The assimilation of brain death to the end of the life of the BDPD is, nonetheless, the indispensable and difficult first step to take together with the relatives, before the question of organ donation and retrieval can be raised. Once this step has been taken, new difficulties arise in a context that interviewees depict as structurally adverse, and where parameters external to the issues of donation, retrieval and transplantation often dominate the discussion with relatives, and eventually determine the final decision.

Chapter 5
Unpredictable Situations

While families need time to hear what they are told, to digest and reflect upon what they are being asked, medical, organizational and institutional times are constrained. The brain-dead body is unstable and needs close monitoring. The procurement process requires tight organization: a number of organs and tissues can be extracted from the body of a single donor, each organ or tissue will be retrieved by a different team, often coming from different hospitals all over the country, and all this needs to be coordinated with the central transplantation agency which allocates the organs. To the strain imposed by these tensions, informants add the difficulty of being at the centre of a process they are not fully in control of. The number of actors involved in procurement processes is high, from the relatives of BDPDs to administrative workers of the hospital or members of the police. The reactions and actions of any of these are likely to break the inherently weak communicational equilibrium with the relatives.

The Problem of Time

The Technical Tensions

Informants stress that the brain-dead body is most of the time at risk of becoming *just* dead, and hence no longer a potential source of organs. The major reason for this is that the hemodynamics of the organism in such state is unstable.[1] Keeping it stable until it reaches the operating room is the most important technical task for the intensive care team. A BDPD thus involves a major investment of work for an intensive care unit: it requires nurses to carry out regular controls that involve careful attention and, if the brain-dead state is particularly unstable, the attention of an intensivist will also be required who may even have to undertake *resuscitative* efforts. The following quote, taken from a chapter by two French intensivists, summarizes the type of technical control the brain-dead body is submitted to in order not to become a normal corpse:

1 Hemodynamics refers to the condition of blood circulation. Pressure, flow, speed, vasomotricity, vascular resistance and so forth are, in a brain death state, the main factors intensive care professionals must control in order to keep the body's vital functions working. These parameters are continuously monitored and, to maintain the required values, various drugs may regularly be administered (Carvais and Sasportes 2000: 974).

> The main purpose of the treatment of patients in state of brain death, apart from respiratory assistance, is to maintain the perfusion of the transplantable organs. Hypovolemy may be corrected by perfusions of colloid and crystalloid solutes. If the urine flow is high, the insufficiency in diuretic hormone must be corrected to avoid volemic loss and ionic disorders. It is also necessary to treat an anaemia caused by haemorrhage, if that is the case. If the correction of the hypovolemy is not sufficient to restore the hemodynamic situation, agents that reinforce the contracting power of the myocardium must be administered. All of these therapeutic interventions illustrate the intensity of the medical care these patients require …. (Bonnet and Cohen 2000: 307)

The fact that the state of brain death is likely to shift into normal death, informants note, puts professionals under pressure not to take too much time with the decision process about organ retrieval.[2] As one informant explains:

> … we are obliged to rush because, if someone is in [a state of] brain death, well such trouble begins to take place in the entire body that inevitably, with time, and this happens with some brain death cases in minutes, with others in hours, at best in 24 hours; there the microbes develop, the oxygenation of the blood becomes less and less good, er, the heart works less and less well, so the entire perfusion, the oxygenation of all the other, all the organs which could be potentially removed, then transplanted, is [at risk]. So there's a race against time: you must be quick …. (Referent Physician 10)

Another reason for professionals to rush is that the process of retrieval disrupts the regular activity of the hospital. An operating room will be occupied for many hours of which no amount has been taken out of the planned schedule. The transportation of the organs extracted also requires activities that have not been planned for, such as booking planes and requesting a police escort if all or part of the transportation is done overland so that the organs can travel faster.

While there is thus functional pressure to rush, the procurement process needs time. The medical features of the potential donor must be investigated: tests must be made to check the possibility of transmission of diseases, the physiological age and medical history of the potential donor must be established to exclude possible medical contraindications, and so forth. There may be, for instance, a heart that has been arrested for too long before it was resuscitated, a cardiac massage that may have damaged the heart or fluids that could have damaged the lungs. The person in charge of the whole coordination and organization of the process is the hospital coordinator, whose denomination as *coordinator* now becomes fully apparent.

---

2 The absolute instability of the brain death state has become questioned in the medical literature in the last decade or two. Yet it seems admitted that brain-dead bodies are most unstable in the first hours. It is if and once the initial instability has been overcome that the organism is more likely to stabilize (Shewmon 1998; Truog 1997).

Although interviewees point to such medical, technical and organizational aspects as sources of stress, the most difficult part remains for them relations with the relatives of potential donors. Families need time to process both brain death and the request of organ donation. However, as has been noted in the previous chapter, another reason why professionals prefer to limit the period of presence of the BDPD in the unit is that it disrupts the sentimental order of the unit. Dominant in the way they describe their experience is the image of professionals trapped between an organizational, technical and sentimental race against time and the need to give time and attention to the relatives: 'you must be quick and … things must not be done in a rush, so that the dialogue with families is not broken' (RP 10).

Time, Trust and the Knowledge Divide

Since time is constrained, trust becomes indispensable if a constructive dialogue is to be possible between hospital coordinators and intensivists, on the one side, and relatives of BDPDs on the other. For the relatives of a BDPD the entire organ procurement process is about trust: trust in the intensive care staff who have failed to save their loved one, in the diagnosis of brain death, in the professionals in charge of the extraction of organs, and in the transparency and probity of the allocation system. The problem is that the intensive care unit is a sort of back stage, generally closed to relatives who are usually not present when their loved one is brought to hospital and given treatment.

But the need for trust goes much further than the physical inability to watch what the professionals do. Trust also relates to the division of knowledge, especially with regard to the treatment given to the BDPD as a patient. Relatives may indeed ask themselves if the professionals in charge are competent enough. Trust is also required in the idea of brain death. All of the informants for this study believe that, even though the idea of brain death is counter-intuitive, lay people can grasp it. Brain death is not particularly difficult to understand or to explain under normal circumstances, namely with people who have time and who do not have a loved one who looks alive but is said to be dead. Therefore, the problem is above all situational: relatives are not in a position to process the idea, whether cognitively or psychologically.

In the absence of trust relatives will reject the diagnosis of brain death, as well as the extraction and allocation of the organs of their BDPD; if they trust the hospital professionals and the allocation system, they may be able to consider the possibility of donation. As one of the interviewees sums up: 'It's necessary for us to have created ties of confidence with them for them to be able to believe us' (RP 6).

Strauss et al. have coined the term 'trust work', which, they argue, is functional to hospital efficiency. The work of building trust, they write, is usually complex, 'involving much time, much talk, demonstration of competence, many subtle gestures and the like' (Strauss et al. 1982: 261). If one considers this list of items and the analysis of the situation made by the informants, it becomes clear that the context is not a propitious one for trust: there is little time, the sudden death of a person who was rather young and seemed to be in good health is not an obvious demonstration of competence in the eyes of relatives, and the efforts and technical gestures that professionals have performed before realizing there was nothing else to be done to save her will remain hidden to relatives in most situations.[3]

Unpredictable and Difficult Situations

It was noted at the beginning of the previous chapter that the first question in all interviews was: Can you tell me about a typical situation from the beginning to the end? Namely from the admission of the patient to the intensive care unit until the body is returned to the relatives? Professionals reacted without exception by saying that there is no such thing as 'a typical situation'. One intensivist corrects herself on just this point when describing the moment when the question of organ donation is raised: '… the second phase [after having announced the brain death diagnosis] is … raising the problem of organ donation. Then normally – well, normally, you can't say normally …' (RP 2). All interviews contain sentences such as 'it's always a different story' (Hospital Coordinator 3), 'there are no two identical families' (HC 4), 'we never know how things will go' (RP 10).[4]

One of the main reasons for the unpredictability of these encounters is that, in spite of attempts to control the content of the discussion, both acceptance and refusal are frequently motivated by factors that do not necessarily reflect the wishes of the deceased and even by factors completely alien to the issue of organ donation for transplantation. As one hospital coordinator explains: 'It's so unpredictable, it depends on what people have experienced, it depends on the circumstances of the accident, it depends, it depends on so many things' (HC 11). Among such extraneous factors are the relatives' judgment of the treatment and care they and the BDPD have received since the moment of the accident; their deepest beliefs about life, death and personhood; and their degree of trust in public and medical institutions. Furthermore, each group of relatives is a complex and unique combination of the psychological characteristics of its members, the relational dynamics among them, and their history as a group (the importance of family structure and relatives' beliefs is discussed more fully in Chapter 6). Professionals consider thus that the only thing they can anticipate as they start talking to a specific group of relatives is that nothing should be taken for granted. 'We walk on eggs', an intensivist notes.

---

3 It is interesting to refer here to Timmermans' description of how intensive care staff may sometimes perform what they consider futile resuscitation efforts in cases of sudden death in order to make relatives feel that all actions available to the professionals had been taken (Timmermans 1999: 90–114, 184–205).

4 Clark and LeBeff (1982: 370, 376–7) write that this is a feeling generally shared by those who announce death. According to the informants the 'problem' of brain death (Chapter 4) and the issue of organ donation push the unpredictability of the situation to an extreme.

However, in retrospect, informants do classify situations into a few types. In that sense their statement that every situation is unique refers more to the feeling that how a specific situation will unfold is unpredictable, than it does to a belief that each situation is absolutely unique. It also has to do with their feeling that these situations are special. Indeed they 'mark' the professionals involved. It is striking how each interviewee illustrates her discourse with very precise and clear memories of the circumstances of specific cases. In that sense one can say that BDPD situations belong to the group of 'striking stories' that 'are never forgotten' by intensive care professionals (Glaser and Strauss 2007: 120). Long after a case, those involved could recall, for instance, the month and/or year of a case, the age and/or the family situation of the BDPD, the relational dynamics among the relatives, the precise cause of brain death and the hospital trajectory of the patient, the names or surnames of some relatives, and so forth. Such situations strike them because they are instances of what social scientists have described as social breakdowns, where routine understood as 'The pre-established pattern of action which is unfolded during a performance and which may be presented or played on other occasions' falls apart (Goffman 1959: 16; see also Maynard 2003). The temporary suspension of taken-for-granted reactions and categories that the breaking of routine entails is known to be a powerful source of anxiety for all participants in such situations (Giddens 1991). In fact, if there is one common feature to all situations around a BDPD it is that they are psychologically unsettling.

'It is Always Difficult'

We saw in the previous chapter how disturbing and shocking brain death situations are for relatives: these deaths are perceived as undue and, at the level of immediate perception, the state of brain death is counter-evidential. This context can cause relatives' response to grief to take extreme forms, as put by one intensivist:

> … it always happens in an atmosphere of, of psychodrama, of, even often of shouting, of mourning behaviour that is extremely, extremely difficult [for us to cope with] …. With scenes that, that are always hard to take for everybody … When you have a young woman, 22 years old, at the feet of her husband, who has had a motorbike crash, who has a crying fit, who, there's an unbelievable agitation, and whom in addition you have to take calmly and tell her 'you know … [we think of him as a potential donor]'. (RP 10)

One of the hospital coordinators recalls one of her first cases, when she had found it difficult not to break into tears:

> I had a lady who, who was sitting there once, a young woman, married, three children of young age, the first was eight months old, the two others were hardly any older. And she was telling me 'it's my husband who gave them the bottle,

> it's my husband who did this, it's my husband who did the shopping, it's my husband who did that …'. Then after a moment I looked at her … and I tell myself 'but my god, this woman, how is she going to get along now?!' (HC 12)

A hospital coordinator whom I encountered several times – without interviewing her formally – told me about her first case: the potential donor was a young woman who became brain dead while giving birth; only her mother was present at the hospital. When the moment came to raise the issue of organ donation the hospital coordinator hesitated, thinking this would be 'too much' for the woman to take. Eventually she decided that she had to have a 'professional attitude' and not be selective. But what she saw as a *professional request* received an outraged response from the mother who accused the hospital coordinator of insensitivity. The woman finally calmed down and agreed to discuss the retrieval of her daughter's organs before eventually refusing.

The situations that affect hospital coordinators and intensivists most are those where the BDPD is a child. This is because the death of a child is always perceived by the staff as unfair and undue, but above all because of the extreme shock, sorrow and despair displayed by the parents. One head of an intensive care unit describes the death of a child as follows:

> … the death of a child is something dreadful.
>
> – [GN] Yes.
>
> Dreadful, dreadful so … it's … it's something you can't imagine.
>
> …
>
> … [for the parents] it's, it's like ripping out their guts [c'est leurs tripes qu'on leur arrache] …
>
> – [GN] Yes.
>
> … the death of an adult is dreadful, especially if it's the young mother of a family … the death of a child remains beyond comprehension. (RP 6)

Apart from the intensity of the sorrow that they witness and are supposed to try to sooth, the length of the meeting with relatives is itself a source of anxiety for professionals. Another hospital coordinator who was not interviewed but who engaged in several long conversations remembers the case of a young couple who had lost their baby in an accident. After they refused organ donation the corpse was returned to them at the morgue, where they stayed for hours, the mother holding her child in her arms and endlessly crying while the father aggressively addressed the nurses who were working there. The hospital coordinator stayed until they left, both, she explains, for the parents and to enable her colleagues to keep up with their work.

Another hospital coordinator tells about four hours spent with the mother of a 12-year-old boy:

> It happened to me that I stayed here [she shows the room where the interview was being conducted], four hours with a mother who had just lost her 12-year-old boy who shot himself in the head. Four hours! Four hours. Here. It's it's, it's hell. Hell.
>
> For anybody. For anybody. It's HELL! It's, it's, HORRIBLE.
>
> Well, it's just one particular case, but that doesn't mean that the other cases don't have their emotional part too, like a burden! their affective part which, hmm, you return home you're bound to think a little about it. (HC 6)

As these examples show, before beginning a discussion about organ donation hospital coordinators and physicians need to feel capable of coping with the display of dramatic feelings and of violent or outraged reactions. Convinced as most of them are of the importance of obtaining organs, they do in most cases raise the question of organ donation. But the feeling that in doing so they are being harsh with a family who, were the organs of their deceased not suitable for transplantation, would be seen as deserving care and support continues to bother them. This tension is at the core of the difficulty of their task and at the source of a feeling of guilt that will be treated in more detail in Chapter 6.

If cases involving children are seen as the most difficult, the difference between them and other cases is of degree, not of nature. At the other end of the scale professionals place what they call 'non-problematic' situations. Interestingly, the categorization of a situation as more or less problematic does not relate to the outcome, namely to whether organ retrieval is accepted or not, but to (i) the idea of brain death being accepted without much difficulty by relatives; (ii) the issue of organ donation having been discussed in advance by the family;[5] (iii) the family as a group being able to focus on the questions of organ donation and retrieval without the discussion being contaminated with relational tensions. Unfortunately, note professionals, things are often not so simple.

---

5 A survey from 2003 by Eurobaromètre shows that 41 per cent of respondents in France declare that they have discussed organ donation or transplantation within their family. 'Le don et la transplantation d'organes' (*Eurobaromètre* 2003: 2). Informants note that the majority of families they meet say they have never discussed donation in the family, although they add that the ratio of those that have to those who have not is slowly changing.

It is Often Complicated

It can, for instance, be very difficult to find any relatives at all, as in the following case:[6]

> … there was a young man who had had … a motorbike accident, and in fact he had a telephone number, but on this number there was an answering machine. … it said on the answering machine 'we are not in'. So it says 'we', so one immediately supposes that there's at least one other person. So I had left several messages but then nobody was calling back …. I found some mail in the wallet, with a name and a telephone number, so I called, I had the chance of finding someone. No! Not even. There was no telephone number, there was just a name. So through the white pages I look for the telephone number, I find a telephone number, I contact this person who in fact was the employer. OK. So the employer tells me 'yes indeed, he has parents, but his parents live in the Pas-de-Calais [area in the north of France] but I can't tell you where.' So I look in the Pas-de-Calais. So we find people who have the same name. So there were two of us doing the search, and we telephoned everyone having the same name: NONE of them were the family. We do the nearby departments, but there wasn't anybody from the family either. OK, I call back the employer who tells me 'hey listen, I can't really see what I can do for you but if it may help you, I know that recently he bought a motorbike from his brother.' And there you go: we found his family though the police and through the vehicle registration!
>
> So, and all that obviously at 7 o'clock in the evening when most offices are closed etc., so we found the family this way!
>
> And in fact his family did really live in the Pas-de-Calais but his mother was divorced and so didn't have the same name any more, etc. (HC 7)

All interviewees had examples of this kind, where they had had to make considerable efforts to find relatives before taking any decision about organ retrieval. This is in effect a rule of practice respected all over France, as far as has been possible to verify. If no relatives are found in time, it is most likely that a brain-dead body will not be considered a potential source of organs. (There is one exception to this to which we will return in Chapter 8). None of the successive versions of the law of presumed consent makes consulting with the family mandatory. The only legal requirement is that an effort be made to find them. Nevertheless, the importance that professionals give to consulting the relatives is sometimes quite extraordinary,

6 This section and the following contain longer quotes than others in this book. It seems this is the best way of communicating the feeling, expressed by professionals, of sometimes being overwhelmed by the situations they face. It is also the only way of showing the level of detail with which professionals recall these situations, which reflects the impact they make on those involved.

as in the following example given by a head of unit, where the BDPD was an immigrant from northern Africa who had no relatives in France:

> I'll give you an example: to go look for people at the Maghreb, the relatives of a patient deceased in the unit … people who are not French, who, who haven't been in France for a long time …. [You call them and] You ask them 'do you know whether he agreed or not to have his organs removed in the case of [brain] death?' You can imagine that [the answer] is already 'no'. (RP 7)

This intensivist added that, from a strict legal perspective, her team had perhaps gone too far, but confirmed that the usual rule is to do as much as possible to find at least one relative with whom to raise the question of organ donation. The reasons why such an obligation weighs so heavily will emerge in the following chapters.

Bad Memories

Almost all interviewees evoke cases that have left them with bitter memories. These are situations where things go wrong, they say, because one of the numerous professionals involved in the procurement process acts inappropriately; or because staff and relatives fail to establish good communication. What is common in all these cases is that relatives leave the hospital angry and resentful, feeling they have been treated with levity, lack of consideration or, worse, with disrespect. Three examples will illustrate this type of situation.

Here is what a nurse evokes as one of the most unpleasant cases of her ten-year career as hospital coordinator:

> … it's a young man who had had a car accident and we had seen his two brothers. So his two brothers had told us: 'it's OK [for retrieval] but we don't want our parents to be aware.' And so the police,[7] the morning after they called the parents …, it was to find out his parents' exact civil status, the name of the parents, their place of birth, etc. Well OK, let them telephone to have this sort of information, but stop there! They call FOR THIS: they don't call to say: 'organs have been removed from your son!' There the parents not being aware … then obviously the sons call me back, absolutely furious … despite the fact that I had ALL ALL ALL prepared, except that the, the police officer that I had seen [and whom the hospital coordinator had warned that the parents were not aware about the retrieval of organs], it wasn't him who was there the day after, and so he hadn't told his colleague! And it's US, it's us who find ourselves afterwards in conflict with the relatives, [with whom] we have, we have in a way concluded a contract, and, and for them we haven't respected the contract despite that in fact it's a third party who hasn't respected it.

---

7 With traffic accidents, cases are transmitted to the public prosecutor and the police are in charge of part of the investigation of the causes of death. They can for that reason contact relatives.

> So that day I became bloody furious …! I called that police officer all sorts of names [nervous giggle]. (HC 7)

Hospital Coordinator 6 remembers in detail a very difficult situation with the father of a young man in his early twenties who had also had a car accident. The father had accepted the retrieval of his son's organs, although in the end retrieval was impossible because the son's heart stopped beating before he could be taken to the operating room for extraction:

> The young man, we didn't, we didn't remove [the organs] from him because … he suffered a cardiac arrest ….
>
> Well, no removal is carried out, and nothing is said to the father. We didn't tell him because he seemed to gradually transform this removal of organs in a hope, a resort of consolation for him. …
>
> And, there was a problem … I don't know what happened, we sent, three weeks, a month later a bill for this man to pay, to pay a little over a 1,000 francs [the law states that no bills should be sent to relatives for acts performed in the context of organ retrieval for transplantation]. OK. He didn't come to see me immediately, he tried to write by himself: he explained that his son had had his organs removed [and that for that reason he must not pay] …. And, one evening, SIX MONTHS LATER, there's a intensivist who tells me, 'hey I've seen a man crying in the, in the corridor there, he's looking for someone to talk to, he has his son whose organs were retrieved, a thing is sent to him asking him for two, 2,000 francs, and he can't pay because he doesn't have the means to.'
>
> It was 6pm and he tells me this. OK. I tell him 'Listen sir I will, er, I'll see what I can do.'
>
> I'm a bit surprised because normally we shouldn't have made him pay because, when someone comes for a removal of organs, even, since there's been an INTENTION to … we MUST NOT charge for anything. So there had been a bungle.
>
> OK. … the morning after I go to see the person in charge of hospitalization expenses, she says to me: 'There was no extraction, so …' I tell her: 'NO! when there has been intention to have the organs removed … !' It lasted two hours, and in the end I showed her the [legal] texts and then well …
>
> So they [administration employees] don't know, they don't know.
>
> She [the employee] tells me 'Well OK we'll try to straighten this', there were 2,000 francs to pay, and, she's a very nice lady … so, she gives out the instructions to her assistants …

> For me: problem solved.
>
> Fifteen days ago, telephone rings. The secretary comes into my office: Mister whatever is on the phone for you, he has just received a letter, the bailiff is going to seize his furniture, Monday morning …
>
> …
>
> So what had happened? The girl who should have done her job properly had still not done it properly. And, the complaint the, the, how should I say, the procedure has, continued, and so this man, on Friday afternoon, in panic, FALLEN APART, had received a letter for the Monday: SEIZURE OF FURNITURE.
>
> …
>
> IT'S A SCANDAL
>
> OK, then, I went down, I left everything, I went to see, they searched, they retrieved the computer thingies and realized that [somebody had sent a document to the wrong office] ….
>
> Do you understand?! A thing like this, it becomes, it's, it's HORRIBLE! Horrible.

The last two examples are of situations that evolved badly after a rather unproblematic first phase. Other bad memories include situations where the relatives show absolute distrust of the intensive care staff and particularly of the hospital coordinator and the physician with whom they interact directly. In such cases the levels of aggressiveness exhibited by relatives can become very difficult for professionals to cope with. Referent Physician 9 evokes with a lot of bitterness her interaction with the relatives of a six-year-old boy diagnosed brain dead very soon after being admitted to the hospital:

> It was … a family from a very disadvantaged background. When I met them, it was very quick: the child came and, two, two or three hours later he had reached brain death …. And I met the parents, I discussed with them, first to tell them that it was serious … and then, I'm, an hour later, I'm, I'm told that the father wants to talk to me again. I talk again with the father who in fact tells me that he's not the father but rather that he is a MAGNETIST.[8]

8 A magnetist is a healer who is supposed to cure people by his power upon magnetic fluids or forces.

> And there if you like, the, the relation was suddenly a little twisted, all in all, because, I hadn't talked to the parents but, in fact, only to the mother, but the man was a, some sort of, I don't know, a magician … who explained to me that he was there because, if the father got to know right away about the death he would kill everybody, anyway, well, you see.
>
> So, under these conditions if you like, it's a little bit difficult to …
>
> So, in any case we tried: we made the nurse coordinator come to try to, to see [about the donation of organs]. And then, it went very very badly: the older brother of, of this little child threatened me, telling me that he would kill me if I ever touched the child, that it was us who had killed him in order to remove his organs … So it went very badly and it didn't go beyond, beyond brain death.

Encounters of this kind call into question the personal and professional integrity of the professionals, who remember them with considerable bitterness. As one of the intensivists puts it: '… there have been a certain number of, of relatives of patients who have really had some very aggressive reactions: "you only think about using the patients" …. Anyhow. Things that are not very pleasant to hear when you are a doctor and you try to just heal people' (RP 12).

One nurse recalls one such case as one of her most painful experiences as a hospital coordinator. The BDPD was a man with adult children. The encounter was conducted with an intensivist. Both the hospital coordinator and the intensivist felt that they had not managed to communicate with them in a positive way, that the exchange was sterile and lasted far too long. One of the daughters repeatedly reproached the staff in an aggressive way, insinuating that they had not done all they could to save her father:

> … the daughter … attacked us, I have the impression that she attacked society, the entire society, for this death, but anyway. So it wasn't pleasant …. I had trouble getting over, … this was one, one of the cases I really had trouble getting over … because, well, I think that we [intensive care staff] were there from the start but … [we did not manage to save the patient]. (HC 1)

Informants note that they may need some time to get over this type of encounter. Remembering one such situation a hospital coordinator said that after the relatives were gone she took half a day off and walked around Paris, with no aim but to let the unpleasant feelings pass and to regain the energy to cope with her personal and professional life.

In some cases, stiffness becomes open aggressiveness, as in the case of the boy above. All interviewees tell personal or second-hand stories about the risk of physical threats, which they say they have in the back of their minds when they approach families. In cases where the professionals in charge perceive a risk of verbal or physical aggression, they may decide not even to raise the question of organ donation with relatives and simply let the BDPD *die a normal death*. None of the interviewees considers it her duty to raise the question of organ donation with relatives if there is a risk of physical violence:

> ... if you have in front of you people who are super aggressive, who don't listen to ANYTHING AT ALL, and that you feel that it's going to degenerate, so, I mean ... Honestly there was one time I told myself: 'I'm not going to take a punch in order to, to get a kidney.' Even if I'm aware that the kidney could serve to ... but hey, I'm not going to take a punch on the face, simply because the family must donate! (HC 12)

In such situations, they stress, there is not much to be done to change the attitude of relatives: 'You may present [the case] brilliantly, [but] you are never going to convince the family that [things are] done in the right way' (RP 11). In the words of a hospital coordinator:

> ... sometimes we can't go beyond a certain point. You get people who are there, who are completely CLOSED .... If the people are closed, are obtuse or whatever you want to call it .... I'm no masochist ... I really do want to do my job and to put in as much as possible but ... when it's 'NO NO NO, don't you touch him, I don't want him to be touched, if you touch ...!' and you feel that really if you touch him it's going to be VERY BAD, so listen, too bad, too bad for those who are waiting. (HC 12)

After going through such a situation professionals' feeling of frustration is doubled, for neither have they obtained a positive answer to their request for organ retrieval nor have they been able to convince the relatives about the probity of medical practice and of the procurement system. The feeling among hospital professionals that their social authority has significantly waned in the last decades repeatedly comes up in their discourse. Beyond the general context of decreasing paternalism, they attribute the loss of authority to blameworthy behaviour that took place in hospitals in the past and so to the scandals that ensued in the media. These events led hospital professionals to develop a more inclusive communicational approach to relatives whereby the latter are informed about the possibility of retrieving organs and asked if they know about the wishes of the deceased (see Chapter 3). Formally speaking such changes do not entail the active participation of relatives in the decision making, let alone their having the last word. But in practice it does, professionals observe, for in a context of waning paternalism, broadening the space for communication with relatives implies the sharing of decision-making power: '... the more one communicates, the more one cedes power. If not it's, it's not communication; and so it's a delegation of power, and so this means that, well, people simply have a right to have another opinion' (RP 5).

Chapter 6
Whose Gift?

Family Structures and Relational Dynamics

Family or Close Persons?

Let us recall that the law of 1994, which was regulating procurement activities at the time this research was conducted, stipulated that: 'If the physician is not directly aware of the will of the deceased, he must seek to obtain the evidence [témoignage] from the family.'[1] Before the adoption of the law of 1994 a discussion took place in parliament about whether the notion of 'close persons' [proches] was not more appropriate than that of 'family', the question being who is the most likely to have information about the wishes of the potential donor. In the end the term family was preferred, it being seen as more restrictive and less vague than close persons, which, it was argued, did not have any precise legal meaning (Thouvenin 1997). In the law of 2004, however, 'family' was replaced by 'close persons'. How are such fine distinctions supposed to translate into practice? What emerges from the interviews is that even before the modification of 2004, hospital coordinators and physicians have tended to apply a non-restrictive interpretation of the idea of family, closer in fact to the idea of close persons.

In November 2000, I attended the annual meeting of the Etablissement français des Greffes in Paris. One of the plenary sessions was addressed by a sociologist who described the evolution of nuclear family relationships in France over the last decades. She explained that the general relational trend in French families had passed from distant and rigid bonds to closer ones allowing easier communication on personal issues such as organ donation. Thus, she concluded, French families at the beginning of the twenty-first century constitute a propitious *locus* for talking about donation, and encouraging discussions in homes should facilitate organ donation decisions in hospitals, for the relatives will be more likely to know about the wishes of BDPDs.

Many of the informants in the research for this book attended this conference. Among them was a nurse whom I interviewed the following day. She expressed her disagreement with such a generalization and observed, drawing from her experience in a hospital located in a socially disadvantaged area, that the sociologist was ignoring the reality of some social groups – especially those of immigrant families where parents are often culturally and relationally at odds with

1 Loi n° 94-654 du 29 juillet 1994, article L. 671-7.

their French children. In such cases, she explains, it is friends who may be the persons closest to a BDPD:

> To say that people communicate with each other at the table, during their family dinners, it's so false, so false! Here we see the patients … the young ones, [arriving due to] a gunshot wound, a knife wound, a scooter accident, the parents do not have the right to go in, it's the friends who, when we ask them, the patients: 'who is the person [you want to see]?' It's the FRIENDS! And often, if there were knives and guns, it's the gang leader. And they give orders to their friends. You have to see the setting! It's, it's not at all the cosy family gathering of, of mine, of my home. Because when I'm home I speak to my children. But … French society it's now very diverse! (Hospital Coordinator 3)

This rejection of generalizations made by outsiders to the field such as the sociologist is not an exception. Interviewees exhibit a strong defensive attitude against what they consider to be illegitimate intrusions in their activity by sociologists, philosophers, legislators, members of the Comité Consultatif National d'Ethique, and so forth. The point here is not whether the sociologist or Hospital Coordinator 3 had the most accurate view of social reality, but that actors in the field feel that they are confronted with situations where general categories (like 'the family') and rules about who legitimately represents a deceased, do not necessarily apply. The general trend described by the sociologist did not take the specific demography of brain death into account, where a significant number of cases are the result of violence with weapons.[2] If one adds to this the fact that what emerges from the interviews is that difficult encounters mostly do not take place with 'normal' families, like the one described by the sociologist, the rejection by the hospital coordinator of the sociologist's generalization becomes more than just a defensive reaction. Professionals in charge of decisions to retrieve organs consider such generalizations not just useless, but a potential source of problems, since the variability of cases they face in practice requires them to be responsive to specific situations and not to blindly apply pre-established categories or rules. From this perspective, the concept of 'close relatives' is looser than that of 'family' and hence more operational.

2 The distribution of cases of brain death by cause of death in 2001 was as follows: 50 per cent vascular accident, 20 per cent trauma by traffic accident, 16 per cent trauma other, 8 per cent anoxia, 1 per cent intoxication, 5 per cent other (Etablissement français des Greffes 2002). Cases of violence with weapons are included in the category 'trauma other'. It is worth adding here that some traffic accidents are motorcycle or car accidents that involve the same group of young men likely to be involved in cases of violence with weapons; thus individuals belonging to the sub-population where 'friends' or members of a gang are said to be more important than the members of the family.

'What is a Family?'

However, informants agree that in the majority of cases their principal interlocutors are members of 'the family' of the BDPD. But, as one intensivist notes: '… the family, what is that for legal purposes?! What's a family?' (Referent Physician 10). They have no doubts about who the relevant family members are when the potential donor is a child, for its parents have the exclusive legal and social legitimacy to decide about the fate of the corpse.[3] The same clarity applies in cases of incapable adults, for whom a legal representative must authorize the retrieval of organs. Usually, however, the potential donor is an autonomous adult, for whom the concept of family may translate into diverse practical arrangements. One intensivist, reflecting on the meaning of the term, proposed an interesting – because incomplete –taxonomy: 'So, [to ask] the family, what does that mean? That's also one of the difficulties, because: what is a family? So, there are all types of families: legal ones, official ones, shattered ones, recomposed ones …' (RP 2).

In a similar vein, another intensivist refers, not without confusion, to the array of possible situations:

> Now with the, the, the single-parent families, and then often the, the recomposed families, with, the, the, … the 20-year-old young man who's there, his mother is there, but she is remarried – often one or two remarriages – there's the father who's there … So we face a whole bunch of people to talk to, we no longer know, we no longer know, who, who, who's the main interlocutor. (RP 10)

The end of this quote clearly shows why a classic family structure is seen as making things easier for hospital coordinators and intensivists: it allows them to identify those who are to be included in the discussion and those who are not; and it permits the identification, within the legitimate group of interlocutors, of authority figures. Indeed, as another intensivist explains, seeking the consent of the family implies looking for someone who, at the end of the day, is in a position to come to a decision or to settle differences that may emerge:

> So, the consent of the family, in the TRADITIONAL conception of, of, of the family, husband-wife, parents-children [it's simple], but all of this doesn't really correspond at all any more to, to today's reality, it's no longer the case. In 2000 it's no longer as it was … the family, it's broken up, the family. And then, WHO bears the family authority?! Who? Who's the person who will be able to say yes or no? (RP 10)

The discourse of informants here echoes Attias-Donfut et al. who write that the evolution of families in contemporary French society has been marked by changes

3 This right of parents is actually limited in the case of children over 13 who can opt out from organ donation by registering in the Registry of Refusals.

in the character of relationships and the locus of authority. Furthermore, the nature and form of family bonds are no longer given once and for all but are exposed to change.[4] In principle, however, if one were to consider only the letter of the law, the question is not who has authority to speak for the family but who, among the close circle that surrounds the BDPD, is most likely to know about her views on organ donation. Listening to professionals, however, it quickly becomes clear that the ultimate decision will eventually be highly dependent on the views of the family as decider rather than as a vector for information its members may have about the wishes of the BDPD.

Another difficulty professionals say increases their feeling that no pre-established protocol can be followed in these situations is related to the contingency of who is present at the hospital when brain death is announced and the question of organ donation raised. Sometimes the professionals decide to wait until a significant relative can reach the hospital, as in the case to which reference was made in the previous chapter where the father of the BDPD lived overseas. He seemed to be the ultimate authority figure in the family and professionals suspended everything for 24 hours until his arrival. However, this is not always possible: the stability of the BDPD cannot be maintained in all circumstances; physicians may consider that the bed occupied by the BDPD must be made available for other patients; the behaviour of the family may be perceived as too disturbing for the sentimental order of the unit, and so forth. Thus the discussion may sometimes have to take place with relatives who, in the eyes of professionals, are not fully legitimate.

Another problem related to who happens to be present is that of the size of the group with which hospital coordinators and intensivists will raise the issue of organ donation. Professionals concur that there is a critical threshold beyond which they risk losing control of the situation. The more interlocutors they have to face at once, they note, the bigger the risk of having a negative outcome and a long, unpleasant and infertile exchange with relatives. As one hospital coordinator comments:

> … And you sometimes find yourself with, you arrive, the family arrives, you have 20 people!
>
> IT'S NOT POSSIBLE TO HOLD A MEETING WITH 20 PEOPLE.
>
> It's not possible! It's not possible: there are too many things that clash, there are also a significant number of families who are, who are recomposed families, there are those that are divorced, there are the ex-partners, the current one, there are the, hmm, hmm, it's … And then in addition … often in these occasions, in, in, you may get a conflict that's developed inside a family, which is going to

4 Giddens argues that the increasing weight given to 'emotional autonomy' in interpersonal relationships is at the core of the potential for change that characterizes families in post-traditional societies (Giddens 1994: 74).

> come out, and, and the differences between the members of a family are going to resurface there, old stories etc. To have a meeting with an entire family, anyway with a, 20, 20 people it's, it's almost impossible. (HC 1)

Apart from the fact that a 'no' is more likely to be the outcome of an encounter with a big group, professionals consider such a 'no' illegitimate, since it reflects neither the wishes of the BDPD, nor the views of those who counted most for her and who will be most affected by her loss and by the fate of her corpse. In short, the hospital coordinator and the intensivist in charge of a specific situation have the difficult task of detecting who among those present were close enough to the deceased to be included in the decision making, and of getting an idea of the nature of the relationships between these closest persons. Then, they are confronted with the next problem: the values, beliefs and backgrounds of each of their interlocutors.

Families' Values and Beliefs

As in the example quoted in Chapter 5, where an intensivist was confronted with a 'magnetist' brought to the hospital by the mother of a boy, informants say that, even though the law in principle excludes the personal views and values of the relatives from the decision-making process, these are inevitably present. As one hospital coordinator explains:

> The contact with the families, it depends totally, it depends totally on the experiences of the family and on the reaction of the family. … Here we've had it all. We've had, from the people who proposed SPONTANEOUSLY … who proposed spontaneously the removal … until, over to the family of, of, of foreign origins, with beliefs more or less, Catholic, you know, a little bit not extremist but, who told us 'no, no, you, for you she is dead but God has spoken to me tonight she's going to come back …'. (HC 11)

Thus relatives may sometimes express a belief in a miraculous recovery from brain death, or in the possibility that the donor will not die completely if her organs continue living in someone else's body. More exceptionally, they may try to invoke some extraneous consideration, for example a racist concern, as in the following remark by a relative reported by a hospital coordinator: 'if [the organs we donate are going to be] transplanted into an Arab! No question of that!' (HC 7).

According to the Etablissement français des Greffes, the results of a survey conducted in 1997 and published in 2000 showed that neither religious beliefs nor religious practice influence the acceptance of organ donation.[5] The professionals

5 *Journée Nationale de la Greffe*, 22 June 2000. Available at: www.sante.gouv.fr/htm/actu/34_000622.htm#ENQU%CATE (accessed: 12 March 2008). This conclusion is shared by Waissmann and Couteau (2000).

seen during this research have a different perception: they see religion as the only factor with some predictive value. They agree that there are more chances of opposition to donation among Jews and Muslims than among Catholics, and even less among Protestants. But this is not a reason not to ask, they add, for it is far from being an absolute rule. Moreover, it is their view that when the relatives of a BDPD refuse organ donation on religious grounds, they are most often *mistaken* about their own religion. This seems to reflect the position of the Etablissement français des Greffes, which states that only extreme – and thus in its eyes non-legitimate – versions of Islam and Judaism are opposed to organ donation for transplantation. Indeed, what is told to the nurses and physicians who follow the training course and other events organized by the Etablissement français des Greffes is that only the Orthodox Church absolutely opposes organ donation for transplantation.

It is on the basis of such *knowledge* that, when Muslim and Jewish relatives of a BDPD raise their religion as an argument against organ retrieval, professionals sometimes try to argue against this view so that, at least, relatives leave the hospital 'better' informed than when they arrived. From this perspective thus there are wrong religious discourses that need to be corrected. Furthermore, hospital professionals add, religion can be 'an excuse' when relatives can think of no other reasons to refuse. As one of them says: 'in their grief people hide behind [their religion]' (HC 12).

Interestingly, a different approach is considered appropriate when a relative refuses organ donation because, for example, she says she cannot stand the idea of her loved one continuing to live in somebody else's body. However scientifically unfounded they may find such objections, hospital coordinators and intensivists say they do not argue too much against them. Although the topic of religion was not treated in depth during this research, it seems that the religious argument against organ donation is thought to be less legitimate than ones professionals label as 'psychological', even if they are fed by what for them are 'magic' views of the world.

According to informants, however, cultural factors other than religion have a greater influence on decisions to donate.[6] The cultural factors they have in mind are not so much specific views about organ donation or transplantation but factors relating to family structure. The importance they attribute to such factors influences the way they approach the relatives. One of the hospital coordinators working in an area where a significant part of the population is of foreign origin notes that when the BDPD is a North African man, the widow, especially if she is young, is likely to be relegated to a secondary position by the BDPD's family. It is usually the blood relatives of the BDPD who actively participate in the process of decision making, rather than his widow. Among these, she adds, the brothers of the BDPD are particularly important:

6 On this point their discourse coincides with survey results (see Herpin and Paterson 2000; Waissman and Couteau 2000).

> … in the Maghreb … the daughter-in-law, she has NO say, and the daughter-in-law, she's scared, she's very scared of the masculine circles, cousin, uncle, dad, anyway, or brothers, especially brothers. She is very scared of the reaction that all of this group is going to have, against her, who's nothing but a foreigner to the family. And so the, the notion of spouse [as main interlocutor] doesn't exist AT ALL. (HC 3)

She adds that in such a case the hospital coordinator, who is usually a woman, should be accompanied by a male intensivist, because as a female she will not be seen as a legitimate interlocutor by the relatives.

As with religion, whether these observations correspond to sociological facts is not the most important question here. What is relevant is that the professionals in charge of meeting with the relatives of a BDPD believe that certain social groups are more likely to behave in certain ways, and this belief can have an influence on the way they address them (that is, the hospital coordinator taking a male intensivist to a meeting which she would otherwise have conducted alone).

Other Factors that May Affect Relatives' Behaviour

Interviewees note that the medical history of a group of relatives of a BDPD, especially if linked to transplantation, is likely to influence the outcome of an encounter. 'Simple' cases are frequently those where some member of the family has, in one way or another, been exposed to organ donation or transplantation. In such a case the group will have discussed organ donation and therefore the issue will not come as a complete surprise. According to professionals these families generally accept donation. Nevertheless, nothing should ever be taken for granted, as is illustrated by the following cases.

In the first case the BDPD was a girl who became brain dead while on the waiting list for transplantation. Contrary to the expectations of the intensive care team, her mother refused organ donation. The painful existence of her daughter while on the waiting list combined with the sorrow felt by the mother at the loss of the girl lead to her immediate and firm refusal of donation. The intensivist and the hospital coordinator did not argue back. In the second case the BDPD was a man who had had a car accident. Two years earlier his wife had been brought to the same intensive care unit after a car accident and had become brain dead as well. Her husband, who was at the hospital with his sisters, had then accepted the retrieval of her organs. When the man became brain dead two years later the encounter took place with his sisters and mother. Knowing the story, the hospital coordinator and the intensivist initiated the discussion rather confidently: the question was not new to relatives, who were familiar with the idea of brain death and who had already agreed once to the retrieval of the organs of a close relative. Considering all this, together with the particularly tragic aspect of the situation, the hospital coordinator and the intensivist decided to let the relatives raise the question of organ retrieval themselves, after the announcement of brain death. To their surprise nobody did. It came out during the meeting that the mother of the BDPD had never been informed about the retrieval of the organs of her daughter-in-law. Her daughters only told her about it in the unit where her son had just been diagnosed brain dead. The hospital coordinator says that the mother appeared shocked by the unveiling of this secret, and that she refused the retrieval of the organs of her son even though she knew by then that he had agreed to donate those of his wife, and that he would most probably have been willing to donate his own. Nobody felt like going against the mother's opposition and so no organs were retrieved.

As in many other situations described by interviewees, this last case nicely illustrates the general proposition that organ retrieval will often be determined by factors related to the personal characteristics of the members of a family or to the nature of the relationships among them rather than to whatever the BDPD may have wanted or thought. In that sense the decision is very often a family decision, which explains why professionals search for a figure of authority within the group of relatives. The following is a good illustrative case described by an intensivist. The BDPD was a male adult who had had a stroke. His wife reported with certainty that her husband was not opposed to organ donation and that he would have agreed to it. However, the parents of the BDPD opposed the position of their daughter-in-law, giving arguments that concerned themselves and the funeral, not the wishes of the deceased:

> The wife of the patient, who was French, agreed [with organ donation], but the parents who were Portuguese refused. They said: 'I don't want it because if the corpse is going to return to my village of origin, I don't want people to know that organs have been removed from him ….'
>
> If we had been, if we had been very rigorous about [the law], … in this specific case we would have the right to remove the organs. Why didn't we do it?
>
> … it's an interview that had a big impact on me because I found it very interesting. … We had the wife, French, she said: 'I'm not against it and my husband wasn't against it.' OK. If we hadn't taken into consideration the opinion of the parents this young woman would have found herself rejected by the family of her husband after the death of her husband. … you must bear in mind that this young woman had a six-month-old baby, so with an even more significant psychological burden …. (RP 7)

This example points to a factor that plays a crucial role in the final outcome of many cases: the professionals' assessment of the future evolution of the grieving process of the relatives and of how a decision to retrieve organs may affect future relations among them. The following example also illustrates this point. The BDPD was a middle-aged male. A hospital coordinator and an intensivist announced brain death and raised the issue of organ donation with the adult daughter and the widow of the BDPD. The daughter was born from a previous marriage of her father and had lost her mother years before. Her father had re-married, with the woman who was present at the hospital:

> … we see in the first place in an interview his wife. … Then, she tells us 'listen I think that yes. However it is absolutely necessary that you ask … his daughter and then … above all do not tell her that I've said yes. It ought to be her who really says what she thinks because, you know, she doesn't like me, she doesn't like me a lot, and I wouldn't want the situation to become worse, especially, especially now.'
>
> So it was very difficult for us … So, we met both of them together. There was the medical team, the wife and the daughter. And then, the daughter who at first says 'no', and then 'it's according to what he wanted! But no, in the end it's no! do not touch him!' She leaves the room shouting and collapses in the corridor. That's what happened.
>
> And then, we talked for a long, long time, the situation calmed down a little, and then she says: 'Listen, no! I don't know what he wanted, but I can't bear the idea that you do that to my father, it's too much! I lost my mother, now it's my father! It's too much it's too much!!!' And, we felt that she was truly on the brink. Really on the brink.
>
> So in the end we didn't carry out the removal.
>
> And then, the wife [the widow-stepmother] tells us 'Well OK, we don't do anything. What his daughter says must, must be respected.' And she told us again, to us in a clear loud voice, what she had told us before, during the private interview.
>
> And, when they were leaving, I accompanied them back to the lift, and then the, the wife [the widow-stepmother] holds out her hand to me and – pulls me as she holds my hand – and then leans towards me and tells me 'listen I'm sorry for what we haven't been able to do, really I'm sorry!' and cries.
>
> So I took her aside and I told her, 'listen, concerning what he, what he would have wanted, I think that what he would have wanted above all else is that you get on well with his daughter, and only then to be able to donate. So there you've chosen, well, not to let that get in the way, not to let that get in the way of your future relations …, so that's that.' (HC 2)

In these last two cases, informants are aware that, according to the law, it was the information from the widows, who reported that their husbands were in favour of organ donation, that should have been decisive. However, they acknowledge that the preservation of family bonds is to be privileged to the point of overrunning the known willingness to donate of the BDPD. The last two cases also show that when there is a divergence of views among relatives who seem to occupy equivalent positions of authority and legitimacy to decide, the outcome will tend to be a decision not to proceed with organ retrieval. Informants add that, even though patients on the waiting list may die as a consequence of such decisions, it would be unethical to impose organ retrieval in such cases. As one hospital coordinator observes:

> It's true that [in such cases] we tell ourselves that it's four organs that we haven't been able to retrieve, maybe four people who are going to die …. I think that there too one ought to put things into perspective: well certainly that's maybe four people who are going to die but what, what kind of life was this woman going to have after all for the rest of her days because she had been put under so much pressure for the organs to be donated, really? (HC 7)

Approval of Organ Donation

Professionals explain that in the simplest cases relatives know that the potential donor wanted to donate her organs and that in most of these cases they appear to feel a moral duty to fulfil such a wish and will not seek to prevent organ retrieval. However, they note, in a majority of cases the answer to the question 'Do you happen to know whether your father, sister, son, was opposed to organ donation?' is 'No, we don't.' It is precisely to facilitate organ retrieval in such situations that the law has always been supposed to have been enacted. The problem is that from this point on the script followed by professionals is very different from the legislative one. As they describe these encounters, they try to encourage reflection among the group of relatives about what the potential donor *might have wanted.* A switch is thus made from the initial question – focusing on a possible opposition to donate – towards a reflection about a possible wish to donate. The response of the relatives is, they observe, usually a sincere effort to try to figure out what the position of the deceased might or would have been.

This discussion generally leads to an exploration of the personality of the deceased, structured around the question frequently asked by professionals: 'Was she generous?' If things go well from the professionals' perspective, the discussion will develop into a positive obituary: '[He] was generous. He used to donate blood …' (HC 4), she was active with NGOs, she used to train the children's football team in the neighbourhood, and so forth. However, in the professionals' view the border between orienting the discussion toward the generosity of the BDPD and manipulation of the sorrow of relatives is thin.

Moreover, the lines between the relatives' reconstruction of the personality of the BDPD, their feeling that they must protect the BDPD and their immediate needs as persons at the beginning of a grieving process are not always neat. Thus, for instance, the idea – borderline, many observe, with a pathological grieving process – that the BDPD will somehow continue to live through transplantation can be a reason why relatives agree to organ donation. This is, in the view of informants, a response to the confusion caused by the sudden loss of their loved one, confusion rendered more acute by the contrast between the brain death state and the classical image of cardio-respiratory death. Thus, in what can sometimes be read as a denial of death, relatives will accompany their acceptance with words to this effect: 'the fact that his organs serve to make other people live, it's him who is going to continue to live' (RP 4). Sometimes acceptance is read by professionals as an attempt by relatives to make sense of something that has no sense – to produce something positive out of what appears as pure tragedy. This is very clear, they note, when brain death is the result of a suicide attempt, a situation in which the acceptance of organ donation is according to them more frequent.

In other cases the relatives somehow assume the ownership or a right to dispose of the corpse and see organ donation as a way of introducing themselves into the donation-transplantation system. This movement of the donating entity from the BDPD to the relatives entails the passage from donation as renouncement with no return (that is, as sacrifice) toward donation as exchange, so that the relatives enter the transplantation chain as donors now and as potential receivers in the future. In the following example, given by a hospital coordinator, the BDPD is a woman and the discussion is with her husband and their adult son: '… [the husband] agreed because he is cardiac, he has a heart condition. He told me: "It may happen that I will end up needing a heart, I'm totally for it"' (HC 12).

There are also those who, having assumed a sort of right over the corpse, donate in an act of solidarity with their fellow citizens and of restatement of their belonging to the community. One hospital coordinator observes that some people ask her whether many people donate, and agree to it after she answers positively:

> … the fact of knowing that someone else has done the same act, this brings some comfort somehow …
>
> Of, of, of thinking that they are not the only ones, and that they belong to a solidarity … or to a body of citizens, or to a national solidarity, anyway something, something of the sort. They go beyond themselves. They transcend themselves, in fact they transcend themselves when they agree to donate. (HC 3)

Thus relatives can accept donation because they feel they belong to a greater whole and, by donating, feel that they become greater. The verb used in French and that I have translated as 'to transcend' is *sublimer*, the root of which refers to something that is bigger than the individual but not inaccessible; and when reached, its force becomes that of the individual as well. The idea of going beyond oneself by a gesture of solidarity clearly recalls Durkheim's writings about the sacred. In his *Elementary Forms of Religious Life* (1995 [1976]), the French sociologist, argues that what is held sacred in a society are symbolic representations of society, namely of a force that pre-exists the individual and is external to her as well as bigger than herself. By participating in the collective individuals feel that they belong to something that is more than themselves and that takes them beyond themselves.

Vetoes of Organ Retrieval

Whether the agreement of families to organ donation is expressed as a way of keeping the BDPD alive or as a way for relatives to include themselves in the system of organ circulation, the physicians and nurses met during this research do not seem to consider it worth spending time and energy in clarifying that it is not the relatives' personal views that are being sought. This approach also applies to families' refusals.

According to all the information gathered during this research, the rule in practice is that opposition from relatives is respected by hospital coordinators and intensivists even when it goes against the known wishes of the BDPD.[7] This type of opposition is said to be of two kinds: relatives claim that they cannot cope with the idea of organ retrieval and/or transplantation of the body parts of the person they have just lost, or they put forward a feeling of responsibility to protect the body and thereby the person of the potential donor. In fact whether relatives appear to be talking in their own name or in that of the deceased, they are often believed to operate a cognitive appropriation of the body of the latter: 'one could say that the relatives assume ownership of the, the, the deceased, if I may, almost like a material possession, if I may say, or an emotional possession. In any case like a possession' (RP 2).[8]

In some cases the relatives voice adamant and inflexible refusals that appear to professionals to leave no room for discussion. These are frequently posed in clear and straightforward utterances, such as 'Don't you dare!', 'I can't bear to imagine it!', and so forth. The case, discussed in the previous section, where the BDPD is a man and the meeting is held with his adult daughter and his second wife (the daughter's step-mother), is a good illustration of this type of situation. Last but not least, images of the process of organ extraction can be paralysing for relatives. If they think about it, they will associate extraction with ideas of 'mutilation',

7 To the contrary, the willingness of relatives to agree to organ retrieval is never imposed against a known opposition to donate by the BDPD (this would put professionals at risk of criminal prosecution).

8 Research conducted with recipients of organs shows that they think in much the same terms and feel indebted to the relatives for the organ they have received. Fox wrote that recipients of kidneys feel both extremely grateful and guilty *vis-à-vis* those who have, in a moment of extreme sorrow, given to someone they did not know part of the body of a person they loved (Fox 1979: 115–21. More recent research shows that this is also the case in France (Vaysse 1993)).

'butchery' [charcutage], 'skinning' [écorcher] and 'cutting up' [dépeçage]. To this professionals add that, whatever the intensivist and the hospital coordinator tell them, relatives sometimes express the fear that the BDPD will physically suffer during the extraction. Less dramatically, relatives may reject the idea of organ retrieval with expressions such as 'she's had enough' or 'she didn't like hospitals, let's not prolong this'.

All informants describe cases of this kind at length and in detail that clearly illustrate their reluctance to do something that could make the grieving process for the relatives more difficult. They all say that they tend to back away and to accept the position of the person(s) who oppose(s) organ retrieval. Hospital coordinators and referent physicians stress the need for organs for transplantation does not morally justify taking the risk of psychologically damaging those who survive the BDPD.[9]

Interviewees note that, when relatives adamantly refuse donation, they often feel incapable of finding the words and the gestures to communicate. In most cases, however, a form of constructive dialogue can be established. It is indeed the view of informants that in most cases the relatives make a sincere effort to try to work out what the wishes of the deceased might have been, as well as to give a reasoned response to the request addressed to them. The problem is that they are asked to respond to the question of organ retrieval on the basis of wishes that they usually do not know and to take a decision about a body they feel responsible for. By agreeing to organ retrieval they take the risk of violating the possible but unknown objection of their loved one and/or of betraying their duty to protect that body.

Hospital coordinators and intensivists interviewed observe that asking relatives to produce the mental and family work needed to answer the question of organ retrieval is, in the state of cognitive and psychological shock they are in, asking 'too much' from them: 'I am the first to say and to think that IT'S NOT THE RIGHT TIME, the time when a person is in intensive care and he becomes brain dead. … Because it's too much for the family, it's too much' (HC 11). 'Too much' because they suddenly have to carry upon their shoulders the responsibility of guarding the wishes of their relative; because they feel responsible for protecting her interests and dignity; because their personal immediate reaction is to reject the mental operations implied by the request of organ retrieval; because, once the loss of their loved one has been accepted, the taken-for-granted next step is arrangements for the funeral, not a new intervention on the body of the person they have just lost.

---

9 This is also the approach of the Etablissement français des Greffes. The psychotherapist in charge of the psychological part of the training given by the transplantation agency to procurement professionals confirmed in a personal communication that one of the aims of this training is to familiarize professionals with the grieving behaviour that relatives of potential donors can display, and to warn them about what not to do or say in order not to provoke a pathological grieving process. I shall come back to the policy of the Etablissement français des Greffes in Chapter 8.

In such a situation, their responses are not always formulated, one head of unit notes, according to the *rational* arguments that legislators said inspired the presumed consent legal device (see Chapter 2): 'we realize that people, they're therefore going to express the consent, the refusal, at a given moment, not necessarily according to Cartesian rules, because there's, they are experiencing the shock of very strong emotions' (RP 2).

Depending on how the encounter evolves and on the influence of external factors such as the information the relatives have about donation and transplantation issues, their family history and so forth, the relatives may be able to overcome their immediate rejection of the idea and eventually accept the retrieval of organs. But the acceptance may be partial and subject to 'restrictions' on some tissues and/or organs. Hearts, skin and corneas are the organs and tissues that informants mention as being most often protected by relatives. With skin and corneas the main fear seems to be disfiguration: a visible and outrageous transformation of the external appearance of the corpse. On the uneasiness of relatives in imagining the extraction of corneas, one intensivist says: 'there's a violation of the tissue integrity that seems to them … absolutely impossible to bear. That they could not bear it psychologically later on' (RP 3). About the skin, one hospital coordinator notes: 'Often I've been told: "but, he, he's going to turn all pink like, like a pig"' (HC 1).

The image of the extraction and transplantation of the heart of the BDPD can also be problematic, for this organ can be closely associated with the person of the potential donor. Hospital Coordinator 6 notes for instance that the heart is for many people 'the index of the soul'. From that perspective the idea of the heart of the loved person beating inside someone else's chest can seem unbearable for the relatives, who may feel that something of the person of their loved one is located in the wrong place, or that she will not be at rest.[10] One hospital coordinator reports a case where one of the daughters of a BDPD imposed a restriction concerning his heart:

> … I saw a young woman not long ago, they agreed to the removal, and, the daughter, one of the daughters, posed a restriction for the heart because she said that she couldn't picture it, and she wasn't able to imagine that it would be possible to live with the idea that the heart of her father was beating … in the, inside the body of another person! And for her the idea was something just unbearable! (HC 4)

Informants say that they sometimes feel that the relatives are not sure that the restrictions will be respected and that 'more is going to be taken than what has

10 The special position of the heart can play in the opposite direction with relatives insisting that the heart be transplanted. This happens according to professionals for two reasons: denial of death – through the graft of the heart the BDPD will continue to live – or the donation of this organ is seen as additional proof of the generosity of the BDPD.

been agreed' (HC 1). Some of them have had the experience of relatives trying to check, after the intervention, that the restrictions they imposed have been respected. While this is difficult to verify with internal organs, restrictions on corneas and the skin can be more easily checked:

> … there are families that check, who are really going to verify afterwards. … they've agreed, they are certainly in tears, when they come to see the corpse they are falling apart but … at the morgue or at the undertaker's they sometimes check. Because there's a lady who came back to tell me: 'Thank you for not touching the eyes.'
>
> I was a bit surprised and she tells me 'yes we've verified, we've checked, we've had a look around'. So I tell myself, despite there being the idea of loss and of mourning, there's nevertheless the idea 'have they really kept their word?' Because in fact it's a little bit this, eh, it's 'I trust you but …' (HC 12)

Professionals see such restrictions as a compromise relatives make between the moral duty to accept the donation of the organs of the BDPD, and the immediate profound resistance they can experience when forced to contemplate the possibility of the retrieval and transplantation. As with absolute refusals, informants say that they tend to accept restrictions without much discussion, even though they believe that these more often reflect the wishes of the relatives than of the BDPD.

They actually add that they even accept refusals they read as obvious lies. It seems from the way informants describe their encounters with relatives that a tacit agreement between all participants is that relatives can legitimately expect transparency on behalf of professionals whilst the latter cannot expect relatives to be transparent about their reasons for accepting or rejecting organ retrieval.[11] Indeed, informants explain, whether donation is accepted or refused, taking part in the decision is not an easy task for the relatives. While it is rather easy to decide for oneself on the fate of one's corpse, it is not for that of a loved one:

> … it's difficult for someone close to allow that the donation of organs is carried out.
>
> – [GN] What do you mean?
>
> I, I don't know why it is. People, people say: 'As far as I'm concerned I would like to, concerning my husband or my daughter I wouldn't want to' … (HC 2)

11 In that sense the encounter between intensive care professionals and relatives of the BDPD reverts the communicative model that is dominant in French hospitals where it is taken for granted that physicians can avoid being completely transparent while relatives are supposed to share what they know about the patient with hospital professionals. For recent illustrations about this model see (Castra 2003; Fainzang 2006; Paillet 2007).

In fact, as professionals depict it, relatives feel responsible for protecting the body and the person of the potential donor, they feel responsible for respecting the wishes of the deceased, or at least the supposed wishes; they also generally find the idea of the body of their dear one cut into pieces and used to save others' lives difficult to cope with. At the same time, it seems inconceivable for them not to play an active part in the decision process. This does not mean that the views of the BDPD are taken completely out of the picture, but that a hierarchy operates so that when it appears that relatives cannot cope with the idea of retrieval and/or transplantation, the views of the BDPD – known or imagined – take a secondary position.

PART III
Law and Policy

In the previous three chapters I tried to capture the main themes in the description professionals give of the way organ retrieval decisions are made on the intensive care shop-floor. At a formal level, and concurring in this with the analysis made by legal scholars, hospital professionals understand that the law – and related statutory texts concerning its application – excludes the interests of the relatives of a BDPD from the set of factors to be taken into account. At the same time, all of them acknowledge that: '… IN PRACTICE the notion of presumed consent never comes into play when you have a family in front of you, BECAUSE it's they who in the end are going to decide' (Hospital Coordinator 6). An intensivist observes:

> … we ask families for information about the will of the deceased but in fact it's not that information that they give, it's their agreement, and when they refuse it's not because they think that the patient would have objected, it's that they don't want to donate. (Referent Physician 8)

All interviewees, after having described how decisions are taken together with the relatives of BDPDs, conclude that their own behaviour does not conform with the letter of the law, and even, in a sense, violates it, as in the following quote from a head of unit:

> – [GN] … this view [of the family] is followed, no matter what …?
>
> It's followed, no matter what.
>
> – [GN] Yes?
>
> This is where we are somewhat in violation of the law.
>
> The law is one of implicit consent, not of explicit consent. Thus, normally the law should, should allow us to, when the deceased has not clearly expressed her opinion, to conceive, implicitly, that she was in favour of organ donation. … IN PRACTICE we hold to the opinion expressed by the relatives, whatever their motivations may be, whether we think they are good or not. (RP 2)

Every informant expressed the view that the systematic non-mobilization of the law is the rule in all hospitals involved with organ procurement activities in France. They see their own practice as exemplifying a standardized approach that has become uniform throughout France after the more disordered first ten to fifteen years of organ retrieval.

Chapter 7
The Regulation of Generosity by the State

The Violence at the Core of the Presumption of Consent

Against Everyday Assumptions

The legal presumption of consent is seen by all the informants involved in the research for this book as going against a number of basic assumptions about social life. As one intensivist puts it: '"He who keeps silent [consents], he who has not said no in fact, he agrees." Pffff, well hey that goes against everyday life' (Referent Physician 4). The first assumption is that, for something as important for most individuals as the fate of their corpse, a presumption should not be so clearly unfavourable to the person about whom something is presumed. Reflecting this idea is the argument developed by Hennette-Vauchez (2001) in her criticism of the presumption of consent from a legal perspective, where she argues that presumptions in French law are usually to the benefit of the person whose opinion is presumed. In the case of organ donation the general view is that it entails the mutilation and thus the desacralization of the dead body. This is why the presumption of consent to organ donation is generally seen as not in the interest of the dead person.

The second assumption said to be violated by the legal presumption is that the individuals are part of a relational network and that what is done to the body of a person is likely and legitimately to be of concern to her closest relatives. From this perspective the law appears to usurp a prerogative that belongs to the relatives. Playing with the word *droit*, which in French refers to both law and subjective rights, a hospital coordinator explains that the law/rights that legitimately apply to organ retrieval are not those stipulated in the law:

> … in 99 per cent of cases – I do mean 99 per cent, I'm not saying 100 per cent – in 99 per cent of cases you would make a dreadful blunder, heavy with consequences, if you told the relatives that it's you in that case, who makes the decision because the law authorizes you.
>
> The law [droit] at that moment is the RIGHT [droit] OF THE FAMILY:
>
> The right to decide, the right to speak, the right to decide what TO DO with the body … From an emotional perspective, a rational perspective, a psychological perspective, a family perspective, a social perspective, the family feels, understands, that the body belongs to them. (Hospital Coordinator 6)

For the relatives, the request for organ donation also means that, instead of getting back the corpse of their loved one after the announcement of death, instead of it being returned to the private sphere where it is seen as ultimately belonging, it is to be entrusted to the medical institution. In this sense, the request for organs introduces an abnormal sort of activity around the newly dead: the corpse should be released to grieving relatives but it is not; the corpse should no longer be treated but it still is; the corpse should interest no one but the family but it does interest hospital professionals, anonymous patients and society as a whole. Moreover, the retrieval intervention is particularly unsettling for the relatives because it is perceived as suspending everything, explains one hospital coordinator:

> … they are lending something to us … We are borrowing it in order to take something from it, and there's a sort of vacuum: for them eight hours in the operating room … it's a vacuum. It's timeless! What's happening during that time? Where is he?!
>
> … [Once the intervention is finished] I go together with them to the morgue and give back to them what they just lent me. And there they will have their corpse back. They have it, THEIR dead one. And then, at that moment, they can start their mourning process, because so far they hadn't started it. (HC 3)

Last but certainly not least, hospital professionals are of the view that the legal presumption of a gift is from the perspective of normal social assumptions an oxymoron. They strongly express the idea that *someone* has actively to say *yes* to legitimize a decision to retrieve organs from a BDPD:

> … once again, I think that we need, for various reasons, it's either because of the collective unconscious or of individual conscience, [we need to] hear a 'YES'. That's how it is, we need it. It's obvious! (RP 4)

It is the idea that a *real* gift is essential that, combined with the perception that relatives are the natural protectors of a corpse and the legitimate representatives of a person who can no longer express her wishes, puts the relatives at the centre of the decision process. More down-to-earth, a head of unit asks what can be so surprising about relatives being at the centre of decision-making? After all:

> … even if we talk about the other one [the BDPD], it doesn't mean that we aren't dealing with the family, even if we talk about the other person's will.
>
> OK, we get into some kind of psychological transference, but we no longer address the deceased since he's dead. Therefore we address the family. … we can dress this up whatever way we want, but in reality it's the family that we are addressing …. (RP 4)

Thus the situation where presumed consent legislation should formally apply, namely an adult in a state of brain death, is in practice close to that where the brain-dead subject is a child, where the consent of the legal representatives is needed to proceed and their opposition respected: 'so in the end we find ourselves, even in the case of adults sometimes in the case of children, … in a situation where the consent of both parents is obligatory' (RP 9).

Abusive Application of the Law

As mentioned in Chapter 6, one of the main factors leading to negative decisions about retrieval is the fear among the professionals in charge that their behaviour may endanger both the relatives' incipient grieving process and the equilibrium of family relations. Most of them seem to believe that they have a significant psychological advantage over relatives: they are not in a state of psychological shock, the announcement of death does not have consequences in their personal lives, and they are not caught by surprise by the notion of brain death or by the question of organ donation. From such a position, informants explain, they may be able to exert psychological pressure upon the relatives, to take advantage of their psychological weakness and try to obtain organs – or more organs – for transplantation.

Another advantage they say they have over relatives has to do with their knowledge of the law and the discretionary power it gives them.[1] They know that the letter of the law is to their advantage, which allows them to confront the relatives with difficult questions and to make the final decision about retrieval or about withdrawal of treatment when a decision not to retrieve is taken. In short, they are aware that the law gives them the power to ask and to act (Foucault 1998): to make the relatives confront certain questions and to engage in otherwise socially and legally unacceptable behaviour.[2] Hospital coordinators and referent physicians thus conclude that it would be possible during many of their encounters with relatives to push them into accepting donation. But apart from the scandals that a more authoritarian-legalistic behaviour might lead to, they fear that it would be the source of 'serious' psychological harm and of 'appalling' effects upon the mourning process:

> … ONE SHOULD NOT go against what the relatives want … First because really I mean we don't know, with regards to the mourning, aren't there, aren't there people who, whom this can really impede their achieving closure?

1 Power is here understood as domination in the sense of the ability of a participant in a specific situation to control the course of events, to determine or influence the possibilities of action available to other participants in the situation. On this aspect see Gould (2003: in particular chapter 2, 27–66).

2 For a broader reflection on the control exerted by the medical profession in end of life processes in French hospitals see Hennette-Vauchez and Nowenstein (2009).

> … I mean we may cause after all SERIOUS things to happen to people at a psychological level. (HC 4)[3]

Why would that cause harm? Because the taking of organs from a dead body with the aim of perpetuating somebody else's life remains a transgression from the point of view of common conceptions of the relationship between personhood and body, and private and public interests; and of the duties of families with regard to the corpse of one of their members.[4]

Individuals, the State and the Law

Solidarity or Generosity?

As we saw in Chapters 3 and 6, informants associate the active role of the relatives in organ donation decisions with a broader process whereby medical paternalism as the dominant trend organizing medical encounters has lost strength. Within the paternalistic model the authority of the physician in public hospitals was related to that of the state and, in fact, the physician often played the role of an arm of state policy. This process of change is presented as part of a long crisis for republican values. Among these, interviewees stress the crisis of the idea of republican solidarity, namely of the way in which the relation between the state and individuals is conceived in French society. The idea of a duty of solidarity that gave legitimacy to the initial project of presumed consent legislation in France came together with the assumption that it is the role of the state to give shape to the institutions that allow the expression of such solidarity by individuals.

3 This seems to be confirmed by the national survey I conducted with hospital coordinators in 2002. To the question 'Do you think that the hospital coordinator can influence families' decisions?' 31 per cent answered 'Yes, a lot'; and 57 per cent 'Yes, a bit'. To a subsequent question: 'Do you try to convince relatives that they should accept donation?' respondents had to answer from 0 (not at all) to 10 (absolutely). 35 per cent answered 0, and the cumulative percentage from 0 to 5 was 78 per cent. Although one cannot infer from these answers that hospital coordinators do not try to influence families in practice, they do show that the idea that it would be wrong to do so is very strong. As far as practice is concerned, all the information gathered during my research suggests that professionals are very cautious about putting families under pressure.

4 As mentioned in Chapter 6, professionals are of the view that the question of organ donation exposes family bonds that are today inherently fragile to a particularly strong strain. At the core of this fragility we find the historical trend whereby these bonds have passed from being rather fixed and given to being more chosen and unstable. For that reason they are more likely to be weakened or broken (Peletz 1995: 364). About how relatives feel after the donation of the organs of a loved one see Lock (2002), Sharp (2006), Waissmann (1996).

One intensivist speaks explicitly in terms of a breakdown of the republican model, where the hierarchy between the three pillars of 'liberty', 'equality' and 'fraternity' is evolving from the dominion of the latter to that of the first. He explains that the community is becoming less important than the individual:

> … We are half-way between an Anglo-Saxon culture towards which we're probably tending more and more, and then the remains of a culture, I would say, rather Napoleonic really, I mean, I wouldn't say Latin …. I don't know much about other legal systems …, but I have the impression that in France we have a legal system that's more like, that comes out from the Republic really, from the Enlightenment, so, every man is a citizen … and so finally the community of citizens has a lot of power over each citizen individually. We may, we may sum it up this way really.
>
> – [GN] So the law in this sense, it embraces …
>
> It embraces somehow the republican ideals. But the republican ideals are becoming in my opinion slightly those of a minority in France …. (RP 12)

This idea, formulated in different ways by many informants, does not imply that the French are seen by them as less generous than before. The main implication is that people do not want to be presumed generous by the state – which is seen as a contradiction in terms – but want to be generous because they have decided to be. Here we come to the core of the tension between solidarity and gift systems. The former fits better with the state taking a central and directive role, with hospital professionals representing public authority, and with relatives and citizens acknowledging the legitimacy of the guidance of the state in the area of organ donation. Gift systems, by contrast, regard the fate of the corpse as a matter for the private sphere – consisting of individuals belonging to affective networks – and are organized around the autonomy of individuals and their relatives.

Within a less and less republican context, to put it in the terms of the intensivist just quoted, a gift system seems more natural than a solidarity system. Like the medical profession, informants note, public institutions have lost their once unquestioned position of authority. This is why applying the law of presumed consent is seen as almost certain to lead to conflict with the relatives of BDPDs in hospitals, and to public scandals in the public sphere. A long quote from a unit head summarizes the general view of the informants in this respect. She starts by rephrasing the saying 'Ignorance of the law is no excuse'[5] that some supporters of the law raise to legitimize the application of presumed consent legislation:

> 'He who has not said no, in fact he agrees.'

5 In French: 'nul n'est censé ignorer la loi.' For a discussion about possible translations see Harvey (2002: 178).

> …
>
> Well, this already creates a very hard, confrontational relationship.
>
> But, the family from whom the organs of the deceased are going to be taken, but what's going to happen afterwards? If the person, if the person has an impact, contacts, such and such, the media hype is going to be UNBELIEVABLE! Saying: 'we were against it.' … Obviously there's going to be publicity in the media and the result is that, the next time, when there will be someone in a state of brain death, there the family will intervene and block everything! By every possible and unimaginable way! … We saw in Amiens [see Chapter 2] …. There was this story of the corneas that were taken from a child [he was 19], without the parents being told about it. The law permitted it.
>
> And you saw the impact that this had: immediately … pfffff. Because all of a sudden there's no longer TRUST in the health system, and so people they're going to write themselves into the register of objections, saying: 'you see what doctors do: they don't warn us … they mutilate the bodies and everything. So we say, we write ourselves into the register of objections.'
>
> And so I believe that this type of attitude … which would consist in using the law the hard way, as transplantation surgeons suggest, could very well have a negative effect with the number of people that would join the register of objections which would grow considerably. Because you can be sure that certain journalists will take advantage of this, because, well, this will be a very attention-grabbing subject. … And all this has a disastrous effect on public opinion. In the same way that there was a considerable dive in blood donation when there were the stories about the contaminated blood! (RP 4)

Avoiding negative public reactions from families is, in fact, one of the main reasons put forward by informants to justify their behaviour. A hospital coordinator states this very clearly: 'I think that my objective [as hospital coordinator] is that there should not be, there should not be any complaints at the hospital …. You see what I mean?' (HC 2).

However, the idea expressed by the professionals that the solution proposed by legislators to the tension between community interests and individual-family autonomy is no longer *natural*, is not to be understood as meaning that they regard it as morally illegitimate. They express sympathy for the notions of social solidarity and state responsibility that they identify as the foundation of the opting-out system. Hence, it is not their view that the law is, in principle, a bad law; but that it is not applicable in the present context.

Within this context, they insist, they are doing as much as possible to obtain organs for transplantation. They stress that they are aware that organs are badly needed and that the lives of many patients in the waiting lists are at risk. They say that each refusal makes them think of the patients that could have been saved who may now die, or whose painful existences will not be relieved.[6] Because most of these professionals have intensive care and anaesthesiology backgrounds, they have been confronted with the suffering of patients in need of organs, as well as with the relief of those who have received a graft. One head of unit thus claims:

> Intensivists do not forget. In any case, that's my experience, … doing liver transplantations and seeing these [patients] who wait, suffering, and these families who wait. I KNOW WELL that [a vital need of organs exists], [but] that's the way it is. (RP 6)

They are thus outraged by the accusation that some surgeons sometimes make, that they do not really care about transplantation. Indeed, as regrettable as they can be, refusals are an inevitable element of gift systems, for they come together with the freedom to donate. They add that, as soon as one takes into consideration the circumstances under which the issue of organ retrieval is raised, it is impossible to blame the relatives who refuse because they do not manage to give under such difficult circumstances. Several informants even express doubts about what they themselves would do were they one day to be in the position of these families. One head of unit openly acknowledges that:

> … even if I am convinced about the GOOD REASONS for transplantation, I'm not sure that if this concerned my family, I would accept.
>
> There you go. I'm very clear, huh.
>
> It's very easy to put the blame on others … but when it concerns YOU, deeply, you, yourself, I'm not sure that, how I would react to a request for organs. (RP 6)

At a Distance from the Shop-Floor

Although they often show some understanding for the frustration of some surgeons, intensive care professionals consider their complaints ill-informed and sometimes fed with arrogance. Those who call for a strict application of the legal texts are thought to believe that because the law makes organs formally available, the situation of loss is less painful for relatives and the organs are less charged with meaning. One hospital coordinator notes that some nephrologists in her hospital regularly accuse her and her colleagues of not being firm enough with relatives.

6 Almost 70 per cent of the respondents to the survey conducted for this research in 2002 said that they have patients awaiting transplantation in mind during their encounters with relatives; and 73 per cent noted that they usually undertake a critical self-evaluation after each encounter with families, especially if the outcome is negative.

She complains: '... a kidney, it seems like for them you can buy it at the chemist's .... They ... don't share at all in this notion of, of bereaved family, of a person who donates, of violent death' (HC 7). One intensivist recalls having heard surgeons at meetings at the Etablissement français des Greffes insisting on the necessity to apply the law of presumed consent: 'to hear the surgeons ... saying "we only need to apply the Caillavet Law", it's ... They're completely crazy!' (RP 6).

One of the interviewees drew a parallel between the discourse of some transplantation surgeons and an exchange she had had with a group of judges not long before her interview. She reports that the judges were shocked by her statement that neither she nor her colleagues were resorting to the presumption of consent in practice:

> I gave some talks to some judges not too long ago, a couple of weeks ago, and they told me 'Madam, you have the law, why do you make things with families so difficult?!'
>
> I said 'But sir, say you had someone close to you, you learnt later that organs had been removed from him, how would you react?' He answers me 'Well, I would ...' I tell him 'yes, but you, you are a judge, you have the law inside you. But ordinary mortals, they are not at all like that, they, they think that it will be ... it's, it's frustrating, and it's going to be, it's not going to be normal. In their eyes the body belongs to them, they ignore everything about the inalienability [non-patrimonialité] [of the body].[7] These people don't think at all in terms of laws, in their eyes it [the body] belongs to them. It's something that, coming from them, especially when it's a child! That's theirs. It's, it's, something that belongs, to a family or a group, well anyway, I don't know it's ...'
>
> But it's because of this that we find the law difficult to apply. (HC3)

The law of 1994 put transplantation surgeons at a distance from organ donation decisions because, it was then argued, their interest in obtaining organs was too strong. This seems to have limited the incidence of abusive behaviour that some families denounced in the 1990s. But it also seems to have increased the lack of understanding about the procurement process between procurement specialists and transplantation surgeons.

7 The French concept of 'non-patrimonialité' has a variety of meanings, the closest of which here is surely inalienability. Other meanings are non-transferability or non-relinquishability. For a discussion in English of the various legal meanings of the concept see Radin (1987).

The Body and the State

Beyond the idea that presumption of consent invalidates the possibility of giving, some informants express the view that the strict application of opting-out legislation would imply breaking a basic agreement about the relationship between the state, on the one hand, and individuals and their families on the other. It would amount to an oppressive form of state rule:

> Medically … one ought to be content, one ought to be content with the law and then there wouldn't be any problems.
>
> – [GN] Yes?
>
> But, at a personal level, it's true … what's … the right of the state to dispose of a body, more than the right of the family? What's the answer? … [laughs] I don't really know.
>
> I don't know. I somehow am bothered by a comprehensive and powerful right of the state. Because we are close to, to something that resembles dictatorship. (RP 1)

This quote clearly reflects two ideas shared by all the informants and that are central to understanding how decisions to retrieve organs from BDPDs are made in French hospitals. First, Referent Physician 1 does not assimilate the system of presumed consent to a gift system but to one where the state has 'the right to dispose of a body'. Second, she contrasts it with a system where such a right belongs to 'the family' of a BDPD. In a nutshell, presumed consent systems are not donation systems and, as a matter of fact, most decisions to retrieve organs in French hospitals are family decisions.

Explaining the distinction between what can be legitimately at the disposal of the state and what should belong to the private sphere, one hospital coordinator sees the donation of organs as an act expressing personal 'virtue' and continues:

> … WHAT is a law doing in a terrain where it's a question of personal inclination?
>
> The gift is to me an inclination of the soul.
>
> … Law is there to organize society … but not to TRY TO MAKE PEOPLE VIRTUOUS. (HC 6)

So far it has been shown that it is both for pragmatic reasons (relatives are the BDPDs actual interlocutors, risk of scandals and so forth) and for moral reasons (it is in most situations appropriate to give the final word to the relatives) that procurement professionals accept and justify the central role played by relatives of BDPDs. But there is more to it than that: in their view, it would be unfair to expect them to be in effect the arm of the law by adopting a stronger position with the relatives of BDPDs. They feel that their crucial and difficult contribution to transplantation medicine is not acknowledged, and complain that they are unjustly stigmatized by their peers and by the media.

Lack of Acknowledgement and Consideration

The Difficulty of the Task

The abundance of expressions such as 'it's difficult' (256 times, in all interviews), or 'it's hard' (139 times, in all but two interviews) in the discourse of professionals reflects how deeply they feel affected by their participation in organ procurement activities. The most difficult aspect of the task to cope with is the sorrow they face and the need to juggle empathy and detachment, to find a balance between protecting themselves from getting too close with relatives and showing enough concern. Finding and keeping an equilibrium between the two is not easy, as one hospital coordinator notes:

> … sometimes it's, you find it hard not to have, not to, not to cry with them too. Because sometimes it has happened to me that I had tears in my eyes because, I mean, there are people who, who affect you and then the, the emotions are transmitted to you and it's, it's difficult. … this doesn't mean that you are less serene but in any case you feel more affected. … it's true that it's difficult. … Besides, after the interviews, sometimes it's true that there's a point, whew, where one feels sort of a bit empty. (HC 4)

Similarly, informants stress, it is not easy to avoid having thoughts like 'if this happened to me, how would I react?' (HC 12).

It is often at the beginning and the end of the process, professionals explain, that they find themselves incapable of maintaining a self-protective distance. At the beginning of the process, it is the encounter with the relatives that is said to be most upsetting. At the end, it is when everything has been achieved and the level of stress falls that a feeling of sadness can overcome those who have been involved. The end of the process in the operating room is said to be emotionally particularly draining, not only because the brain-dead body has become a cold cadaver, but also because it has been emptied out. One hospital coordinator remembers the first time she was confronted with this:

> The anaesthesiologist had … cleaned everything around the head, had taken off all the tubes, all the organs had been removed, the surgeon was preparing the organs, BEFORE closing up the body again.

> – [GN] Yes.
>
> Which means that, well at one point I found myself in the operating room with, with in front of me this vision of: a face, so SOMEONE, really, a face; the surgical site, and THERE, a belly opened up and empty … (HC 2)

Interviewees explain that the presence in the operating room of a corpse, as opposed to a living body, is particularly difficult to cope with. It is unusual that death occurs there, and when it does, it means that something has gone wrong:

> The final picture is, is tough. … DEATH in the operating room, the fact of having a corpse on the operating table, is always something that is, that, that goes down very badly. To have a dead body in an emergency unit, in an intensive care unit, those are places where you often see dead people. A corpse in the operating room is something EXTREMELY rare! …
>
> Very rare! In scheduled anaesthesia [remember that French intensivists are also anaesthesiologists], this would be proof of, of a very serious accident. … 'Death on the table', as it's called, is something that's psychologically terrible! That, that people don't forget. The death of the same injured person in intensive care two hours later, it's a place, intensive care is a place where dying is normal. … in our discipline, to have someone come out, come out of the operating room, as is said 'feet first', whew, this, this doesn't go down well.
>
> Then … the last image of the presence of, of this corpse in the operating room, at 2 o'clock in the morning with people tired, when there's almost nobody left, except the nurse coordinator, the surgery nurse, and then the youngest of the surgeons who's there, who's there to close [the body] up. And then cleaning up the floor, with the corpse in the middle …
>
> The final image … stays such that you, you don't forget it soon …. (RP 10)

A hospital coordinator notes that, notwithstanding her almost 20 years of experience:

> It's tough. … When I leave, I'm nevertheless quite tired, because eight hours at the operating room is in any case quite long. From time to time I do feel quite shattered, I get a small tear in the eyes saying to myself: 'the poor, poor relatives'. (HC 3)

If health professionals in charge of organ procurement seem to be particularly sensitive to external criticism of their unwillingness to apply the law or to do more to obtain more organs, this is because they feel that the psychological difficulties that they endure are not acknowledged. Such situations are inherently moving, they note, and there is no way any participant can remain unaffected. Those who will tell you the opposite, states one head of unit, have just 'superficial brains' (RP 4). Yet, although negative judgements from transplantation specialists appear to irritate the informants a great deal, the most difficult criticism to take, especially for hospital coordinators, is that from their peers.

Stigmatization by Peers

Hospital coordinators note that awkward reactions and even negative remarks about organ retrieval are not infrequent among their nurse colleagues in intensive care, who can be very negative about the fact that it is when a family has just lost a loved one that the question of organ retrieval is raised. This makes them hostile not only to organ donation, but also towards those directly in charge of it. Some hospital coordinators complain that they are regularly stigmatized as 'birds of prey' or 'gravediggers' by other members of staff, who accuse them of waiting for diagnoses of brain death to 'jump upon' BDPDs' bodies and their desperate families. As one hospital coordinator puts it:

> There are people here, we should not talk to them about donation eh!
>
> Not, not long ago I was talking with a nurse who was telling me: 'it's inhumane what you do' …
>
> – [GN] Oh yeah?
>
> 'Because,' she tells me, 'don't you realize?! You lose a close relative, you are in grief, you are there weeping about his death and you are told: "he's dead but you've got to give up his kidney". Don't you realize!' she tells me, 'IT'S INHUMANE WHAT YOU DO. [If you did such a thing to me] I, I would throw a punch at you!' (HC 12)

In fact, note the informants, quite different from the generally highly positive image of transplantation medicine, everything connected with the procurement phase is somehow dark and 'inhumane'.[8] It is because of this dark side of organ procurement, they explain, that it is crucial that the procedures are respectful of the feelings of the relatives of BDPDs and that the allocation system is fair. In fact the system has to be irreproachable. And how exemplary the system and practice are, must also be evident to all hospital personnel. Professionals in charge of procurement activities feel that they are continuously on stage, performing in front of a difficult public. As a consequence, one hospital coordinator explains: '… the staff should not live this like some kind of, of MAD, mad atmosphere. Everyone [involved] should behave

8 Fox and Swazey write about the 'predatory' aspect of transplantation medicine (Fox and Swazey 1992: 206).

calmly. It can't be a circus ….' She adds that everyone should behave in a way that shows respect for the situation: 'It's something that should be done in due respect of what goes on, because it's not something fun!' (HC 3). In such a context of surveillance, those involved conclude the application of presumed consent legislation would have serious internal negative consequences in hospitals.

Doing the Dirty Work

This feeling of being presumed guilty of blameworthy behaviour extends to the way in which the media report their participation in the transplantation chain. First, they note, while their contribution to transplantation medicine is crucial, it is not publicly acknowledged. It is concealed behind the dramatic technical achievements of transplantation surgery:

> Often the media make a spectacular drama of things, like: 'they [surgeons] succeeded in taking the aorta, folded it in four, turned it around, they did all sorts of unbelievable magic.' But it's just, it's just whitewash. In terms of technique, it's necessary to have, it's necessary to be skilled, obviously, … to do a technical operation. But, technique is ONLY technique. … the aspect that I think is most delicate, it's the interpersonal aspect in this kind of situation. That's it. For instance to announce something which is not good. To announce a cure is always great, to announce that someone is better is always great, but, but to announce a death, … it's always very DIFFICULT. (RP 4)

Second, hospital coordinators and referent physicians resent the fact that the media rarely report on the importance of organ procurement. When they do, this is usually in the context of a 'scandal' and it is without consideration for the difficulties involved. But they also understand why this is so. It is inevitable, they explain, that a large part of procurement activities remains in the shadow. Their part in the transplantation chain is all about death and body parts, and contemporary Western societies tend to avoid direct confrontation with death; it is therefore not surprising that those who deal directly with it tend to be marginalized. As one intensivist explains:

> We hear a lot more talk about, about transplants than about, about donation. Why? Well, because, in the understanding of everybody, transplantation means life and donation means death, donation means death. Behind this there's a dead person and behind a transplant there's life. And then the, the dirty work, the dirty work is nevertheless …, it's all that there is UNTIL the end of the donation, dirty work. It's all there is! … it's, it's dirty work.
>
> …
>
> And then comes the glorious work depicted by the media …. (RP 10)

All this echoes sociologist Hughes' (1984) conceptualization of *dirty work*. All societies have spheres of activity that, while being functional in some way, entail the breaking of certain basic values or norms. The work done by prison guards is according to Hughes a good illustration of dirty work, but prestigious activities can also have their share of dirty work. Star, applying the concept to the medical profession, refers to doctors performing examinations of intimate parts of patients, seeing and touching unhealthy bodies, performing abortions, and so forth (Star 1995). Procurement activities are of the same kind: they are thought of as necessary for the good of society, but their accomplishment entails the breaking of a number of fundamental social assumptions.

A second feature of dirty work according to Hughes is that, because the activities concerned are functional even though they violate basic social assumptions, they need to be enclosed and concealed by silence. In fact, adds Hughes, social actors need to know enough about them not to do anything that would bring them into the light of day. In a nutshell, to divert one's gaze from something that is implicitly accepted one needs to know enough about it, so that one knows where not to look. Hence the avoidance, in the public and political spheres, of talk about the origin of organs, while transplantation is praised and celebrated. Seeing organ procurement as dirty work also helps us understand the functionality of the position of the nurses and intensivists specifically in charge of procurement activities in a hospital. They perform most of the dirty tasks and take responsibility for them. To put it in more Douglassian terms, part of the functionality of the procurement specialists is that they keep the polluting potential of the procurement activities from spreading too much (Douglas 1991).

The problem, however, with organ procurement activities is that they cannot be fully insulated from view. They take place in hospital units and require the participation of other colleagues. Thus organ procurement is dirty work that it is impossible to hide from the gaze of intensive care personnel and nurses in the operating room. Because dirty activities are transgressive of basic values, once they become visible it is difficult for most actors who are confronted with them to remain silent, to continue as if nothing has happened. From this perspective one can understand better the negative remarks and the stigmatization that those responsible for it are exposed to. Indeed, they are in the difficult position of having to perform dirty work in highly exposed circumstances.[9]

At this point, the question one may want to ask is: since participating in organ procurement is not a formal obligation for nurses or physicians, why do some of them take up the function of hospital coordinator and referent physician, often with much eagerness?

9 The analysis of procurement as dirty work appears to be also useful with regard to the media scandals in the 1990s. When certain features of procurement behaviour became visible, the public blaming and condemnation of the transgression became probably almost inevitable. For an analysis of the relation between visibility and scandals in France see de Bic and Lemieux (2005).

Personal Achievement and Public Interest

None of the informants expressed a wish to cease being involved with procurement activities. Although many of them are not necessarily as blindly enthusiastic about transplantation as they were in the early years, all show a strong commitment to taking part in its further development. And most of them add that they find their participation in the transplantation chain satisfying. The national survey conducted with hospital coordinators in 2002 confirmed the high commitment of hospital coordinators. To the question, 'If you had to give up coordination today, would you regret it?' 64 per cent of respondents said that they would.[10]

We need to qualify what has been said so far with regard to the early years of organ transplantation. This was the period when intensivists involved with the activity felt, together with transplantation surgeons, that they were making medical history. The shared excitement among specialists is one of the factors that appear to have facilitated the mobilization of presumed consent legislation in some hospitals. As the activity grew and spread to involve an increasing number of hospitals and of physicians and nurses, the participation of a few pioneers was no longer enough to keep the activity developing. This was accompanied by an increasing division of labour between intensive care and transplantation teams.

As was mentioned above, the law of 1994 confirmed this separation between the spheres of transplantation and procurement. While this contributed to avoiding tensions between intensive care staff and surgeons – as well as between surgeons and relatives of BDPDs – it also had the consequence of removing the strong motivation of surgeons from intensive care units, where decisions to retrieve organs are taken. Even more important seems to be the fact that with time the novelty of the activity decreased and routinization took over from the excitement of the first years. Thus, the part played by intensive care professionals in the transplantation chain became mostly that of the management of organ procurement and hence of death, sorrow and brain-dead bodies.

It emerges from the interviews that the specific motivations of hospital coordinators nowadays have to do with a strong interest in the relational part of the function, with being in charge of an activity from the beginning to the end and with having at some stages the same level of responsibility as physicians. Both hospital coordinators and intensivists encountered during the research say that, in spite of the difficulties they encounter, they see their participation in organ procurement activities as enriching in personal terms, and professionally

10 Twenty-one per cent said they would not; among these, 3.5 per cent said that they were now satisfied with what they had done, another 3.5 per cent that the management of their hospital was not sufficiently supportive, and 10 per cent that they had had enough. It is internationally acknowledged that the task of the hospital coordinator (and by extension of those who are regularly involved with procurement activities) often leads to situations of burn-out (Lloveras 1999; Matesanz 2001).

rewarding. They express a sense of both duty and pride in contributing to the development of an activity that is important from the perspective of public health. One head of unit adds that this feeling helps them to overcome the difficult aspects of their task:

> … it must be sublimated, how could I say this … the purpose of what we do … [it must be sublimated] in the sense of, of a service to the community. Meaning not necessarily to the hospital community, but to the whole community, to society. Actually, it's an activity that has this meaning for the people who are there at the moment of removal.
>
> … [otherwise] how could I say, the recognition for my unit, it's really quite indirect [open laughter]. (RP 2)

Similarly, while the contact with families can be painful and difficult, it is also often personally rewarding. Here is how one hospital coordinator presents the trade-off between the psychological difficulty and the satisfactory relational side of her participation in the organ procurement process:

> … it's true that psychologically I've learnt a lot, from all these people that I've met, so much, so much. This is something fascinating, I think.
>
> – [GN] Yes?
>
> Oh yeah! Even if in fact it doesn't last long, the interview with the family takes 20 minutes, three quarters of an hour, one hour at most. But it's really rewarding. It's something that's sometimes deeply moving and that, that astonishes you profoundly … that's really interesting.
>
> – [GN] Hmm.
>
> Even if it's tough, it's one of the most beautiful aspects of the job of coordinator. (HC 3)

Professionals seem to understand the functionality of their backstage role, and even to accept it as something to some extent unavoidable. Although they generally dislike the approach of journalists, they also show understanding for their tendency to focus on transplantation rather than on procurement, and to describe procurement in rather biased ways. They appear to believe that families who respond aggressively to announcements of brain death or to requests for organ donation unfortunately have their reasons. They even often express some understanding for surgeons who complain about them not doing enough for transplantation. There is one important exception to this attitude: the conviction that the health authorities have not assumed their share of responsibility for the dirty work that has to be done in the area of organ procurement. In other words, from discussions with professionals it seems clear that they resent the fact that the responsibility for the dirty work rests exclusively and unfairly upon their shoulders.

Chapter 8
The Law as Policy

The Passivity of Health Authorities

The general impression that emerges from the discourse of hospital professionals that were encountered during the course of this research is that the content of the law of presumed consent is, in principle, socially positive and politically daring. Their view is also that the law cannot be said to be inapplicable in absolute terms. The problem, as they present it, is that the measures that should have been taken to render attempts to apply the law legitimate have never been taken by the authorities. The reason for that has been, in their view, a lack of political courage and sense of responsibility. They complain that they have for decades been left to their own devices in the handling and management of a complicated and delicate activity. One hospital coordinator comments that political work to enhance organ procurement has focused on the enactment of legislation and ignored the necessary policy follow-up: ‘they [politicians] prefer to pass a bill and [expect that] we, in hospitals, are just going to manage that’ (Hospital Coordinator 7).

In the opinion of hospital coordinators and intensivists, the information and communication policy of the Etablissement français des Greffes has been insufficient in terms of the content, number and regularity of campaigns. According to them the resistance to the idea of engaging in a regular and transparent public discourse about these matters is strong within the team at the head of the Etablissement français des Greffes.[1] Its members are said to be fearful about the possible reactions of the general population, and particularly worried that campaigns might result in a considerable increase of registered refusals. Nevertheless, professionals argue, without such a policy any attempt actually to implement the opting-out system will be perceived by the general population and by the hospital personnel involved in procurement activities as fundamentally illegitimate, and will therefore be ineffective.

It makes no sense in a democratic society, they argue, to try to apply a law that goes against basic social assumptions about social life when one knows that most of the population is unaware of its existence and content. Their reasoning is more or less as follows: generally speaking most people are not knowledgeable about most laws; such ignorance is not a problem for most laws, whose content expresses views broadly shared by members of society; when the content of a law

1 Their sayings refer to the team in charge until July 2003 when Carine Camby took over from Didier Houssin as Director General of the Etablissement français des Greffes. Having said that, the communication policy has not changed substantially since.

goes against common views but not necessarily against fundamental values, it may be legitimate to impose it in practice; but it is completely illegitimate to do so in the case of disposition over corpses because this would involve breaking a sort of basic agreement between individuals and the state. This reasoning does not lead professionals to conclude that the law of presumed consent is illegitimate, but that the general population must be informed about it and that health and political authorities have not fulfilled their duty to do so. As one intensivist explains:

> … the phrase 'ignorance of the law excuses no one' is well known …
>
> Except that nobody knows the law! That's clear: the civil code, the criminal code, that's altogether I don't know how many thousands of pages. I would like to be introduced to someone who knows all of that, apart from lawyers. Nobody knows the law!
>
> People do know that one must not jump the traffic lights, that one must not murder his neighbour. However, I mean, people don't know all of the articles of the law! It's obvious! (Referent Physician 4)

Another intensivist extends the argument to the role of authorities:

> … 'Ignorance of the law excuses no one' …
>
> It's a, a very French phrase, the French use it often: no one is excused for ignoring it …, from the moment that those in charge …, our government for instance, those responsible for the information, in particular the Ministry of Health, will have made the necessary effort. (RP 3)

However, they note, since there is no political will to see the law of presumed consent applied, the focus of public communication policy should be on organ donation and on informing the public about the nature of the concrete situation where decisions to retrieve organs are taken, and thus about the state of brain death, about when a person can become a potential donor and about the difficult position of the relatives. Indeed, hospital coordinators and referent physicians stress that the lack of preparation of the general population is observable in most of their encounters with the relatives of a BDPD. Above all, they explain, the relatives appear completely unprepared to confront the questions of organ donation and retrieval following the announcement of the (brain) death of a relative. If they were better prepared, the number of rejections would decrease, since many of the rejections are imputable to the situational shock of the relatives rather than to an unwillingness to donate or to a negative view about transplantation medicine.

In the professionals' view the need for a proactive approach by the public authorities is all the more crucial because the media coverage of these matters is insufficient and frequently negative. As one intensivist explains:

> … we must admit that, spontaneously, the law of the media market doesn't result in having this type of programme being chosen by those in charge of TV channels or [radio] stations or by the news editors of the press. And well it's up to the state, through the Ministry of Health, or to the Etablissement français des Greffes … to campaign to promote this – that's the way it is – by saying: 'Transplantation is a therapeutic method, but for there to be a transplant it's necessary to retrieve organs.' That's why it's therefore necessary to do some communication on this. And the communication is insufficient. (RP 4)

A consequence of the passivity of health authorities regarding public information is, according to hospital professionals, that those specifically in charge of organ donation and retrieval are too often the only serious source of information that people are likely to be exposed to.[2] In this way the information is delivered too late and at the worst of moments.

They therefore complain about being frequently in charge of everything – informing citizens, soliciting relatives, caring for grieving families and organizing the retrieval of organs. Returning to the vocabulary of dirty work evoked in the previous chapter, one could say that they reproach the Etablissement français des Greffes for not accepting responsibility for its share of the dirty work involved in organ transplantation, which is to disseminate clear and transparent information about organ procurement.

The Communication Policy of the Etablissement français des Greffes

A look at the communication policy of the Etablissement français des Greffes since its creation in 1996 seems to confirm the complaints of hospital coordinators and intensivists. This national agency launched its first major campaign in 1998, after the Registre National des Refus had been created in 1997. The campaign consisted mostly of the distribution of brochures in pharmacies across the country. The slogan on the front page of the brochure was: 'Take a stand for or against.' The brochure contained information about corpses as a source of organs for transplantation, about how to oppose organ donation via the Registre National des Refus, and about the importance of each person discussing these issues with his or her close relatives. The brochure also contained a donor card that could be detached.[3] Although interviewees praised the content and form of this campaign,

2 This was before the vote of the law of 2004, which provides in article 7 that general practitioners should ensure that their patients between the age of 16 and 25 have been informed about organ donation for transplantation. Because this law was enacted after research for this book was completed, it is not possible to judge what effect, if any, the new legal provision has had in practice.

3 Legal scholar Hennette-Vauchez (2001) has criticized the distribution of donor cards with this campaign, arguing that it is incoherent and misleading to do this in the

they lamented that the absence of continuity had contributed to weakening, if not cancelling, its mid- and long-term effects.

After this first national campaign, the Etablissement français des Greffes concentrated its efforts on coordinated local initiatives, of which the most important is to this day the annual donor day on 22 June, when the coordination team of every hospital authorized to retrieve organs organizes information sessions for the staff and the public. Hospital coordinators also organize, if and when they have the time, information sessions in intermediate and secondary schools, as well as in town halls within the catchment area of their hospitals. Unlike the annual donation day, the last two kinds of events are not formally coordinated by the Etablissement français des Greffes but are left to the initiative of the coordination teams of hospitals. As a consequence, the regularity with which they are organized varies, depending on whether, in a given hospital, there are one or more hospital coordinators; and on whether coordinators work full-time or part-time in this function, or are full-time intensive care nurses who do coordination shifts.[4] While all interviewees note that these local initiatives are likely to have positive effects, especially those in schools, they regret that they do not reach enough people. For the message of such local activities to become rooted among the general population, they explain, a continued national communication policy lead by the Etablissement français des Greffes is needed.

The reasons that procurement professionals give to explain why the team at the head of the Etablissement français des Greffes has been so timorous about public campaigns are confirmed in public statements made by the director of the agency, either in the media or during parliamentary hearings. He also confirmed them in an interview with the author in 2001, when he emphasized the negative effects that repeated national public campaigns could have. He praised the local approach based on meetings between hospital coordinators and members of the general population. The advantage of such meetings, according to him, is that they open a space for discussion between the informant and the recipient while public campaigns are more likely to engender misunderstandings and thus opposition to organ donation.

His central idea was that it is intrinsically risky to communicate about organ donation because 'people' do not want to hear about death, and even less so when such a discourse emanates from public institutions (see also Houssin 2003). To limit the risk of defensive reactions, it is wiser to be discreet and local, on the one hand; and patient with regard to the pace at which attitudes and behaviour

---

context of presumed consent legislation. She concludes that this is one more sign of the unwillingness or inability of health authorities in France to take real responsibility for a law presuming the consent of the dead.

4 According to the information gathered through my survey, the percentage of hospital coordinators working as part-time nurses and being the only hospital coordinator of their hospital was 9.7 per cent; those who fulfilled the coordination function next to a full-time job as a nurse, 34.5 per cent.

are expected to change on the other. Trying to change the present state of affairs with a strong communication policy would most likely be counterproductive. The question of organ donation must be perceived by the people as being left up to them; thus, the public communication must not be perceived by the general population as too insistent. The aim must be to communicate 'without any excess' in order to contribute to enhancing a 'serene' dialogue about organ donation within households.[5]

Having considered the idea that such a cautious approach is likely to make the situation for the family of a BDPD more difficult, the director of the Etablissement français des Greffes answered, in his interview with the author, that one might indeed prefer preventively to expose the whole population to a small amount of distress by mounting national campaigns about organ donation instead of imposing a large amount of distress on the relatives of BDPDs, but his conclusion was that the possible counter-effects of the former approach are to be 'feared' more than those of the latter.

During the interview the director expressed himself very carefully. The same prudence can be found in an article he published in *Transplantation Proceedings* in 2003, where it is stated:

> Modifying positively the public opinion supposes first that *negative forces* are kept under control. All elements that are likely to cause *distrust* among the public should be *feared*. One should particularly *be afraid of* arguments in the media that a deceased person was in fact not dead, that allocation rules have been broken, or that organ trafficking is present.[6]

One of the reasons for such extreme caution, he explains, is that society is still very ambivalent about transplantation medicine: 'Adaptation of a human society to this type of medicine will take time. … a long mutation is necessary, … which requires the adaptation of habits, harmonization of beliefs, evolution of the language' (Houssin 2003: 1157).

Like the procurement professionals interviewed about their encounters with relatives, the direct of the Etablissement français des Greffes seemed to have the feeling of walking on eggs as far as the communication policy of the agency was concerned. Hospital coordinators and intensivists acknowledge that public

---

5 In 2002 brochures were distributed in hospitals on the occasion of the national donation day (22 June), which had been relabelled as 'The Day for Reflection on Organ Donation and Transplantation'. The message of the campaign was: 'organ donation: talking about it is to do something about it.' On this occasion a number of activities were also organized (a scientific conference in Strasbourg on 24 June, launching of balloons in 25 towns on 22 June, TV spots broadcasted on the 20, 21 and 22 June). See about this campaign: http://www.agence-biomedecine.fr/presse/en-preparation-de-la-journee-de-reflexion-sur-le-don-d-organes-et-la-greffe-du-22-juin-2002.html [accessed May 2010].

6 Emphasis added.

communication about these issues is difficult because it implies confronting the general population with matters one does not want to hear about: one's own death and that of those we love, and the use of corpses as healing material. As one of them puts it: 'I think that it's difficult to reflect on one's own death! … in everyday life one does not think about this and, and one tends more to make projects for life than to make a project for death!' (HC 10).

Nevertheless, drawing on their personal experiences with relatives, colleagues, medical students and lay people, the view of professionals is that the public agency overestimates the difficulties. First, they note, one should always remember that most people have a very positive perception of transplantation medicine. Second, while most people would prefer not to be confronted with the idea of death or with that of using human bodies as healing material, most are ready to listen if the topic is addressed in an open and transparent way. Last and certainly not least, while they find themselves in a highly delicate position when dealing with the relatives of a BDPD, they usually manage to overcome their own reservations and their sympathy with the difficult situation of the family and raise the difficult issues of brain death and organ donation.

Thus hospital coordinators and intensivists do not consider the passivity or cautiousness of the Etablissement français des Greffes justified. This leads them to conclude that as long as systematic and transparent information campaigns about organ donation, procurement and transplantation are not conducted, the responsibility for France not having a higher donation rate will lie primarily with the health authorities. They disagree with the idea, propagated in the media and that structures policy discussions, that the level of organ donation in France results from the unwillingness of people to donate. The problem, they stress, derives from the conditions under which the question of organ donation is raised. Policy should therefore focus on preparing people so that the diagnosis of brain death and the question of organ retrieval do not come as a complete surprise.

Their diagnosis is the same when it comes to the non-application of opting-out legislation in hospitals. While they regard the current context as unfavourable for the application of the law, they do not exclude that, if it were changed, the law might be applied. The only way to improve the situation, notes one head of unit, is to be transparent:

> … politicians should simply assume their responsibility. They only have to vote in favour of a bill, saying: 'Well OK listen here, there's a problem in public health, there are people for whom the only treatment is a transplant, so we're going to make things easier, we tell you: "we want to pass a bill."' I, a deputy, when I run for election, I announce while campaigning at the market, where I go to see the fishmonger, the baker, the whatever, that I'm going to have a bill passed, saying: 'when someone dies his body belongs to the community.'
>
> And, let them do it! At that moment, well if people vote for him and they get a majority, that will be law and it will be applied. But it's too easy to do it on an

> individual basis afterwards. If society therefore decides to vote – because really it's up to society to decide, up to the nation – if a nation decides this, very well, no problem with me. The idea in theory doesn't shock me too much, actually it doesn't even shock me at all, but we don't have the right to do it on the sly! It must be done in the open. I actually think that a lot of people don't have the courage, won't have the courage, to say, while they campaign at the markets to get votes for the upcoming elections: 'I'm going to build highways, a swimming pool, I'm going to lower taxes, and, on top of that I'm going to have a bill passed saying that when someone dies his body belongs to the whole of society, to the community to save other lives. Vote for me.'
>
> I'm waiting for the day that someone says this. (RP 4)[7]

Changing the Law?

In 1999 the French parliament began the process of re-evaluation of the Bioethics Laws of 1994, and thus of the legal mechanism presuming the consent of the dead to organ donation. As was noted in Chapter 2, this process was prolonged until August 2004. Contacts with professionals took place in a period that coincided with most of the re-evaluation process, that is between 2000 and 2004. This chronological coincidence made it easy to raise and explore with them the question of the suitability of modifying the existing legislation. During interviews this question was raised toward the end, after they had talked about organ donation decisions in their own way. They were asked, in connection with the re-evaluation of the Bioethics Laws in parliament, whether they could think of anything that should be changed.

A return to the situation of 1976, where relatives were not always included in the decision making, would in their view make no sense, neither ethically nor pragmatically. Would it then be sensible to adjust the law to actual practice? In most cases this question led to one of the most interesting moments in the interview. Although the interviewees had until then presented sophisticated arguments about the distance between law and practice, they seemed surprised by the question. In fact, in almost all cases the first reaction was silence.

Breaking the Law? A Question of Perspective

We have seen that the hospital coordinators and intensivists are knowledgeable about the letter of the law and acknowledge its non-application in practice; they

7 This quote illustrates how far removed presumed consent for organ donation is from the idea of a gift. Actually, my informants assimilate the latter to a right of the state to dispose of corpses. As we saw in Chapter 2, legal scholars have also criticized the successive laws on the basis of this argument.

offer a set of justifications for their behaviour that range from pragmatic reasons to fundamental values. But although they admit to regular 'transgression' of the law, they give no evidence of feeling deviant in a negative sense. Just the opposite: as we saw in the previous chapter, it is the strict application of the law that would be perceived as fundamentally deviant.

The way in which organ retrieval decisions are made in hospital has been analysed in a different light by legal scholars, some of whom have even written about *contra-legem* behaviour (Carvais and Hermitte 2000: 855). Others have referred to the non-mobilization of presumed consent legislation as adding to the list of factors that, taken together, lead them to conclude that the law lacks legitimacy and should therefore be revised (Hennette-Vauchez 2001). The picture presented by hospital professionals is less black and white regarding two important points. First, looking at the question through the prism of everyday practice, the law appears in their discourse as one element in a setting of normative pluralism, in which a legal rule is not *per se* more constraining than other, non-legal, rules. In other words, the assumption that all laws are made to be strictly applied or to stick to reality, which underlies the approach of most legal scholars, is simply absent from the professionals' discourse. Their perspective is in that way closer to a more sociological approach to deviant or non-conforming behaviour, which can only be understood in context, that is, in relation to co-existing normative orders. For, as Becker puts it, 'Undertaken in pursuit of legitimate interests, the deviant act becomes, if not quite proper, at least not quite improper' (Becker 1973: 29).

After initially displaying surprise when asked about the suitability of modifying the law, interviewees said that they could not think of major modifications, except maybe that it could be provided in the law that everyone above a certain age should be asked officially about their wishes, and that those who wanted could register them on their identity cards, driving licences, or health insurance cards. The point, they explain, is not to force everyone to state a position, but to make them aware of the possibility of donating their organs for transplantation while they are still alive. This type of initiative would in their view enhance reflection and discussion among groups of close relatives, and thereby prepare them for the possibility of one of their members becoming a BDPD. But, this sort of measure should not be expected to eliminate the part played by relatives in the decision-making process; it should contribute to make the interaction between hospital professionals and relatives smoother by slightly reducing the surprise element for relatives when suddenly confronted by the question of donation. Apart from this, the interviewees suggested only minor organizational changes.

At this point, with most of them not having raised the issue themselves, they were asked whether the non-application of presumed consent legislation could be seen as a reason to change the law. This question almost always led to a subtle shift in their discourse, sometimes even to the point of slightly defensive responses, while they had exhibited no tension before. Here we reach the second important difference of approach with legal scholars. It concerns the professionals' understanding of the aims of the law of presumed consent. They would argue that it was not really correct to say (as they in fact had) that the law is never applied or that it is of no use at all. First, they stress, the law is not *only* about presumed consent, but also about how to obtain information about the wishes of the deceased. In that respect legislators have qualified families as the most important source of such information. For the professionals the centrality of the relatives as a source of information in the law makes it less obvious that their own behaviour is clearly transgressive of the law.

Indeed, they continue, while legislators in 1976 had succinctly and clearly relegated the relatives to a peripheral role in decisions to retrieve organs, the laws of 1994 and 2004 give them a more central position. Those who drafted and voted in the Bioethics Laws intended that relatives of BDPDs be given the opportunity to be consulted when it came to deciding about organ retrieval. It is not easy, hospital coordinators and referent physicians observe, once this door has been opened, not to take their views into consideration. From this perspective, one hospital coordinator notes: 'I don't feel like an outlaw' and explains that the law can, under a certain reading, be understood as putting most of the responsibility on the relatives:

> [the law says that] 'the medical team must seek to ascertain the wishes of the deceased from the family': it's, it's a bit, it's a bit, it's not very good because we leave it to the family to bear THE RESPONSIBILITY of saying yes or no, but on the other hand this also gives them THE FREEDOM, to say yes or no. (HC 2)

As to the policy of the political authorities and the Etablissement français des Greffes, procurement professionals make it very clear that there is no pressure put on hospital coordinators and intensivists to apply the presumption of consent. Actually, informants stress that the directives they receive from the Etablissement français des Greffes go in the opposite direction. Written confirmation of this can be found in the guide that professionals received in 2001 during training sessions organized by the Etablissement français des Greffes, in which one can read the following about the meeting with the relatives of a BDPD: 'After consulting the Registre National des Refus, every possibility and the greatest possible liberty must be offered to the relatives to report the possible objection of the deceased to the removal of his organs and tissues' (Etablissement français des Greffes 2001: 102).

No mention is made even of the possibility of mobilizing the presumption of consent in the absence of information about the wishes of a BDPD. Furthermore, according to my informants, although the instructors of the Etablissement français des Greffes stress during these training sessions that the dialogue with the relatives should focus on the wishes of BDPDs, they insist that even if the relatives' opposition to donation is clearly an expression of their own wills, their veto should not be opposed:

> We, we are told that if the relatives say no, we don't go beyond it, even if the law says that if the person hasn't said anything his consent is presumed. We never go against the family, because we are told that THEY are the ones who are going to live afterwards with THIS burden, inevitably, they will live with this, all of their life, and NOT us. (HC 10)

In previous chapters we saw how a certain feeling of guilt weighs upon procurement professionals when they think of the questions they ask of the relatives of a BDPD. The Etablissement français des Greffes appears to be in part the source of this feeling, or at least to reinforce it, when it teaches professionals that merely raising the question of organ donation and retrieval is likely to be seriously traumatizing for the relatives.

Direct or Indirect Rule Following?

If professionals point to the ambiguity of the law, if directives from the health authorities urge them in most cases to respect the views of relatives, why do they spontaneously label (before being directly asked about it) their behaviour as transgressive of the law? In fact, the two ideas are not necessarily contradictory. The feeling of transgression relates to what they understand as the inspiring philosophy of the law – that of a society united behind the ideas of solidarity and progress – and the means initially mobilized with the aim of enhancing the development of transplantation medicine – presumed consent legislation. At the same time, they consider that the principal aim of legislators in the 1970s, 1990s and 2000s has been to increase the supply of organs, presumed consent legislation being just a means to achieve it.

Thus the paramount aim that hospital professionals appear to be bearing in mind in practice is that of obtaining, in the current context, as many organs as possible. If, as they believe, the mobilization of the presumption of consent would lead to a decrease in procurement rates – not to mention the damaging effect it would have for the whole medical profession and for public health institutions – it becomes clear that literal conformity to the law would go against the main aim of the law (Griffiths 2005a: 9–11). This explains the only exception to the rule of non-application of presumed consent legislation that I have heard of: the law can be mobilized on the very rare occasions when the hospital professionals in charge are certain that the BDPD has no relatives. This occurs with a very limited number of homeless potential donors who have no relatives who accompany their stay in hospital or might complain afterward about the retrieval of organs. As one hospital coordinator explains:

> … the notion of presumed consent … comes into play when there aren't any relatives and you've done some research and you haven't found any indication in the register [of objections] nor in his personal belongings nor through indirect relations. It's then that the notion of presumed consent comes into play. (HC 6)

This is confirmed by one intensivist:

> But that doesn't mean that the law ought to be changed, because, the law also makes our work easier: if for instance the, the patient doesn't have any relatives, doesn't have … [we can assume that] a priori, if he hasn't objected then he has consented, well, in the end it, this stops you from torturing yourself.
>
> – [GN] You remove the organs in those cases?
>
> Oh, well, if the patient doesn't have any relatives … well, we get, we get some research done by the police, but if there's no family, it will happen: if he has no children, no collaterals, etc. Oh yes! We do do it. (RP 12)

If there is a suspicion that some relative may be found later, the retrieval will not take place, for it is always feared that if a relative finds out later, this may cause distress or complaints. This exceptional application does not appear as ethically problematic for interviewees, not even when it is suggested that the chance that a homeless person knows about the law or the registry of refusals is certainly very low.

It is likely that the differential treatment applied to the homeless is partly explained by a certain contempt for this marginal group. However the discourse of the professionals suggests that it is the absence of relatives that is really central. A hospital coordinator puts it limpidly while talking about the case of a homeless BDPD she was responsible for: she describes her failure to trace any relatives, after having checked that the name of the BDPD did not appear in the Registre National des Refus and how, together with the intensivist in charge they decided to proceed with organ retrieval:

> … in fact we didn't know what his will was and we could imagine that [he could have been opposed to organ donation]. Now, who are we going to harm? … all in all, who could it possibly hurt, and who, who, who could suffer from this situation? … well, it's true that everyone has, can have their own convictions, religion etc. … [But, in such cases] he's going to go off to a cemetery as a pauper, with no relatives behind him who could possibly suffer from, from, from this act. Anyway it isn't something that bothers me a lot. In a way I think that, for this in any case the law allows us, [regarding] this sort of people to, to, end up by removing the organs and I don't think that this is bad. (HC 4)

Thus the special status of these persons with regard to the presumption of consent seems due to the fact that they do not belong to any protecting network: in the absence of close relatives, all the care described in Chapters 4, 5 and 6 disappears. They are, to use Castel's concept, 'disaffiliated', namely disconnected from the basic networks of community and family (Castel 1995). Durkheim (1950) has written about the increasing exposure of the individual in modern societies to state institutions, due to the absence of intermediate institutions between the two. From this perspective it seems that the relatives of a BDPD play the role of protective mediator for an individual who, alone, would be overwhelmed by the presumption of consent imposed by the law.

This very exceptional application, one might think, is a good reason for keeping the law as it is. And informants did indeed argue in this sense. But asked more directly – and despite their awareness that every single organ obtained may save a life – they consider these cases so exceptional that they acknowledge that they are quantitatively insignificant. As they reflected on these issues, interviewees mentioned that the existence of the law of presumed consent to organ donation may be having another minor yet positive effect in the few cases when the relatives ask about the content of the law. However, having given it some more thought they acknowledge that the effects of mentioning the content of the law are probably marginal. The following quote from an interview with a hospital coordinator illustrates this type of reasoning:

> … we find the law difficult to apply.
>
> – [GN] But why then do you say that it's nevertheless a good law?
>
> Because it's very permissive, so it's possible, it's possible, it's nevertheless possible, when the relatives talk to us about the law, to tell them 'hey listen, the law says we can [remove the organs]'.
>
> – [GN] And that helps you, you think?
>
> That doesn't help at all, no, hmm … no, we can't say that it's of any help. (HC 3)

Does support for maintaining the law boil down to the idea that it cannot be excluded that it may be useful in exceptional circumstances?

Why Changing the Law?

The professionals interviewed have stronger views on the cons of modifying the law of presumed consent than about the pros of keeping it. Their attachment to the law as it is can perhaps be best understood if one connects it to a certain form of conservatism. Two of the three arguments that according to Hirschmann are characteristic of the 'rhetoric of reaction' feature in the way professionals discuss possible changes in the law: perversity and futility (Hirschman 1991).

The argument of perversity is to the effect that change will only worsen the situation. With the exception of one intensivist, all interviewees observe that their position in the discussion with relatives is slightly strengthened by the legal background of presumed consent. They explain that the question 'do you happen to know whether the BDPD was against organ donation?' allows them to explore the personality of the deceased in a positive light: once an opposition to donate has been discarded, it can be presumed that the deceased was a generous person who, most probably, would have wanted to donate her organs. Changing the law in the direction of express consent would tend to reverse this way of raising the question. A negative answer to the question 'do you happen to know whether she was in favour of organ donation?' would seem to suggest that she was against it.[8] All this said, the professionals acknowledge that the positive effect of the phrasing of the main question is probably marginal.

Their scepticism about the pros of keeping the law as it is contrasts with stronger ideas about the cons of any substantial change in the law. Thus, the possibility of giving formal responsibility for the decision to the relatives is opposed with a double argument. The first is that the endorsement of such responsibility is too big for relatives to cope with. The second is that such a change would give them an illegitimate right. Here is a long quote summarizing quite well the position of most of the informants:

> It seems to me nevertheless that this should be maintained. This means that the beginning of the discussion shouldn't be: 'well OK madam, your husband has deceased, it's very unfortunate, but you have the possibility of donating, etc. What do YOU think?' Because to start a conversation like this, it's to make someone carry DIRECTLY, to make someone directly bear an extremely heavy responsibility and not only that, I mean, carry it himself, while facing those he has to talk to, but also regarding the family circles who are behind him. So in this discussion, it seems to me – that's my personal view – important to keep to starting like this: 'What was the will of the deceased?' This seems to me a good beginning for the discussion. AND, on the other hand, the person talked to – the father, the mother, the son, the spouse etc. – whatever the answer may be, the important thing is nevertheless the way he's going to receive the, the, the question and that's therefore going to determine his way of thinking about it. This means that he's going to think about it by asking himself 'but what did the deceased want?' He won't be able to avoid this question. I must tell you next that, actually, the feeling is that it's the relatives who end up by giving THEIR OWN decision and that in this sense we move away from, from the law, it's this way, it's the truth. They end up by giving their decision, but at least after having probably recalled, even if he didn't mention it, the, the, the will of, of the deceased. So, in this sense I think that we ought to maintain this policy. (RP 2)

8 The same reasoning was presented by a Frank van Gelder, hospital coordinator in Belgium (another country with presumed consent legislation), in an intervention at the 2002 annual conference of the European Transplant Coordinators Organisation in Lyon. 'Round table: Issues in Tissue Procurement and Family Approach' (from fieldwork). Neades (2008) reports the same kind of argument given by Norwegian hospital coordinators.

Professionals think adapting the law to practice would be morally undesirable, for it would give formal recognition to the power of the relatives to block organ retrieval. Indeed, while they all agree that the relatives should usually have the last word – especially when they veto organ donation – giving legal recognition to such a position would give a positive value to a power that is in practice not always used for legitimate reasons. They note that they can be confronted with cases where they come to know that the relation between the BDPD and her relatives was not good, or even that the BDPD had not been in touch with her relatives for years. One hospital coordinator, reflecting upon her 14 years of experience, notes that, although very rarely, it has happened that she has opted not to consult relatives, but friends or colleagues of the BDPD, as in the following case:

> … I've probably done more than 300 retrievals in total during 14 years more or less: I've had to, I've had to, maybe ten times, not really see any family members, that is dad, mum, brother or sister, but to see mates, friends … A young woman whom I remember very well, it was her colleagues from work who had discussed, who had discussed about organ donation and they had even discussed about getting a donor card. And her colleagues told me 'but she has a card, for sure, we've talked about it, she wanted to.' I never found the card, but …. But this young woman, she left home at 17, she was 27, she had, she had an aneurysm rupture. Her sister [came to the hospital] … that made it ten years that she hadn't seen her sister, so she arrived, I didn't tell the sister that I had done the removal. (HC 3)

Beyond these possible negative effects that a change of legislation may have, hospital coordinators and referent physicians seem more convinced by the argument of futility: adapting the law to practice would not improve donation rates. Informants definitely do not share the postulate, at the core of the reasoning of legal scholars, that the systematic non-application of the law calls for a modification of the text. In fact they are, with one exception, of the view that talking about legislative change is a waste of time. To a question about the desirability of modifying the law, one hospital coordinator replies with another question:

> Yes but change the law to put what in its place? … It's true, it's a law that doesn't suit practice …. But at the same time, what law could we have to bring people to donate? What kind of law? I don't see, honestly, I don't see it …. Honestly I don't see what could make [things] move. (HC 1)

Tolerance versus Autonomy

Summing up, it appears that the professionals in charge of organ donation and retrieval decisions in hospitals; (i) almost never resort to the law of presumed consent to obtain organs for transplantation; (ii) consider that this law is, with very marginal exceptions, of no real utility regarding its original aim; (iii) state that it would be in almost all cases ethically unfair and pragmatically unwise to resort to it. Nevertheless, in spite of all these arguments, they; (iv) stress that it would be at best useless and at worst counter-productive to modify the law in order to adapt it to actual practice. The same sort of discourse can be found in the statements made in the press and in parliamentary commissions by representatives of the Etablissement français des Greffes. In the author's interview with the director of this public agency, he too expressed the view that although opting-out systems have not proved to be more efficient than opting-in ones, it would be better not to change the law, since it is not producing bad results and there is still room for some improvement within the present legal frame.

Asked about the moral status of the presumption of consent and about the opinion expressed by some, that it is not in accordance with society's views, one intensivist argues that the very letter of the law puts professionals in the position of being closer to society for, through the imposition of the consultation of relatives since 1994, the law is indirectly allowing them to let relatives decide. However, the key role played by relatives is not a right, but the result of a policy and a practice of 'tolerance' on behalf of authorities, hospital coordinators and intensivists in charge of organ procurement. Implied by the idea of tolerance of deviation from a rule is the fact that the actors who tolerate deviant behaviour have the power to cease such an approach and the possibility, if only formal, to impose the strict application of the rule (Foucault 1979: 82). Thus, the present situation allows political authorities and hospital professionals to retain a form of power: that of retrieving organs when there are no obvious signs of refusal and without consulting the relatives of the BDPD. The exceptional cases of homeless BDPDs and the example of the young woman whose relatives were not consulted referred to above are clear illustrations of this point.

As a matter of fact, an opting-out system is better than an opting-in one from the perspective of the legal security of hospital professionals (Hennette-Vauchez 2004: 294). Let us imagine, for example, a situation where a BDPD is not found in the registry of oppositions, whose relatives cannot be reached in a *reasonable* time with all *reasonable* efforts having been made and where the professionals in charge decide to proceed with organ donation. Let us imagine that some relatives of the BDPD eventually find out about the retrieval of the organs of their loved-one and that they decide to take the professionals or the hospital to court, arguing that the BDPD had once in a conversation mentioned that she was opposed to organ donation, or even showing written proof of her opposition. We can be quite certain that a French court would rule that the behaviour of professionals had not been unlawful. In the very few cases that have been brought to the courts, of which the Amiens cased mentioned in Chapters 2 and 3 is representative, the behaviour of physicians was found to be lawful.[9]

9 This is a hypothesis, for, as Hennette-Vauchez writes, the number of cases brought to court is too small to draw any general conclusions about the attitude of courts *vis-à-vis* presumed consent legislation (Hennette-Vauchez 2004: 293–4).

Thus, even though practice has followed a process of normalization that is structured around the almost systematic consultation of the relatives and the non-mobilization of the presumption of consent in practice, the margin of discretion of hospital professionals is higher in an opting-out setting than in an opting-in one. The variety of behaviour noticeable in the 1970s and 1980s is probably more likely to take place in an opting-out than in an opting-in system.

Conclusion

A Policy Fiasco?

A great deal of importance is attributed to legal regimes of consent in international debates about organ procurement. Many participants in the discussion argue that opting-out (presumed consent) systems are the most efficient; some have started to observe that their superiority has not really been proved; and others conclude that existing regimes have failed and that market mechanisms or incentives to donation should be introduced. The authors and professionals who state either the superiority of presumed consent legislation or its failure share a common approach to the analysis of law as policy. On this approach the assessment of a policy project is made in terms of accomplishment or non-accomplishment of clearly pre-defined objectives; if these objectives are observed in practice, it is assumed that they result from the policy project, and if they are not, it is concluded that the project has been a fiasco. This type of analysis is sustained by an instrumentalist theory of the relationship between policy and practice that rests on the idea that there is a straightforward and simple connection between the two. However, if one wants to study the relationship between a policy project and the shop-floor, one must do so by taking into consideration the complexity of the social processes whereby rules about everyday life are formulated by state authorities (here in the form of legal texts) and those whereby the participants to the shop-floor understand, transform and incorporate them.

As was described in Chapter 2 and as noted by French hospital professionals, the 1976 version of presumed consent legislation seems to have been proposed, supported and enacted on the assumption that it would be applied in hospitals. In 1994 and 2004 the presumed consent system was reconfirmed in parliament, even though it was accepted that practice was not in accord with the letter of the law. At this point, if one takes into consideration the disenchantment that accompanied the legislative proceedings of 1994 and 2004, how to read the case becomes less obvious. From the moment that legislators acknowledged that the law was not being applied, treating its subsequent non-application as a failure becomes problematic, to say the least.

Social science research has shown that legislation is not necessarily proposed or adopted in order to be implemented, which does not mean that it is enacted with no aim or that it has no effect in practice. Bovens and 't Hart justly write that:

> Sometimes laws are enacted and policies endorsed which clearly will never be able to reach their stated objectives. But this does not turn them into instant

> failures. They can be meant to convey a message to particular groups and interests, to take the pressure off a particular issue, to delineate boundaries, or to instigate a change of social attitudes. (Bovens and 't Hart 1996: 40)[1]

The lack of sympathy among French hospital professionals for proposals of legal change, as presented in the last part of this book, can be partly understood from this perspective. As we have seen, support for the presumed consent rule coexisted with the idea that the imposition of presumed consent upon relatives would be illegitimate and unfair because non-democratic and authoritarian. It is the ideology behind the opting-out system that was supported, since it was seen as conveying a stronger message of solidarity than an opting-in system. Similarly, political authorities and medical institutions support the law because it sets the ideal standard for organ donation. The same seems to apply to the media, where one finds no critical discourse about the consent regime.

What can the influence of this kind of message be in practice? What any law produces in the first place is categories, namely a way of framing and interpreting a specific area of social life and a way of opening and closing specific possibilities of action (Thompson 1975). Thus, even if legal texts may not be applied, they have, as classificatory schemes, a potential for shaping everyday practice (Garth and Sarat 1998; McCann 1998; Gilliom 2001). Let us first consider what the main ideas of the presumed consent approach are. The very enactment of legislation about organ donation rests on the idea that this sphere of social life must be regulated by the state. More generally, the French Bioethics Laws convey the idea that biomedical activities must remain under tight legal control. We also find in the law the ideas that the practice of organ donation should exclusively develop in a system based on gratuity and anonymity; that the donor at the core of the regime is the individual BDPD; that the default ethical, social and legal option for individuals is donation and not the opposite.

The extent to which present practice has been shaped by these ideas seems limited and difficult to prove, especially for the last two points which are the centre of this study. According to survey data, most of the French population is unaware of the existence of the opting-out rule; and most believe that the law gives a central role to the relatives of a BDPD. Furthermore, the law is rarely mentioned by hospital professionals in meetings with relatives.[2] With regard to this last point, hospital professionals believe that mentioning the law is, in most situations, likely

1 See also Aubert 1967. For two interesting studies about the enactment of regulation with other aims than application in practice, see Castel (1988) and Foucault (1973) about the regulation of madness in France.

2 Recent work done by economists (Abadie and Gay 2004) explores the idea that the default legal options for donation may influence donation rates. In a nuanced way, they argue that opting-out legislation creates a more enhancing setting for organ donation than opting-in legislation. The problem with their argument is that they seem to take for granted that relatives of BDPDs know about the law.

to provoke negative reactions among relatives who would consider the legal presumption of donation an illegitimate intrusion of the state into their private sphere.

This study shows that if there is any relation between legal regulation and practice in the sphere of organ donation in France, it is rather circular than unidirectional, and it is exposed to historical change. The values carried by the 1976 version of the law can be said to have influenced the behaviour of certain professionals by providing legal security to those who extracted the organs of a BDPD without informing her relatives or letting them play an active role in the decision-making process. But the situation was soon reversed. In the early 1990s legislators, influenced by the process of normalization that had taken place in hospitals, accepted the fact that such decisions are taken in a different way. The continuity of French legislation presuming the consent of the dead since 1976 coincides neither with continuity in the motivations or intentions of lawmakers and health authorities, nor with continuity in hospital practice.

The relationship between law and practice is also rarely straightforward in terms of meaning. This is very clear in the decade that followed the enactment of the 1976 law, where different hospital professionals understood differently the concepts at the core of the law, and above all balanced in different ways what they saw as contradictory ethical imperatives that they perceived, implicitly or explicitly, as part of the law. In sum, while a system of categories is likely to influence how individuals and groups understand social situations and how they act, it is theoretically and empirically unfounded to assume, when it comes to the relationship between law and everyday life, that the meaning of the legal categories is given once and for all in the text of the law. On the contrary, the process of construction of meaning of any rule continues after its enactment; it is flexible and likely to evolve (Bloor 2002).

There is yet another kind of so-called 'symbolic effect' that the law of presumed consent may have had in practice in the years after its first enactment: that of making health institutions and hospital professionals believe that the problem of organ shortage had been solved with the enactment of the law.[3] It is likely that the absence of policy measures during the late 1970s and 1980s resulted from this belief. A decade later, the creation of the Etablissement français des Greffes, the diffusion of public campaigns and the institutionalization of the roles of the hospital coordinator and the referent physician, seem to acknowledge that the law had not had the effects initially expected.

3 Rosenberg (2008: 228–46) mentions this kind of effect in his study of the effect of the American Supreme Court *Roe v. Wade* decision on abortion. He contends that both at the level of the media and of public opinion, and at that of pro-choice movements, the decision seemed to have the effect of diminishing the vitality of the discussion and the level of activism. For a critical discussion about Rosenberg's thesis see Cummings and NeJaime (forthcoming).

Ethics and Professional Identity

This study shows that, in the mid and long term, the legal regime of consent has had, if anything, a tenuous influence in French hospital practice, and that such influence cannot be assumed from the start but depends on the context within which organ donation decisions are taken, particularly on how the participants understand each other's role. The law is just one element in this context, which is political and public on the one hand, and situational on the other. Practice has evolved together with the growing unwillingness of physicians and nurses to be the main deciding entity and to be the vectors of transmission and imposition of a strong solidarity message when decisions to retrieve organs from BDPDs are taken. This trend is related to their behaviour becoming more visible and exposed to the criticism of colleagues, the media and relatives of BDPDs.

However, this is not to say that visibility should inevitably lead to a retreat when it comes to a project of social engineering. What matters with this kind of project is that the persons crucial to implementation are willing and feel able to play the role state authorities want them to play. For this to happen it is particularly important that they feel they act in an enhancing social context, namely one where the authority inspiring change is legitimate enough among the general population and among those in the position of imposing it to justify their compliance (Rosenberg 2008: 31–5).

According to hospital professionals the general context of hospital practice changed during the 1980s. The relation with patients and their relatives became less clearly one of authority, especially in the sphere of 'ethical' choices. Those who in the early years had made decisions to retrieve organs without allowing relatives to participate, seemed to believe that they were doing the right thing. Their certainty weakened together with the waning of paternalism and of the public prestige of health professionals and institutions. Beyond the sphere of organ donation, relatives and patients gradually were more fully informed about diagnoses and treatment options. The greater the emancipation of patients, note hospital professionals, the more pluralistic the ethical setting where decisions are made. Thus the imposition by hospital professionals of a specific option became less legitimate for the patients and relatives they encountered, and slowly in their own eyes as well.

Writing about genetic counsellors, Rose (2007) notes that the opening of the ethical arena to pluralistic and contradictory discourses is a source of strong self-questioning for most professionals. The same can be said to apply to French hospital professionals in charge of organ retrieval decisions. Together with their confrontation with a more critical public discourse, with fewer complying relatives and with more critical peers in the 1980–1990s, their questioning of their own behaviour grew. Most activities that relate to organ procurement involve contrary ethical imperatives. In her study of neonatology in France, Paillet defines ethical situations as those where participants engage in questioning about what is 'good', 'just' and 'legitimate'. She describes neonatologists as often involved with 'intense' reflexive ethical evaluations and strained between contradictory principles in situations where there seems to be no completely good way out (Paillet 2007: 92–6). Situations where decisions about organ retrieval must be made are upsetting and require participants to make choices that involve the sacrifice of some good. As such these situations are potential enhancers of self-questioning and constitute thus a threat to professionals' feeling of 'ontological security' (Giddens 1991: 52–3).

Ceteris Paribus ...

What is the general scope of the conclusions we can draw from the French case beyond the basic idea that we cannot infer what takes place in practice from the mere existence of a law presuming the consent of a BDPD? What does the study say about national and historical differences in organ donation rates? The way in which decisions to retrieve organs are taken depends on a number of factors, many of which have nothing to do with the law and are not directly related to the question of organ donation for transplantation. The factors that appear to influence organ procurement are organizational, demographic, political and cultural. This study has focused on the cultural and political factors, which have a strong influence on donation and refusal rates, while the organizational and demographic factors have a stronger influence on the size of the pool of potential donors. Among the cultural and political factors three emerge as central: the strength of medical paternalism, the degree of exposure of procurement behaviour, and the amount of autonomy individuals enjoy *vis-à-vis* their group of close relatives.

Medical paternalism concerns the relational triangle patient–relatives–hospital professionals, around which communication is usually organized in intensive care units where patients are often unable to communicate or give consent to treatment. As with any power and authority relationship, it is dynamic: physicians (and to a lesser degree nurses) are authoritative for as long as and to the extent that their authority is accepted by the patient–relatives entity. Paternalism implies giving little information to the patient–relatives while the latter have a duty to be transparent; it also implies taking decisions without the active participation of the patient–relatives. Paternalism further entails that the scope of medical expertise is thought to encompass not only technical knowledge but also ethical wisdom. Non-paternalism implies that medical staff have a duty to inform the patient–relatives, to broaden the space for their participation in decision making and to be less interventionist about non-technical decisions.

The category 'exposure of procurement behaviour' comprehends visibility throughout the media, and exposure to critical ethical discourse in the public and political spheres as well as by peers in hospitals. Criticism by legal scholars of presumed consent legislation has always existed in France, but it became stronger and more visible in the 1990s, when it was also formally taken into consideration in the parliamentary proceedings leading to the legislation of 1994 and 2004. In the early 1990s, instances of allegedly abusive and outrageous procurement behaviour were exposed by the media. Inside hospitals walls and accompanying the decrease of paternalism with regard to the patient–relatives entity, professional hierarchies became slightly looser and a space opened for the critical views of some members of the staff in intensive care units, operation rooms and morgues to be more clearly expressed.

The lower the level of accepted paternalism and the higher the degree of exposure of procurement behaviour, the more active the participation of relatives became. But why does such participation coincide with a significant number of family refusals? Is that inevitable? Two factors are important here: the boundaries that separate what is perceived as belonging to the private and to the medical spheres, and the duties and rights that the relatives feel they have with regard to the body of the potential donor. The waning of medical authority coincided with a stronger idea of patient autonomy and thus of ethical pluralism. As one of the physicians interviewed observed, autonomy implies that you accept that people may make decisions you disapprove of. It also includes the idea that medical expertise does not encompass ethical expertise when it comes to choices that concern the future quality of life of a patient and/or of a group of relatives. Thus the participation of relatives in the context of a more pluralistic ethical setting makes refusals more legitimate in the eyes of hospital professionals, who will tend to avoid trying to make relatives change their mind.

The first step in the direction of a more general explanatory theory of organ donation can be taken by introducing some reflections inspired by the preliminary findings of a comparative study that I am currently conducting, and that includes Spain and the Netherlands. For many years Spain has had the lowest refusal rate in the world (about 14 per cent), France has a medium rate (30 per cent), and the Netherlands have a rate that is among the highest in the world (about 55 per cent). Spain, like France, has had a law of presumed consent since the late 1970s while the Netherlands have an opting-in system. Yet neither in Spain nor in France do hospital professionals apply the law of presumed consent (by contrast with France, Spanish professionals have never applied it). In all three countries families can effectively veto organ retrieval and the meeting with the relatives of a potential donor is therefore a crucial moment in the process leading to retrieval.

It is often argued in the literature and in the Dutch public discussion that the low level of donation in the Netherlands is explained by its opting-in legislation and that the adoption of an opting-out system should result in higher donation rates (Weimar et al. 2008: 460–61). This idea is illusory since the factors that have rendered the presumption of consent inapplicable in France are even stronger in the Netherlands. Could it be that the Dutch are somehow less inclined to donate their organs after death than the Spaniards or the French?

Most interestingly, and with all the due caution that one must have when dealing with public surveys about organ donation, a recent *Eurobarometer* survey shows that the Dutch declare themselves more willing than the Spaniards or the French to donate their organs after death and those of a relative (*Eurobarometer* 2007). Table C.1 shows the percentage of positive answers given by respondents to two questions, as well as effective donation rates:

Table C.1 Percentage of those willing to donate (Spain, France and the Netherlands)

	S	F	N
Would you be willing to donate one of your organs to an organ donation service immediately after your death?	57%	67%	69%
If you were asked in a hospital to donate an organ from a deceased close family member, would you agree?	59%	61%	66%
Donation rate	86%	70%	45%

There is something puzzling about Table C.1: except in the case of France, donation rates do not seem to correspond at all with the expressed willingness of potential donors or their family members. Let us see if variation on the dimensions of medical paternalism, exposure of procurement behaviour, and individual autonomy *vis-à-vis* one's relatives – factors that as we have seen play an important role in the French case – can be useful in explaining the differences between the three countries. We have seen in the French case that the more a family feels entitled to decide in the name of a BDPD, or even in its own name because its members feel that they have some kind of right of disposal over the body, the more room there is for discussion about the decision to be made. On the other hand, when a family acts as a simple vector of information about the wishes of the deceased, the default position appears to be that organ retrieval should not take place. With regard to the degree to which families feel entitled to decide in the absence of information, the data collected position Spain and the Netherlands at the extremes of a spectrum from more to less active participation with France in the middle, probably slightly closer to Spain than to the Netherlands.

The situation in Spain emerges clearly in the conversations held with professionals and the interviews conducted, but it is also prominent in the Spanish literature about the family interview, which supports informing the family in positive terms about donation and strongly encouraging them to donate. A very interesting indicator of the assumption of relatives' central role is the reluctance among Spanish hospital coordinators and representatives of the Organización Nacional de Trasplantes to create a registry where people could register their wishes. It is argued, on the basis of survey data, that a registry might lead to a decrease in the donation rate, since about 40 per cent of Spanish respondents say they are opposed to it. It is argued that the lack of information about organ donation and transplantation among the general population limits the legitimacy of a decision that an individual takes while still alive. Starting from the premise that the natural response to the unknown is refusal, two Spanish authors, López-Navidad and Caballero, argue that lacking information and professional guidance, people are more likely to give a negative response if required to make a decision on organ donation in the event of their death than if the decision were left to their relatives afterwards. The reason being that the relatives would receive proper counselling and advice from a transplantation expert at the moment when the decision to donate must be made (López-Navidad and Caballero 2001: 798).

This idea, combined with the perception that it is legitimate for families to decide in the absence of information about the wishes of the deceased and with a higher degree of acceptance of medical paternalism, produces an interesting picture of the Spanish situation. With regard to paternalism, the authority of Spanish professionals is displayed both in terms of arguments used to encourage relatives to accept donation and of the time that is spent with them. For example, when a group of relatives appears reluctant to accept organ retrieval, Spanish professionals will, more often than in France and much more so than in the Netherlands, discuss the matter at length with them. More families who at first express doubts over or even refuse donation, in the end authorize the retrieval of the organs of the BDPD in Spain than in the other two countries. In sum, of the three countries Spain appears to be the one where what transpires at the hospital is most important.

The point here is not to assess the ethical merits of practice in the three countries. What is important is that the setting is different in each of them and that what professionals and relatives consider acceptable in Spain may not be so in France or in the Netherlands. What can be seen as improper insistence in the Dutch or French contexts is considered normal in the Spanish context. Moreover, the approach of Spanish professionals is not just paternalistic: the emotional involvement of Spanish professionals appears to be stronger than that of their French and Dutch counterparts. A certain degree of insistence, which would be seen as intrusive in other contexts, appears more natural and thus acceptable in a context of strong emotional proximity. Spanish hospital coordinators often refer to their function as one of offering the relatives a 'pillow', that is, as a source of emotional support who can help the family to canalize the flow of emotions at this very difficult moment. This role seems to be appreciated by the relatives of BDPDs.

This takes us to another interesting difference between the three countries. Speaking in general terms, the amount of time that hospital professionals spend with relatives of critical care patients is much more limited in Spain and in France than in the Netherlands.[4] The differences in policies concerning visiting hours in intensive care units are an interesting indicator. Spanish intensive care units are among the most closed in Western Europe, with the French following quite closely, while the Dutch appear to be closer to the other end of the spectrum. In Dutch intensive care units the relatives of patients can be present most of the day, and even of the night in highly critical situations; the relatives of Spanish and French patients only have access to professionals during a limited number of hours per day. In Dutch units relatives are given more support, are informed in a much more continuous and detailed way and are more actively involved in the

4 The same applies to the amount of time spent with the relatives of newly deceased patients who are not potential donors.

decisions that concern their relative.[5] When a patient becomes a potential donor in a Dutch unit, the family's meeting with medical staff follows a whole series of meetings in which families have become accustomed to receiving support and information. Because such practice is more exceptional in Spain and in France, it can be hypothesized that the presence in Spanish and French hospitals of a hospital coordinator who informs the relatives and gives them support at that difficult moment is particularly welcomed and may, for that reason, be a facilitator of positive answers to the question of organ donation.

Furthermore Dutch families seem to receive more complete information about organ retrieval, in particular about the negative aspects of such procedures, which have mostly to do with the delay before the corpse is returned to them, with what will be done to the body during the extraction, and with external signs of the operation such as the colour of the corpse – which changes due to the fact that the body is emptied of its blood – or the loss of weight resulting from the extraction of blood and organs. On the other hand, if they do not ask about it, Spanish and French families receive little information about the practical effects of a retrieval operation. It can be hypothesized that, in such dramatic circumstances, the more a relative is told about this the more she may have a protective attitude with regard to the body of her newly dead family member.

How hospital professionals who discuss donation with the relatives of a BDPD respond to such defensive reactions is related to their different assessments of whether organ donation is likely to have a positive or a negative impact on family members. As has been shown in this study, French hospital professionals and transplantation authorities are of the view that being confronted by the question of organ donation, the operation of retrieval, and the allocation of the organs of the BDPD to unknown receivers, is likely to be traumatic for family members and that this trauma can make their grieving process more difficult. The same idea seems to be common among Dutch professionals. Spanish professionals, by contrast, are confident that decisions to donate are likely to facilitate the grieving process by producing something good out of a tragic event. It seems likely that this difference will influence the attitude of hospital professionals, the arguments they may or may not use in discussing donation with the families, and the length of time they will expect the group of relatives to take to consider the matter.

In turn, their attitude toward the impact of donation on the relatives is likely to be influenced by the way they approach the ethical dilemma at the core of these situations. When Dutch or French hospital professionals hear that Spanish coordinators tend to be more insistent about organ donation with families, they qualify such approach as intrusive and therefore unethical. When Spanish professionals are presented with this argument they reply that what is unethical above all is to let patients die on the waiting list. The self-assurance of Spanish

5 About different levels of information and communication see Hennette-Vauchez (2008) and Peretti-Watel et al. (2003) for France, Díez Ripollés et al. (2000) and Esteban et al. (2001) for Spain, and Griffiths et al. (2008) for the Netherlands.

professionals is supported by a very homogenous public discourse about organ donation and transplantation, both in the media and in the political arena. In France and in the Netherlands, public debate on the matter is far more diverse.

Last but not least, politically speaking, transplantation medicine and organ procurement have been a very clearly stated priority in Spain since the creation of the Organización Nacional de Trasplantes, and even more so since Spain started to become a world model. All the Spanish informants stress that this sector of health policy has overcome governmental and political changes and remains regularly at the top of the priorities of health authorities. One of the Spanish interviewees, a hospital coordinator in a university hospital of a major city, made a cynical comment about this:

> This is something I shouldn't say since procurement is my job, but I often really don't understand why they put so many resources into transplantation that could be dedicated to things that are much more of a priority, I mean hypertension, I mean diabetes, whatever. Actually I do know why, because politically those things don't sell, don't sell a shit, while this [procurement] allows us to be at the top. But it's not fair.

The Organización Nacional de Trasplantes (ONT) has invested massively in public campaigns, which are conducted regularly and are strongly pro-donation. It also devotes significant time and resources to cultivating good relations with the media. At the level of hospitals, it has also promoted highly the image of the hospital coordinator, who is most of the time an intensivist. Rafael Matesanz, director of the ONT, never gives a talk without praising hospital coordinators for being the key to the Spanish success. In sum, the general political context within which organ donation takes place gives less occasion for ethical self-questioning on the part of the professionals dealing with organ procurement activities in Spain than in France or the Netherlands.

These exploratory comparative hypotheses can be nicely summarized using the distinction made in Chapter 7 between a solidarity and a gift approach to organ donation. Practice in some French hospitals in the 1970s and 1980s was inspired by a strong solidarity approach, while it is nowadays closer to a gift approach where the main decider is the individual or the family. Table C.2 gives the main features of the two approaches.

In effect, we can construct two ideal models that do not exist anywhere in their pure form, but that have heuristic value when it comes to analysing specific cases and differences between them. In this way, we can speak of Spain having a solidarity system structured around the family–individual entity, and the Netherlands having a gift system with the BDPD at the centre of decisions to retrieve. France is somewhere between the two, with a public discourse and an ideal representation of organ donation that is largely in terms of solidarity, while practice tends to be structured more around the idea of gift giving. Furthermore, although the deciding entity is often the family–individual unit, the individual seems to have more weight in France than in Spain.

Table C.2 Main features of the solidarity and gift approaches to organ donation

	Solidarity	Gift
Public debate about organ donation	• Homogeneous • Pro donation: donation is rational and it is a moral duty, donation is positive for the grieving process • Pro transplantation	• Heterogeneous • More emphasis on negative aspects of organ donation and transplantation
Ethical assessment of organ donation by professionals	• Homogeneous	• Heterogeneous
Sphere of authority of medical professionals	• Technical • Ethical	• Technical
Autonomy of patient–relatives *vis-à-vis* hospital professionals	• Low	• High
Autonomy of individual *vis-à-vis* family	• Low	• High

The legal regime of consent is just one element in these systems, with solidarity systems being more likely to adopt opting-out legislation, although not necessarily to follow it in practice. The existence of the legal rule may be more or less known by social actors; it may reflect views more or less widely shared by the members of a society; it may be interpreted differently at different historical moments and by different groups; it may be more or less followed in practice. If improving donation rates is the objective of policy and academic debates, variations in degrees of paternalism, of exposure of procurement behaviour and of autonomy of the individual *vis-à-vis* her family, taken together, are much more important factors for understanding differences in donation rates than is the legal regime of consent. If, on the other hand, understanding how legal rules work in practice is the objective, then analysis should focus on the legal regimes, on their meaning as social rules, and on how individuals and institutions integrate them into their everyday behaviour.

Bibliography

Books and Articles

Abadie, A. and Gay, S. 2004. *The Impact of Presumed Consent Legislation on Cadaveric Organ Donation: A Cross Country Study*. Faculty Research Working Paper Series John F. Kennedy School of Government. Harvard University. RWP04-024.

Ad Hoc Committee of the Harvard Medical School to Examine the Definition of Brain Death. 1968. A Definition of Irreversible Coma: Report of the Ad Hoc Committee of the Harvard Medical School to Examine the Definition of Brain Death. *Journal of the American Medical Association*, August 5, 205(6), 337–40.

Agence de la Biomédecine. 2008. *Rapport d'activité 2007*. Paris: Agence de la Biomédecine.

Amnesty International. 2002. *People's Republic of China: The Death Penalty in 2000*.

Ariès, P. 1974. *Western Attitudes towards Death: From the Middle Ages to the Present*. Baltimore, MD and London: Johns Hopkins University Press.

Attias-Donfut, C., Lapierre, N. and Ségalen, M. 2002. *Le nouvel esprit de famille*. Paris: Editions Odile Jacob.

Aubert, V. 1967. Some Social Functions of Legislation. *Acta Sociologica*, 10, 98–120.

Augé, M. 1995. Ce que nous avons perdu, ce sont les vivants, pas les morts, in *La mort, et moi, et nous*, edited by M. Augé. Paris: Editions Textuel, 71–92.

Barnes, B., Bloor, D. and Henry, J. 1996. *Scientific Knowledge: A Sociological Analysis*. London: Athlone.

Beaud, O. 1999. *Le sang contaminé: essai critique sur la criminalisation de la responsabilité des gouvernants*. Paris: PUF.

Beck, U., Giddens, A. and Lash, S.M. 1994. *Reflexive Modernization: Politics, Tradition and Aesthetics in the Modern Social Order*. Cambridge: Polity Press.

Becker, G.S. 1997. How Uncle Sam Could Ease the Organ Shortage. *Business Week*. 20 January 1997.

Becker, H. 1958. Inference and Proof in Participant Observation. *American Sociological Review*, 6, 652–60.

——. 1973. *Outsiders: Studies in the Sociology of Deviance*. New York: Free Press.

——. 1996. The Epistemology of Qualitative Research, in *Essays on Ethnography and Human Development*, edited by R. Jessor, A. Colby and R.A. Schweder. Chicago, IL: University of Chicago Press, 53–71.

Benoît, G. 2000. Les divers degrés de pénurie, in *La greffe humaine. (In)certitudes éthiques: du don de soi à la tolérance de l'autre*, edited by R. Carvais and C. Sasportes. Paris: PUF, 263–278.

de Bic, D. and Lemieux, C. 2005. Le scandale comme épreuve, *Politix*, special issue 'À l'épreuve du scandale', 71, 9–38.

Bloor, D. 2002. *Wittgenstein, Rules and Institutions*. London: Routledge.

Boileau, C. 1997. Ethnographie d'un prélèvement d'organes. *Sciences sociales et santé*, 1, 22–33.

——. 2002. *Dans le dédale du don d'organes. Le cheminement de l'ethnologue*. Paris: Edition des Archives Contemporaines.

Bonnet, F. and Cohen, S. 2000. Recherche des causes de la pénurie. Aspects techniques et organisationnels: le point de vue de l'anesthésiste-réanimateur, in *La greffe humaine. (In)certitudes éthiques: du don de soi à la tolérance de l'autre*, edited by R. Carvais and C. Sasportes. Paris: PUF, 305–20.

Bovens, M. and 't Hart, P. 1996. *Understanding Policy Fiascoes*. New Brunswick, NJ: Transaction Publishers.

British Medical Association. 2007. *Presumed Consent for Organ Donation*. Available at: http://www.bma.org.uk/sc/ethics/organ_transplantation_donation/presumedconsent.jsp (accessed: July 2010).

Bury, M. 2000. On Chronic Illness and Disability, in *Handbook of Medical Sociology*, edited by C.E. Bird, P. Conrad and A.M. Fremont. Englewood Cliffs, NJ: Prentice Hall.

Calabresi, G. 1991. Do We Own Our Bodies? *Health Matrix*, 1, 5–18.

Calne, R. 2006. Essay History of Transplantation. *The Lancet*, 368, S51–S52.

Campion-Vincent, C. 1996. *La greffe, la rumeur et les médias. Les récits de vols d'organes. Etude réalisée pour l'Etablissement français des Greffes*. Paris: Maison des Sciences de l'Homme.

——. 2000. Les récits et la légende des vols d'organes, expression des réticences face à la greffe, in *La greffe humaine. (In)certitudes éthiques: du don de soi à la tolérance de l'autre*, edited by R. Carvais and C. Sasportes. Paris: PUF, 357–72.

Carvais, R. 2000. La transplantation d'organes: histoire sociale des sciences, in *La greffe humaine. (In)certitudes éthiques: du don de soi à la tolérance de l'autre*, edited by R. Carvais and C. Sasportes. Paris: PUF, 31–48.

Carvais, R. and Hermitte, M.A. 2000. Les français attachés au droit commun réticents à l'égard du droit de la bioéthique, in *La greffe humaine. (In)certitudes éthiques: du don de soi à la tolérance de l'autre*, edited by R. Carvais and C. Sasportes. Paris: PUF, 843–69.

Carvais, R. and Sasportes, M. 2000. *La greffe humaine. (In)certitudes éthiques: du don de soi à la tolérance de l'autre*. Paris: PUF.

Castel, R. 1988. *The Regulation of Madness: The Origin of Incarceration in France*. Paris: Polity Press.

——. 1995. *Les métamorphoses de la question sociale. Une chronique du salariat*. Paris: Fayard.

Castra, M. 2003. *Bien mourir. Sociologie des soins palliatifs*. Paris: PUF.

Charatan, F. 2001. Doctor Testifies to China's Reuse of Prisoners' Organs. *British Medical Journal*, 323(69).

Clark, R. and LeBeff, E. 1982. Death Telling: Managing the Delivery of Bad News. *Journal of Health and Social Behaviour*, 23(4), 366–80.

Cohen, L. 1999. Where It Hurts: Indian Material for an Ethics of Organ Transplantation. *Daedalus*, 128, 135–65.

Comité Consultatif National d'Ethique. 1998. Avis n° 60 du 25 juin 1998 sur le réexamen des lois de bioéthique. Available at: www.ccne-ethique.fr [accessed: May 2010].

——. 2000. Avis n° 67 du 27 janvier 2000 sur l'avant-projet de révision des lois de bioéthique. Available at: www.ccne-ethique.fr [accessed: May 2010].

Commaille, J. 1994. *L'esprit sociologique des lois: essai de sociologie politique du droit*. Paris: PUF.

Commission Nationale Consultative des Droits de l'Homme. 2000. Avis portant sur la révision des lois de 1994 sur la bioéthique. Adopté le 29 juin 2000. Available at: www.commission-droits-homme.fr [accessed: May 2010].

——. 2001. Avant-projet de loi tendant à la révision des lois relatives à l'éthique biomédicale. Adopté le 25 janvier 2001. Available at: www.commission-droits-homme.fr [accessed: May 2010].

Conseil d'Etat. 1999. Les lois de bioéthique: cinq ans après. Etude adoptée par l'Assemblée Générale du Conseil d'Etat le 25 novembre 1999. Available at: www.conseil-etat.fr [accessed: May 2010].

Council of Europe. 1999. Recommendation 1399, Xenotransplantation. Available at: www.coe.int [accessed: May 2010].

——. 2002. Additional Protocol to the Convention on Human Rights and Biomedicine, on Transplantation of Organs and Tissues of Human Origin. Available at: http://conventions.coe.int/Treaty/EN/Treaties/Html/186.htm [accessed: October 2008].

Cranford, R.E. 1995. Death, Definition and Determination of Criteria, in *Encyclopedia of Bioethics*, edited by W.T. Reich. New York: Simon and Schuster Macmillan, 529–34.

Cummings, S.L. and NeJaime, D. forthcoming. Lawyering for Marriage Equality. *UCLA Law Review*.

Dagognet, F. 1990. *Corps réfléchis*. Paris: Odile Jacob.

Das, V. 2000. The Practice of Organ Transplants: Networks, Documents, Translations, in *Living and Working with the New Technologies: Intersections of Inquiry*, edited by M. Lock, A. Cambrosio and A. Young. Cambridge: Cambridge University Press, 263–86.

Díez Ripollés, J.L. et al. 2000. *La atención a los enfermos terminales*. Valencia: Tirant lo Blanch.

Douglas, M. 1991. *Purity and Danger: An Analysis of the Concepts of Pollution and Taboo*. London: Routledge.

Durkheim, E. 1950. *Leçons de sociologie. Physique des mœurs et du droit*. Paris: Presses Universitaires de France.

——. 1964. *The Division of Labor in Society*. New York: Free Press.

——. 1967. *Sociologie et philosophie*. Paris: PUF.

——. 1970. *Suicide: A Study in Sociology*. London: Routledge and Kegan Paul.

——. 1995. *The Elementary Forms of Religious Life*. New York: The Free Press.

Erin C.A. and Harris, J. 2003. An Ethical Market in Human Organs. *Journal of Medical Ethics*, 29, 137–8.

Esteban, A. et al. 2001. Withdrawing and Withholding Life Support in the Intensive Care Unit: A Spanish Prospective Multi-Centre Observational Study. *Intensive Care Medicine*, 27, 1744–9.

Etablissement français des Greffes. 2001. *Guide de la coordination hospitalière du prélèvement*. Paris: EfG.

——. 2002. *Rapport d'activité 2001*. Paris: EfG.

——. 2003. *Rapport d'activité 2002*. Paris: EfG.

——. 2004. *Rapport d'activité 2003*. Paris: EfG.

——. 2005. *Rapport d'activité 2004*. Paris: EfG.

Eurobarometer. 2007. Europeans and Organ Donation. *Special Eurobarometer*, May 2007.

Eurobaromètre. 2003. Le don et la transplantation d'organes. *Eurobaromètre spécial*, décembre 2003.

Fainzang, S. 2006. *La relation médecins-malades: information et mensonge*. Paris: PUF.

Fillion, E. 2005. Que font les scandales? La médecine de l'hémophilie à l'épreuve du sang contaminé. *Politix*, special issue 'À l'épreuve du scandale', 71, 191–214.

Foucault. M. 1973. *Moi, Pierre Rivière, ayant égorgé ma mère, ma sœur et mon frère: un cas de parricide au XIXè siècle*. Paris: Gallimard.

——. 1979. *Discipline and Punish*. London: Penguin.

——. 1998. *History of Sexuality*. London: Penguin.

Fox, R.C. 1979. Organ Transplantation: Sociocultural Aspects, in *Essays in Medical Sociology: Journeys into the Field*, R.C. Fox. New York: John Wiley and Sons, 115–21.

——. 1988. The Medicalization of American Society, in *Essays in Medical Sociology: Journeys into the Field*, R.C. Fox. 2nd edn. New Brunswick, NJ: Transaction Books.

Fox, R.C. and Swazey, J.P. 1992. Leaving the Field, in *Spare Parts: Organ Replacement in American Society*, R.C. Fox and J.P. Swazey. New York: Oxford University Press, 197–210.

——. 2002. *The Courage to Fail: A Social View of Organ Transplants and Dialysis*. New Brunswick, NJ: Transaction Publishers.

Frey, B. 1997. *Not Just for the Money: Economic Theory of Personal Motivation*. Cheltenham: Edward Elgar.
Frist, W.H. 1989. *Transplant: A Heart Surgeon's Account of the Life-and-Death Dramas of the New Medicine*. New York: Fawcett Crest.
Garfinkel, H. 1967. *Studies in Ethnomethodology*, Englewood Cliffs, NJ: Prentice Hall.
Garth, B.G. and Sarat, A. 1998. *How Does Law Matter?* Chicago, IL: Northwestern University Press and The American Bar Foundation.
Giddens, A. 1991. *Modernity and Self-Identity: Self and Society in the Late Modern Age*. Stanford, CA: Stanford University Press.
——. 1994. Living in a Post-Traditional Society, in *Reflexive Modernization: Politics, Tradition and Aesthetics in the Modern Social Order*, edited by U. Beck, A. Giddens and S.M. Lash. Cambridge: Polity Press, 56–109.
Gilliom, J. 2001. *Overseers of the Poor: Surveillance, Resistance and the Limits of Privacy*. Chicago, IL: University of Chicago Press.
Glaser, B.G. and Strauss, A. 2005. *Awareness of Dying*. Chicago, IL: Aldine.
——. 2007. *Time for Dying*. Chicago, IL: Aldine.
Gnant, M.F.X. and Muhlbacher, F. 1990. Kidney Transplantation: Getting the Numbers Right. *The Lancet*, 335.
Goffman, E. 1959. *The Presentation of the Self in Everyday Life*, New York: Anchor Books.
——. 1961. *Asylums: Essays on the Social Situation of Mental Patients and Other Inmates*. New York: Penguin Books.
Goodin, R.E. and Tilly, C. 2006. It Depends, in *The Oxford Handbook of Contextual Political Analysis*, edited by R.E. Goodin and C. Tilly. Oxford: Oxford University Press, 3–32.
Gordon, P.C. and Brink, J.G. 2008. Forty Years On: The Anesthetic for the World's First Human-to-Human Heart Transplant Remembered. *Journal of Cardiothoracic and Vascular Anesthesia*, 22(1), 133–8.
Gould, R.V. 2003. *Collision of Wills: How Ambiguity about Social Rank Breeds Conflict*. Chicago, IL: University of Chicago Press.
Griffiths, J. 1979. Is Law Important? *New York University Law Review*, 54, 339–74.
——. 2003. The Social Working of Legal Rules. *Journal of Legal Pluralism*, 48, 1–84.
——. 2005a. An Introduction in Eight Propositions to the Social Working Approach to Legislation, in *Social and Symbolic Effects of Legislation under the Rule of Law*, edited by N. Zeegers, W.J. Witteveen and B. van Klink. New York: Edwin Mellen Press.
——. 2005b. Do Laws Have Symbolic Effects?, in *Social and Symbolic Effects of Legislation under the Rule of Law*, edited by N. Zeegers, W.J. Witteveen and B. van Klink. New York: Edwin Mellen Press.
Griffiths, J., Weyers, H. and Adams, M. 2008. *Euthanasia and Law in Europe*. Oxford: Hart Publishing.

van Gunsteren, H.R. 1976. *Quest for Control: Critique of the Rational Central Rule Approach in Public Affairs*. New York: John Wiley and Sons.

Hamburger, J. 1981. Past, Present, and Future of Transplantation. *Transplantation Proceedings*, 13(1), 41–3.

Harris, J. 1986. The Survival Lottery, in *Applied Ethics*, edited by P. Singer. Oxford: Oxford University Press, 87–95.

Harvey, M. 2002. What's So Special About Legal Translation? *Meta: journal des traducteurs/Meta: Translators' Journal*, 47(2), 177–85.

Healy, K. 2006. *Last Best Gifts: Altruism and the Market for Human Blood and Organs*. Chicago, IL: University of Chicago Press.

Hennette-Vauchez, S. 2001. Le consentement présumé du défunt aux prélèvements d'organes: un principe exorbitant mais incontesté. *Revue de recherche juridique*, 1, 183–228.

——. 2004. *Disposer de soi? Analyse du discours juridique sur les droits de la personne sur son corps*. Paris: L'Harmattan.

——. 2008. France, in *Euthanasia and Law in Europe*, edited by J. Griffiths, H. Weyers and M. Adams. Oxford: Hart Publishing.

Hennette-Vauchez, S. and Nowenstein, G. 2009. Dire la mort et faire mourir. Tensions autour de la mort encéphalique et la fin de vie en France. *Sociétés contemporaines*, special issue 'L'etat et la mort, entre droit et politque, des corps en sursis', 37–58.

Hermitte, M.A. 1993. Consentement et prélèvement d'organes sur cadavres. *Ethique et transplantation*, Club de la Transplantation, 23–24 septembre 1993.

——. 1996. *Le sang et le droit. Essai sur la transfusion sanguine*. Paris: Seuil.

Herpin, N. and Paterson, F. 1992. Centralisation et pouvoir discrétionnaire: la transplantation rénale en France, in *Ethique des choix médicaux*, edited by N. Herpin and F. Paterson. Arles: Actes Sud, 37–61.

——. 2000. Le don d'organes et la perception de la mort par les français: les systémistes et les intégralistes, in *La greffe humaine. (In)certitudes éthiques: du don de soi à la tolérance de l'autre*, edited by R. Carvais and C. Sasportes. Paris: PUF, 797–818.

Hertogh, M. 2005. The Social Making and Social Working of Legislation, in *Social and Symbolic Effects of Legislation under the Rule of Law*, edited by N. Zeegers, W.J. Witteveen and B. van Klink. New York: Edwin Mellen Press, 163–81.

Hirose, R. and Griffin, M.D. 2008. The Development of Modern Immunosuppressive Medications, in *Skin Disease and Organ Transplantation*, edited by C.C. Otley and T. Stasko. Cambridge: Cambridge University Press, 13–21.

Hirschmann, A.O. 1991. *The Rhetoric of Reaction: Perversity, Futility, Jeopardy*. Cambridge: Belknap Press.

Houssin, D. 2003. Possible Solutions to the Natural Limitations of Organ Transplantation: What Is at Stake in the Information of the Public and Education? *Transplantation Proceedings*, 35(3), 1156–8.

Hughes, E.C. 1962. Good People and Dirty Work. *Social Problems*, 10(1), 3–11.
——. 1984. Work and Self, in *The Sociological Eye: Selected Papers*. New Brunswick, NJ: Transaction Publishers, 338–47.
Human Rights Watch. 1994. *World Report 1994*. New York: Human Rights Watch.
——. 1996. *World Report 1996*. New York: Human Rights Watch.
——. 2008. *World Report 2008*. New York: Human Rights Watch.
Iacub, M. 1998. La construction de la mort en droit français. *Enquête*, 7, 39–54.
Irving, J. 2001. *The Fourth Hand*. New York: Ballantine Books.
Isambert, F.-A., Ladrière, P. and Terrenoire, J.-P. 1978. Pour une sociologie de l'éthique. *Revue française de sociologie*, 19, 323–39.
Jain, S. and DeGeorgia, M. 2005. Brain Death-Associated Reflexes and Automatisms. *Neurocritical Care*, 3(2), 122–6.
Kennedy I. et al. 1998. The Case for 'Presumed Consent' in Organ Donation. *The Lancet*, 338.
Kluge, E.H. 2000. Improving Organ Retrieval Rates: Various Proposals and Their Ethical Validity. *Health Care Analysis*, 8, 279–95.
Küss, R. and Bourget, P. 1992. *An Illustrated History of Organ Transplantation: The Great Adventure of the Century*. Rueil-Malmaison: Laboratoires Sandoz.
Landers, S.J. 2004. Transplants: 50 Years of Saving Lives, *amednews.com*. Available at: http://www.ama-assn.org/amednews/2004/02/16/hll20216.htm [accessed: May 2010].
Landowski, E. 1980. L'opinion publique et ses porte-parole. *Actes sémiotiques – documents*, II, 12, 3–35.
Le Breton, D. 1993. *La chair à vif. Usages médicaux et humains du corps humain*. Paris: Métailié.
Lemieux, C. 2007. L'accusation tolérante. Remarques sur les rapports entre commérage, scandale et affaire, in *Affaires, scandales et grandes causes*, edited by L. Boltanski et al. Paris: Stock, 367–94.
Lloveras, J. 1999. What Should Be the Role of the State in the Development of Transplantation? *Transplantation Proceedings*, 31(4), 1765–8.
Lock, M. 1989. Reaching Consensus about Death: Heart Transplants and Cultural Identity in Japan. *Society – Société*, 13(1), 15–26.
——. 1995. Transcending Mortality: Organ Transplants and the Practice of Contradictions. *Medical Anthropology Quarterly*, 9(3), 390–99.
——. 2000. On Dying Twice: Culture, Technology and the Determination of Death, in *Living and Working with the New Medical Technologies: Intersections of Inquiry*, edited by M. Lock, A. Cambrosio and A. Young. Cambridge: Cambridge University Press, 233–62.
——. 2002. *Twice Dead: Organ Transplants and the Reinvention of Death*. Berkeley, CA: University of California Press.
López-Navidad, A. and Caballero, F. 2001. For a Rational Approach to the Critical Points of the Cadaveric Donation Process. *Transplantation Proceedings*, 33, 795–805.

——. 2002. Claves en la obtención de organos de cadáveres para trasplante. *Revista española de trasplantes*, 11(1), 7–18.
Machado, N. 1998. *Using the Bodies of the Dead: Legal, Ethical, and Organisational Dimensions of Organ Transplantation*. Aldershot: Ashgate.
Matesanz, R. 1997. Organización Nacional de Trasplantes. Las razones de un éxito. *Revista de Administración Sanitaria*, 1(4) octubre–diciembre.
——. 2001. A Decade of Continuous Improvement in Cadaveric Organ Donation: The Spanish Model. *Nefrología*, 21, suplemento 5, 59–67.
——. 2006. *El milagro de los trasplantes: de la donación de órganos a las células madre*. Madrid: La Esfera de los Libros.
——. 2008. *El modelo español de coordinación y trasplantes*. 2nd edn. Madrid: Editorial Grupo Aula Médica.
Matesanz, R., Miranda, B. and Felipe, C. 1995. Increasing the Number of Organ Transplants. *British Medical Journal*, 310, 1404.
Mauss, M. 1985. Essai sur le don. Forme et raison de l'échange dans les sociétés archaïques, in *Sociologie et anthropologie*, M. Mauss. Paris: PUF, 145–279.
Maynard, D.W. 2003. *Bad News, Good News: Conversational Order and Clinical Settings*. Chicago, IL: University of Chicago Press.
McCann, M.W. 1998. How Does Law Matter for Social Movements?, in *How Does Law Matter?*, edited by B.G. Garth and A. Sarat. Chicago, IL: Northwestern University Press and The American Bar Foundation.
Memmi, D. 1992. La compétence morale. *Politix*, 17, 105–24.
Merrill, J.P. 1981. Early Days of the Artificial Kidney and Transplantation. *Transplantation Proceedings*, 13(1), 4–8.
Michielsen, P. 1996. Presumed Consent to Organ Donation: Ten Years Experience in Belgium. *Journal of the Royal Society of Medicine*, 89, 663–6.
Mollaret, P. and Goulon, M. 1959. Le coma dépassé, *Revue neurologique*, 101, 3–15.
Moore, S.F. 1973. Law and Social Change: The Semi-Autonomous Social Field as an Appropriate Subject of Study. *Law and Society Review*, 7, 719–46.
——. 1978. *Law as Process: An Anthropological Approach*. London: Routledge.
Müller-Ruchholtz, W. 1999. Glances at the History of Transplantation Immunology. *Transplantation Proceedings*, 31(1), 1443–51.
Murray, J.E. 1981. Early Days of Renal Transplantation. *Transplantation Proceedings* 13(1), 9–15.
Neades, B.L. 2008. Health Care Professionals' Experiences in Applying Presumed Consent Legislation in Organ Donation in Three European Societies: A Phenomenological Study, in *Organ Transplantation: Ethical, Legal and Psychosocial Aspects. Towards a Common European Policy*, edited by W. Weimar, M.A. Bos, J.J. Busschbach. Lengerich: Pabst Science Publishers, 150–54.
Némirovsky, I. 2007. *Suite française*. New York: Vintage Books.
Newsletter Transplant 2008. 2008. International Figures on Organ Donation and Transplantation 2007.

Nowenstein, G. 1999. *Greffe d'organe et société. Une analyse politique du débat public, mémoire de DEA*, Paris: EHESS.

——. 2004. Organ Procurement Rates: Does Presumed Consent Legislation Really Make a Difference?, *Law, Social Justice and Global Health*, 1. Available at: http://www2.warwick.ac.uk/fac/soc/law/elj/lgd/2004_1/nowenstein/ [accessed: May 2010].

Nowenstein, G. and Podyma, E. 2003. Etre coordonateur hospitalier aujourd'hui en France. Compte-rendu d'enquête. *Bulletin de l'AFCH*, June.

Organ Donation Taskforce. 2008. *The Potential Impact of an Opt Out System for Organ Donation in the UK: An Independent Report from the Organ Donation Taskforce*. London: Department of Health. Available at: http://dh.gov.uk/en/Publicationsandstatistics/Publications/PublicationsPolicyAndGuidance/DH_090312 [accessed: May 2010].

Otley, C.C. and Stasko, T. 2008. *Skin Disease and Organ Transplantation*. Cambridge: Cambridge University Press.

Ozinsky, J. 1967. Cardiac Transplantation: The Anaesthetists View. *South African Medical Journal*, 41, 1268–70.

Paillet, A. 2007. *Sauver la vie. Donner la mort*. Paris: La Dispute.

Parsons, T. 1964. *The Social System*. New York: Free Press.

Parsons, T., Fox R.C. and Lidz, V. 1972. The 'Gift of Life' and Its Reciprocation. *Social Research*, 39(3), 367–415.

Paterson, F. 1997. Solliciter l'inconcevable ou le consentement des morts. *Sciences sociales et santé*, 1, 35–73.

Peletz, J. 1995. Kinship Studies in Late Twentieth-Century Anthropology. *Annual Review of Anthropology*, 24, 343–72.

Peretti-Watel, P. et al. 2003. French Physicians' Attitudes toward Legalisation of Euthanasia and the Ambiguous Relationship between Euthanasia and Palliative Care. *Journal of Palliative Care*, 19, 271–7.

Pernick, M.S. 1999. Brain Death in a Cultural Context: The Reconstruction of Death, 1967–1981, in *The Definition of Death: Contemporary Controversies*, edited by S.J. Youngner, A.M. Arnold and A. Schapiro. Baltimore, MD: Johns Hopkins University Press, 3–34.

Plum, F. 1999. Clinical Standards and Technological Confirmatory Tests in Diagnosing Brain Death, in *The Definition of Death: Contemporary Controversies*, edited by S.J. Youngner, A.M. Arnold and A. Schapiro. Baltimore, MD: Johns Hopkins University Press, 34–65.

Pouillon, J. 1982. Remarks on the Verb 'To Believe', in *Between Belief and Transgression: Structuralist Essays in Religion, History and Myth*, edited by M. Izard and P. Smith. Chicago, IL: University of Chicago Press, 1–8.

Price, D. 2000. *Legal and Ethical Aspects of Organ Transplantation*. Cambridge: Cambridge University Press.

Quinio, P. et al. 2002. A Multicenter Survey of Visiting Policies in French Intensive Care Units. *Intensive Care Medicine*, 28, 1389–94.

Rabelais, F. 2007 [1653]. *Gargantua and Pantagruel*. Available at: http://ebooks.adelaide.edu.au/r/rabelais/francois/r11g/book2.30.html [accessed: May 2010].
Radcliffe-Richards J. et al. 1998. The Case for Allowing Kidney Sales. *Lancet*, 351, 1950–52.
Radin, M.J. 1987. Market-Inalienability. *Harvard Law Review*, 100(8), 1849–937.
Ragin, C. 2000. *Fuzzy-Set Social Science*. Chicago, IL: University of Chicago Press.
Randle, H.W. 2008. The History of Organ Transplantation, in *Skin Disease and Organ Transplantation*, C.C. Otley and T. Stasko. Cambridge: Cambridge University Press, 9–12.
Renard, M. 1920. *Les mains d'Orlac*. Paris: Nilsson.
Revue de la Mutualité. 1992. Présomption de consentement. La loi Caillavet. Un entretien avec son auteur. *Revue de la mutualité*, 148, 12–14.
Roels, L. et al. 1990. Effect of a Presumed Consent Law on Organ Retrieval in Belgium. *Transplantation Proceedings*, 22, 2078–9.
——. 1991. Three Years of Experience with a 'Presumed Consent' Legislation in Belgium. *Transplantation Proceedings*, 23, 903–4.
Rose, N. 2007. *The Politics of Life Itself: Biomedicine, Power, and Subjectivity in the Twenty-First Century*. Princeton, NJ: Princeton University Press.
Rosenberg, G.N. 2008. *The Hollow Hope: Can Courts Bring About Social Change?* Chicago, IL: The University of Chicago Press.
Savatier, J. 1979. Les prélèvements d'organes après décès. Travaux de l'Institut des sciences criminelles de Poitiers. *Problèmes juridiques, médicaux et sociaux de la mort*, 19–46.
Schneider, W. 1999. 'Death Is Not the Same Always and Everywhere.' Socio-cultural Aspects of Brain Death and the Legislation of Organ Transplantation: The Case of Germany. *European Societies*, 3, 353–89.
Settergren, G. 2003. Brain Death: An Important Paradigm Shift in the 20th Century. *Acta Anaesthesiologica Scandinavica*, 47, 1053–8.
Sharp, L.A.A. 2006. *Strange Harvest: Organ Transplants, Denatured Bodies, and the Transformed Self*. Berkeley, CA: University of California Press.
Shelley, M.W. 2000. *Frankenstein or the Modern Prometheus*. London: Penguin Classics.
Shepherd-Hughes, N. 1996. Theft of Life: Globalization of Organ-Stealing Rumors. *Anthropology Today*, 12(3), 3–11.
Shewmon, D.A. 1998. Chronic 'Brain Death': Meta-Analysis and Conceptual Consequences. *Neurology*, 51(6), 1538–45.
Singer, P. 1994. *Rethinking Life and Death: The Collapse of Our Traditional Ethics*. New York: St. Martin's Press.
Star, S.L. 1995. Epilogue: Work and Practice in Social Studies of Science, Medicine, and Technology. *Science, Technology, and Human Values*, 20(4), 501–7.

Starzl, T.E. 1981. The Succession from Kidney to Liver Transplantation. *Transplantation Proceedings*, 13(1), 50–54.
Strauss, A., Fagerhaugh, S., Suczek, B. and Wiener, W. 1982. Sentimental Work and the Technologized Hospital. *Sociology of Health and Illness*, 4(3), 254–78.
Sudnow, D. 1967. *Passing On: The Social Organization of Dying*. Englewood Cliffs, NJ: Prentice Hall.
Tesnière, A. 1993. *Les yeux de Christophe. L'affaire d'Amiens*. Monaco: Editions du Rocher.
——. 1996. Où est l'éthique?, *Etudes*, 5, 482–4.
Thompson, E.P. 1975. *Whigs and Hunters: The Origin of the Black Act*. London: Allen Lane.
Thouvenin, D. 1997. Don et-ou prélèvement d'organes. *Sciences sociales et santé*, 1, 75–97.
——. 1999. L'obtention des organes: le don comme finalité et le prélèvement comme modalité, in *Les lois 'bioéthique' à l'épreuve des faits. Réalités et perspectives*, edited by B. Feuillet-Le Mintier. Paris: PUF, 77–131.
——. 2000. L'organisation de l'activité de transplantation d'organes par les règles juridiques, in *La greffe humaine. (In)certitudes éthiques: du don de soi à la tolérance de l'autre*, edited by R. Carvais and C. Sasportes. Paris: PUF, 643–65.
Tilly, C. 2005. *Identities, Boundaries, and Social Ties*. Boulder, CO: Paradigm Publishers.
Timmermans, S. 1999. *Sudden Death and the Myth of CPR*. Philadelphia, PA: Temple University Press.
van Tol, D. 2005. Classifying Physician Negotiated Death, in *Social and Symbolic Effects of Legislation under the Rule of Law*, edited by N. Zeegers, W.J. Witteveen and B. van Klink. New York: Edwin Mellen Press.
Truog, R. 1997. Is it Time to Abandon Brain Death? *Hastings Center Report*, January–February, 29–37.
Vaysse, J. 1993. Cœur étranger en corps d'accueil. *Communications*, 56, 175–81.
Veatch, R.M. 1999. The Conscience Clause: How Much Individual Choice in Defining Death Can Our Society Tolerate? in *The Definition of Death: Contemporary Controversies*, edited by S.J. Youngner, A.M. Arnold and A. Schapiro. Baltimore, MD: Johns Hopkins University Press, 137–60.
de Voragine, J. 1941. *The Golden Legend*, trans. G. Ryan and H. Ripperger. Salem, NH: Ayer.
Waissmann, R. 1996. Analyse des acceptations et des refus du don d'organes; une étude de cas en France. *Sociologie et sociétés*, 2, 109–18.
——. 2000. Donneur, non-donneur: les affres d'une décision, in *La greffe humaine. (In)certitudes éthiques: du don de soi à la tolérance de l'autre*, edited by R. Carvais and C. Sasportes. Paris: PUF, 393–420.

Waissmann, R. and Couteau, M.J. 2000. Les opinions des Français sur la greffe et le don d'organes: l'âge, la famille, la tendance politique et l'appartenance religieuse sont-ils des enjeux?, in *La greffe humaine. (In)certitudes éthiques: du don de soi à la tolérance de l'autre*, edited by R. Carvais and C. Sasportes. Paris: PUF, 831–42.

Weimar, W., Bos, M.A. and Busschbach, J.J. 2008. *Organ Transplantation: Ethical, Legal and Psychosocial Aspects. Towards a Common European Policy*. Lengerich: Pabst Science Publishers.

Wijdicks, E.F.M. 2003. The Neurologist and Harvard Criteria for Brain Death. *Neurology*, 61, 970–76.

Wolstenholme, G. and O'Connor, M. 1968. *Law and Ethics of Transplatnation*. London: J. and A. Churchill.

World Health Organisation. 1991. *Human Organ Transplantation: A Report on Developments under the Auspices of the WHO*. Geneva: WHO.

Yearley, S. 2005. *Making Sense of Science*. London: Sage.

Youngner, S.J., Arnold, A.M. and Schapiro, A. (eds). 1999. *The Definition of Death: Contemporary Controversies*. Baltimore, MD: Johns Hopkins University Press.

Zeegers, N., Witteveen, W. and van Klink, B. 2005. *Social and Symbolic Effects of Legislation under the Rule of Law*. New York: Edwin Mellen Press.

Legal Texts

France

Décret n° 47-2057 du 20 octobre 1947 tendant à modifier l'article 27 du décret provisoirement applicable du 31 décembre 1941 codifiant les textes relatifs aux opérations d'inhumation, d'exhumation, d'incinération et de transport des corps.

Loi n° 49-480 du 7 juillet 1949.

Loi n° 76-1181 du 26 décembre 1976.

Décret n° 78-501 du 31 mars 1978 pris pour l'application de la loi du 22 décembre 1976 relative aux prélèvements d'organes.

Circulaire du 3 avril 1978 concernant le décret n° 78-501 du 31 mars 1978 pris pour l'application de la loi n° 76-1181 du 22 décembre 1976 relative aux prélèvements d'organes.

Circulaire du 14 mars 1986 précisant les conditions d'application du décret 81-460 du 08-05-1981 portant simplification des procédures et des conditions de prise en charge de fournitures et d'appareils au titre de prestations sanitaires.

Loi n° 94-548 du 1 juillet 1994 relative au traitement des données nominatives ayant pour fin la recherche dans le domaine de la santé et modifiant la loi n° 78-17 du 6 janvier 1978 relative à l'informatique, aux fichiers et aux libertés.

Loi ° 94-653 du 29 juillet 1994 relative au respect du corps humain.
Loi n° 94-654 du 29 juillet 1994 relative au don et à l'utilisation des éléments et produits du corps humain, à l'assistance médicale à la procréation et au diagnostique prénatal.
Décret n° 96-1041 du 2 décembre 1996 relatif au constat de la mort préalable au prélèvement d'organes, de tissus et de cellules à des fins thérapeutiques ou scientifiques et modifiant le code de la santé publique.
Décret n° 97-306 du 1 avril 1997 relatif aux conditions d'autorisation des établissements de santé effectuant des prélèvements d'organes et de tissus à des fins thérapeutiques et modifiant le code de la santé publique.
Arrêté du 1 avril 1997 portant homologation des règles de bonnes pratiques relatives au prélèvement des tissus et au recueil des résidus opératoires issus du corps humain utilisés à des fins thérapeutiques.
Loi n° 2004-800 du 6 août 2004 relative à la bioéthique.

Spain

Ley 30/1979, de 27 de octubre, sobre extracción y trasplante de órganos.
Real Decreto 2070/1999, de 30 de diciembre.

Parliamentary Reports and Documents

Auburtin, B. 1976. Rapport n° 58 fait par M. Auburtin, Annexe au procès-verbal de la séance du 16 novembre 1976.
Bianco, J.L. 1992. Rapport n° 2600 présenté le 25 mars 1992 par Jean Louis Bianco, Projet de loi relatif au don et à l'utilisation des éléments et produits du corps humain et à la procréation médicalement assistée, et modifiant le code de la santé publique.
Caillavet, H. 2001. Rapport n° 3208 du 10 juillet 2001, Audition de Henri Caillavet.
Charles, B. and Claeys, A. 2001. Rapport d'information de la mission d'information commune préparatoire au projet de loi de révision des lois 'bioéthiques' de juillet 1994, Tome II, Auditions, volume 3. Available at: http://www.assemblee-nationale.fr/rap-info/i3208-23.asp [accessed: May 2010].
Claeys, A. and Huriet, C. 1999. L'application de la loi n° 94-654 du 29 juillet 1994 relative au don et a l'utilisation des éléments et produits du corps humain, à l'assistance médicale à la procréation et au diagnostic prénatal. Office Parlementaire d'Evaluation des Choix Scientifiques et Technologiques.
Delaneau, J. 1976. Rapport n° 2654 fait au nom de la commission des affaires culturelles, familiales et sociales sur la proposition de loi, adoptée par le Sénat, relative aux greffes d'organes. Par M. Delaneau, député, Distribué le 7 décembre 1976 pour la séance du 8.

Mattei, J-F. 1993. Rapport à Monsieur le Premier Ministre sur l'éthique biomédicale, 15 novembre 1993.
——. 1994. Rapport fait au nom de la commission mixte paritaire chargée de proposer un texte sur les dispositions restant en discussion du projet de loi relatif au don et à l'utilisation des éléments et produits du corps humain, à l'assistance médicale à la procréation et au diagnostic prénatal, Jean-François Mattei, député, Jean Chérioux, sénateur, annexe au procès verbal de la séance du 9 juin 1994.

Press Articles

France

10/01/1992. *Le Figaro*. 'Greffes: ces enfants qui meurent de trop attendre'.
14/01/1992. *La Croix*. 'Les limites du don de soi'.
07/02/1992. *Le Figaro*. 'Greffe et don d'organes, comment obtenir les greffons indispensables? Comment expliquer les "refus familiaux"?'
18/05/1992. *Le Figaro*. 'Le respect des morts face à la médecine'.
17–18/05/1992. *Le Monde*. 'La mort violée'.
18/05/1992. *Le Parisien*. 'Vol d'organes: une famille accuse'.
20/05/1992. *Le Canard Enchaîné*. 'Dernières nouvelles du cannibalisme'.
20/05/1992. *L'Evénement du Jeudi*. 'Plus jamais ça!'
28/05/1992. *L'Express*. 'Les voleurs de regard'.
04/06/1992. *Le Figaro*. 'Les critères ambigus des greffes d'organe'.
04/06/1992. *Le Monde*. 'Evoquant l'existence de "filières de recrutement" un rapport de l'IGAS dénonce la proportion élevée de greffes d'organes réalisées en France sur des malades étrangers'.
04/06/1992. *Le Parisien*. 'Transparence pour la transplantation d'organes'.
04/06/1992. *Libération*. 'Les greffes d'organe sous le scalpel de l'IGAS'.
06/06/1992. *Le Monde*. 'Après le rapport de l'IGAS sur les transplantations, le débat est relancé sur la nationalité des greffés'.
12/06/1992. *Le Figaro*. 'La satisfaction de France-Transplant'.
??/04/1993. *Le Monde*. 'Un nouveau pillage du tiers-monde'.
23/04/1993. *Le Figaro*. 'Bioéthique: la loi en panne. Elle ne sera pas examinée avant l'automne'.
28/07/1993. *Le Canard Enchaîné*. 'La bataille du rein empoisonne le marché de la greffe d'organes'.
29/07/1993. *France Soir*. '30 reins greffés dans des services non agréés'.
29/07/1993. *Le Figaro*. 'Pratiques "interdites" pour des greffes de rein'.
29/07/1993. *Le Monde*. 'Un spécialiste de néphrologie de l'hôpital Tenon est accusé de ne pas avoir respecté la loi sur les prélèvements d'organes'.
29/07/1993. *Le Parisien*. 'Greffes: pratiques édifiantes à Tenon'.
29/07/1993. *Libération*. 'Les greffes peu conformes de l'hôpital Tenon'.

30/07/1993. *La Croix*. 'L'hôpital Tenon fait les frais d'un contrôle'.
30/07/1993. *L'Humanité*. 'Des greffes d'organes loin d'être au-dessus de tout soupçon'.
30/07/1993. *Le Figaro*. 'Greffes de rein à Tenon: l'Assistance publique s'explique'.
30/07/1993. *Le Monde*. 'Des mesures ont été prises à l'hôpital Tenon de Paris'.
04/08/1993. *Libération*. 'Les greffes d'organes victimes de la suspicion'.
21–22/08/1993. *Le Figaro*. 'La crise de croissance des transplantations'.
30/10/1993. *Le Monde*. 'Trafic d'organes et adoption'.
05/12/1993. *Le Monde*. 'Télévision documentaire: voleurs d'organes'.
08/12/1993. *Libération*. 'Trafic d'organes en Amerique latine'.
07/01/1995. *Libération*. 'Quand les yeux ont le prix des yeux'.
17/08/1995. *Le Monde*. 'Un reportage sur les greffes de cornée en Colombie suscite la polémique'.
26/09/1995. *Libération*. 'Suspension du prix Albert-Londres. La mesure vise le reportage "Voleurs d'organes", lauréat 1995'.
20/08/1996. *L'Humanité*. 'Les yeux des enfants d'Amérique'.

UK

16/11/2008. *The Guardian*. 'Chief Medical Officer condemns organ donor decision'.
18/11/2008. *The Guardian*. 'Taskforce opposes "presumed consent" for organ donors'.

Films

P. Almodóvar, *Todo sobre mi madre*, 1999.
S. Frears, *Dirty Pretty Things*, 2002.
A. González Iñárritu, *21 Grams*, 2003.
T. Jones, *Monty Python's The Meaning of Life*, 1983.

Index